CAREER EXAMINATION SERIES

MW00851229

THIS IS YOUR **PASSBOOK**® FOR ...

ELECTRICIAN'S HELPER

NATIONAL LEARNING CORPORATION®
passbooks.com

PASSBOOK® SERIES

THE *PASSBOOK® SERIES* has been created to prepare applicants and candidates for the ultimate academic battlefield – the examination room.

At some time in our lives, each and every one of us may be required to take an examination – for validation, matriculation, admission, qualification, registration, certification, or licensure.

Based on the assumption that every applicant or candidate has met the basic formal educational standards, has taken the required number of courses, and read the necessary texts, the *PASSBOOK® SERIES* furnishes the one special preparation which may assure passing with confidence, instead of failing with insecurity. Examination questions – together with answers – are furnished as the basic vehicle for study so that the mysteries of the examination and its compounding difficulties may be eliminated or diminished by a sure method.

This book is meant to help you pass your examination provided that you qualify and are serious in your objective.

The entire field is reviewed through the huge store of content information which is succinctly presented through a provocative and challenging approach – the question-and-answer method.

A climate of success is established by furnishing the correct answers at the end of each test.

You soon learn to recognize types of questions, forms of questions, and patterns of questioning. You may even begin to anticipate expected outcomes.

You perceive that many questions are repeated or adapted so that you can gain acute insights, which may enable you to score many sure points.

You learn how to confront new questions, or types of questions, and to attack them confidently and work out the correct answers.

You note objectives and emphases, and recognize pitfalls and dangers, so that you may make positive educational adjustments.

Moreover, you are kept fully informed in relation to new concepts, methods, practices, and directions in the field.

You discover that you arre actually taking the examination all the time: you are preparing for the examination by "taking" an examination, not by reading extraneous and/or supererogatory textbooks.

In short, this PASSBOOK®, used directedly, should be an important factor in helping you to pass your test.

ELECTRICIAN'S HELPER

JOB DESCRIPTION

Under direct supervision, assists an electrician in installing, repairing, replacing, and maintaining electric wiring systems, appliances, apparatus and equipment according to the provisions of the Electrical Code and approved plans and specifications; performs related work.

EXAMPLES OF TYPICAL TASKS

Assists electricians in pulling wires and testing electrical systems. Replaces defective light switches, plugs, and lighting fixtures. Checks signal systems. Keeps electricians supplied with materials, tools and supplies. Cleans working areas, machines, tools and equipment. Performs routine machine operations.

SCOPE OF THE EXAMINATION

The multiple-choice test may include questions on materials, tools and equipment used in electrical work; safe working practices; basic electrical skills, good housekeeping practices; maintaining and cleaning machines, tools and equipment; basic principles of electricity; electrical calculations; diagrams, schematics and plans; and other related areas.

HOW TO TAKE A TEST

I. YOU MUST PASS AN EXAMINATION

A. *WHAT EVERY CANDIDATE SHOULD KNOW*

Examination applicants often ask us for help in preparing for the written test. What can I study in advance? What kinds of questions will be asked? How will the test be given? How will the papers be graded?

As an applicant for a civil service examination, you may be wondering about some of these things. Our purpose here is to suggest effective methods of advance study and to describe civil service examinations.

Your chances for success on this examination can be increased if you know how to prepare. Those "pre-examination jitters" can be reduced if you know what to expect. You can even experience an adventure in good citizenship if you know why civil service exams are given.

B. *WHY ARE CIVIL SERVICE EXAMINATIONS GIVEN?*

Civil service examinations are important to you in two ways. As a citizen, you want public jobs filled by employees who know how to do their work. As a job seeker, you want a fair chance to compete for that job on an equal footing with other candidates. The best-known means of accomplishing this two-fold goal is the competitive examination.

Exams are widely publicized throughout the nation. They may be administered for jobs in federal, state, city, municipal, town or village governments or agencies.

Any citizen may apply, with some limitations, such as the age or residence of applicants. Your experience and education may be reviewed to see whether you meet the requirements for the particular examination. When these requirements exist, they are reasonable and applied consistently to all applicants. Thus, a competitive examination may cause you some uneasiness now, but it is your privilege and safeguard.

C. *HOW ARE CIVIL SERVICE EXAMS DEVELOPED?*

Examinations are carefully written by trained technicians who are specialists in the field known as "psychological measurement," in consultation with recognized authorities in the field of work that the test will cover. These experts recommend the subject matter areas or skills to be tested; only those knowledges or skills important to your success on the job are included. The most reliable books and source materials available are used as references. Together, the experts and technicians judge the difficulty level of the questions.

Test technicians know how to phrase questions so that the problem is clearly stated. Their ethics do not permit "trick" or "catch" questions. Questions may have been tried out on sample groups, or subjected to statistical analysis, to determine their usefulness.

Written tests are often used in combination with performance tests, ratings of training and experience, and oral interviews. All of these measures combine to form the best-known means of finding the right person for the right job.

II. HOW TO PASS THE WRITTEN TEST

A. NATURE OF THE EXAMINATION

To prepare intelligently for civil service examinations, you should know how they differ from school examinations you have taken. In school you were assigned certain definite pages to read or subjects to cover. The examination questions were quite detailed and usually emphasized memory. Civil service exams, on the other hand, try to discover your present ability to perform the duties of a position, plus your potentiality to learn these duties. In other words, a civil service exam attempts to predict how successful you will be. Questions cover such a broad area that they cannot be as minute and detailed as school exam questions.

In the public service similar kinds of work, or positions, are grouped together in one "class." This process is known as *position-classification*. All the positions in a class are paid according to the salary range for that class. One class title covers all of these positions, and they are all tested by the same examination.

B. FOUR BASIC STEPS

1) Study the announcement

How, then, can you know what subjects to study? Our best answer is: "Learn as much as possible about the class of positions for which you've applied." The exam will test the knowledge, skills and abilities needed to do the work.

Your most valuable source of information about the position you want is the official exam announcement. This announcement lists the training and experience qualifications. Check these standards and apply only if you come reasonably close to meeting them.

The brief description of the position in the examination announcement offers some clues to the subjects which will be tested. Think about the job itself. Review the duties in your mind. Can you perform them, or are there some in which you are rusty? Fill in the blank spots in your preparation.

Many jurisdictions preview the written test in the exam announcement by including a section called "Knowledge and Abilities Required," "Scope of the Examination," or some similar heading. Here you will find out specifically what fields will be tested.

2) Review your own background

Once you learn in general what the position is all about, and what you need to know to do the work, ask yourself which subjects you already know fairly well and which need improvement. You may wonder whether to concentrate on improving your strong areas or on building some background in your fields of weakness. When the announcement has specified "some knowledge" or "considerable knowledge," or has used adjectives like "beginning principles of…" or "advanced … methods," you can get a clue as to the number and difficulty of questions to be asked in any given field. More questions, and hence broader coverage, would be included for those subjects which are more important in the work. Now weigh your strengths and weaknesses against the job requirements and prepare accordingly.

3) Determine the level of the position

Another way to tell how intensively you should prepare is to understand the level of the job for which you are applying. Is it the entering level? In other words, is this the position in which beginners in a field of work are hired? Or is it an intermediate or advanced level? Sometimes this is indicated by such words as "Junior" or "Senior" in the class title. Other jurisdictions use Roman numerals to designate the level – Clerk I, Clerk II, for example. The word "Supervisor" sometimes appears in the title. If the level is not indicated by the title, check the description of duties. Will you be working under very close supervision, or will you have responsibility for independent decisions in this work?

4) Choose appropriate study materials

Now that you know the subjects to be examined and the relative amount of each subject to be covered, you can choose suitable study materials. For beginning level jobs, or even advanced ones, if you have a pronounced weakness in some aspect of your training, read a modern, standard textbook in that field. Be sure it is up to date and has general coverage. Such books are normally available at your library, and the librarian will be glad to help you locate one. For entry-level positions, questions of appropriate difficulty are chosen – neither highly advanced questions, nor those too simple. Such questions require careful thought but not advanced training.

If the position for which you are applying is technical or advanced, you will read more advanced, specialized material. If you are already familiar with the basic principles of your field, elementary textbooks would waste your time. Concentrate on advanced textbooks and technical periodicals. Think through the concepts and review difficult problems in your field.

These are all general sources. You can get more ideas on your own initiative, following these leads. For example, training manuals and publications of the government agency which employs workers in your field can be useful, particularly for technical and professional positions. A letter or visit to the government department involved may result in more specific study suggestions, and certainly will provide you with a more definite idea of the exact nature of the position you are seeking.

III. KINDS OF TESTS

Tests are used for purposes other than measuring knowledge and ability to perform specified duties. For some positions, it is equally important to test ability to make adjustments to new situations or to profit from training. In others, basic mental abilities not dependent on information are essential. Questions which test these things may not appear as pertinent to the duties of the position as those which test for knowledge and information. Yet they are often highly important parts of a fair examination. For very general questions, it is almost impossible to help you direct your study efforts. What we can do is to point out some of the more common of these general abilities needed in public service positions and describe some typical questions.

1) General information

Broad, general information has been found useful for predicting job success in some kinds of work. This is tested in a variety of ways, from vocabulary lists to questions about current events. Basic background in some field of work, such as sociology or economics, may be sampled in a group of questions. Often these are principles which have become familiar to most persons through exposure rather than through formal training. It is difficult to advise you how to study for these questions; being alert to the world around you is our best suggestion.

2) Verbal ability

An example of an ability needed in many positions is verbal or language ability. Verbal ability is, in brief, the ability to use and understand words. Vocabulary and grammar tests are typical measures of this ability. Reading comprehension or paragraph interpretation questions are common in many kinds of civil service tests. You are given a paragraph of written material and asked to find its central meaning.

3) Numerical ability

Number skills can be tested by the familiar arithmetic problem, by checking paired lists of numbers to see which are alike and which are different, or by interpreting charts and graphs. In the latter test, a graph may be printed in the test booklet which you are asked to use as the basis for answering questions.

4) Observation

A popular test for law-enforcement positions is the observation test. A picture is shown to you for several minutes, then taken away. Questions about the picture test your ability to observe both details and larger elements.

5) Following directions

In many positions in the public service, the employee must be able to carry out written instructions dependably and accurately. You may be given a chart with several columns, each column listing a variety of information. The questions require you to carry out directions involving the information given in the chart.

6) Skills and aptitudes

Performance tests effectively measure some manual skills and aptitudes. When the skill is one in which you are trained, such as typing or shorthand, you can practice. These tests are often very much like those given in business school or high school courses. For many of the other skills and aptitudes, however, no short-time preparation can be made. Skills and abilities natural to you or that you have developed throughout your lifetime are being tested.

Many of the general questions just described provide all the data needed to answer the questions and ask you to use your reasoning ability to find the answers. Your best preparation for these tests, as well as for tests of facts and ideas, is to be at your physical and mental best. You, no doubt, have your own methods of getting into an exam-taking mood and keeping "in shape." The next section lists some ideas on this subject.

IV. KINDS OF QUESTIONS

Only rarely is the "essay" question, which you answer in narrative form, used in civil service tests. Civil service tests are usually of the short-answer type. Full instructions for answering these questions will be given to you at the examination. But in case this is your first experience with short-answer questions and separate answer sheets, here is what you need to know:

1) Multiple-choice Questions

Most popular of the short-answer questions is the "multiple choice" or "best answer" question. It can be used, for example, to test for factual knowledge, ability to solve problems or judgment in meeting situations found at work.

A multiple-choice question is normally one of three types—

- It can begin with an incomplete statement followed by several possible endings. You are to find the one ending which *best* completes the statement, although some of the others may not be entirely wrong.
- It can also be a complete statement in the form of a question which is answered by choosing one of the statements listed.
- It can be in the form of a problem – again you select the best answer.

Here is an example of a multiple-choice question with a discussion which should give you some clues as to the method for choosing the right answer:

When an employee has a complaint about his assignment, the action which will *best* help him overcome his difficulty is to
- A. discuss his difficulty with his coworkers
- B. take the problem to the head of the organization
- C. take the problem to the person who gave him the assignment
- D. say nothing to anyone about his complaint

In answering this question, you should study each of the choices to find which is best. Consider choice "A" – Certainly an employee may discuss his complaint with fellow employees, but no change or improvement can result, and the complaint remains unresolved. Choice "B" is a poor choice since the head of the organization probably does not know what assignment you have been given, and taking your problem to him is known as "going over the head" of the supervisor. The supervisor, or person who made the assignment, is the person who can clarify it or correct any injustice. Choice "C" is, therefore, correct. To say nothing, as in choice "D," is unwise. Supervisors have and interest in knowing the problems employees are facing, and the employee is seeking a solution to his problem.

2) True/False Questions

The "true/false" or "right/wrong" form of question is sometimes used. Here a complete statement is given. Your job is to decide whether the statement is right or wrong.

SAMPLE: A roaming cell-phone call to a nearby city costs less than a non-roaming call to a distant city.

This statement is wrong, or false, since roaming calls are more expensive.

This is not a complete list of all possible question forms, although most of the others are variations of these common types. You will always get complete directions for answering questions. Be sure you understand *how* to mark your answers – ask questions until you do.

V. RECORDING YOUR ANSWERS

Computer terminals are used more and more today for many different kinds of exams.

For an examination with very few applicants, you may be told to record your answers in the test booklet itself. Separate answer sheets are much more common. If this separate answer sheet is to be scored by machine – and this is often the case – it is highly important that you mark your answers correctly in order to get credit.

An electronic scoring machine is often used in civil service offices because of the speed with which papers can be scored. Machine-scored answer sheets must be marked with a pencil, which will be given to you. This pencil has a high graphite content which responds to the electronic scoring machine. As a matter of fact, stray dots may register as answers, so do not let your pencil rest on the answer sheet while you are pondering the correct answer. Also, if your pencil lead breaks or is otherwise defective, ask for another.

Since the answer sheet will be dropped in a slot in the scoring machine, be careful not to bend the corners or get the paper crumpled.

The answer sheet normally has five vertical columns of numbers, with 30 numbers to a column. These numbers correspond to the question numbers in your test booklet. After each number, going across the page are four or five pairs of dotted lines. These short dotted lines have small letters or numbers above them. The first two pairs may also have a "T" or "F" above the letters. This indicates that the first two pairs only are to be used if the questions are of the true-false type. If the questions are multiple choice, disregard the "T" and "F" and pay attention only to the small letters or numbers.

Answer your questions in the manner of the sample that follows:

32. The largest city in the United States is
    A. Washington, D.C.
    B. New York City
    C. Chicago
    D. Detroit
    E. San Francisco

1) Choose the answer you think is best. (New York City is the largest, so "B" is correct.)
2) Find the row of dotted lines numbered the same as the question you are answering. (Find row number 32)
3) Find the pair of dotted lines corresponding to the answer. (Find the pair of lines under the mark "B.")
4) Make a solid black mark between the dotted lines.

VI. BEFORE THE TEST

Common sense will help you find procedures to follow to get ready for an examination. Too many of us, however, overlook these sensible measures. Indeed, nervousness and fatigue have been found to be the most serious reasons why applicants fail to do their best on civil service tests. Here is a list of reminders:

- Begin your preparation early – Don't wait until the last minute to go scurrying around for books and materials or to find out what the position is all about.
- Prepare continuously – An hour a night for a week is better than an all-night cram session. This has been definitely established. What is more, a night a week for a month will return better dividends than crowding your study into a shorter period of time.
- Locate the place of the exam – You have been sent a notice telling you when and where to report for the examination. If the location is in a different town or otherwise unfamiliar to you, it would be well to inquire the best route and learn something about the building.
- Relax the night before the test – Allow your mind to rest. Do not study at all that night. Plan some mild recreation or diversion; then go to bed early and get a good night's sleep.
- Get up early enough to make a leisurely trip to the place for the test – This way unforeseen events, traffic snarls, unfamiliar buildings, etc. will not upset you.
- Dress comfortably – A written test is not a fashion show. You will be known by number and not by name, so wear something comfortable.
- Leave excess paraphernalia at home – Shopping bags and odd bundles will get in your way. You need bring only the items mentioned in the official notice you received; usually everything you need is provided. Do not bring reference books to the exam. They will only confuse those last minutes and be taken away from you when in the test room.
- Arrive somewhat ahead of time – If because of transportation schedules you must get there very early, bring a newspaper or magazine to take your mind off yourself while waiting.
- Locate the examination room – When you have found the proper room, you will be directed to the seat or part of the room where you will sit. Sometimes you are given a sheet of instructions to read while you are waiting. Do not fill out any forms until you are told to do so; just read them and be prepared.
- Relax and prepare to listen to the instructions
- If you have any physical problem that may keep you from doing your best, be sure to tell the test administrator. If you are sick or in poor health, you really cannot do your best on the exam. You can come back and take the test some other time.

VII. AT THE TEST

The day of the test is here and you have the test booklet in your hand. The temptation to get going is very strong. Caution! There is more to success than knowing the right answers. You must know how to identify your papers and understand variations in the type of short-answer question used in this particular examination. Follow these suggestions for maximum results from your efforts:

1) Cooperate with the monitor

The test administrator has a duty to create a situation in which you can be as much at ease as possible. He will give instructions, tell you when to begin, check to see that you are marking your answer sheet correctly, and so on. He is not there to guard you, although he will see that your competitors do not take unfair advantage. He wants to help you do your best.

2) Listen to all instructions

Don't jump the gun! Wait until you understand all directions. In most civil service tests you get more time than you need to answer the questions. So don't be in a hurry. Read each word of instructions until you clearly understand the meaning. Study the examples, listen to all announcements and follow directions. Ask questions if you do not understand what to do.

3) Identify your papers

Civil service exams are usually identified by number only. You will be assigned a number; you must not put your name on your test papers. Be sure to copy your number correctly. Since more than one exam may be given, copy your exact examination title.

4) Plan your time

Unless you are told that a test is a "speed" or "rate of work" test, speed itself is usually not important. Time enough to answer all the questions will be provided, but this does not mean that you have all day. An overall time limit has been set. Divide the total time (in minutes) by the number of questions to determine the approximate time you have for each question.

5) Do not linger over difficult questions

If you come across a difficult question, mark it with a paper clip (useful to have along) and come back to it when you have been through the booklet. One caution if you do this – be sure to skip a number on your answer sheet as well. Check often to be sure that you have not lost your place and that you are marking in the row numbered the same as the question you are answering.

6) Read the questions

Be sure you know what the question asks! Many capable people are unsuccessful because they failed to *read* the questions correctly.

7) Answer all questions

Unless you have been instructed that a penalty will be deducted for incorrect answers, it is better to guess than to omit a question.

8) Speed tests

It is often better NOT to guess on speed tests. It has been found that on timed tests people are tempted to spend the last few seconds before time is called in marking answers at random – without even reading them – in the hope of picking up a few extra points. To discourage this practice, the instructions may warn you that your score will be "corrected" for guessing. That is, a penalty will be applied. The incorrect answers will be deducted from the correct ones, or some other penalty formula will be used.

9) Review your answers

If you finish before time is called, go back to the questions you guessed or omitted to give them further thought. Review other answers if you have time.

10) Return your test materials

If you are ready to leave before others have finished or time is called, take ALL your materials to the monitor and leave quietly. Never take any test material with you. The monitor can discover whose papers are not complete, and taking a test booklet may be grounds for disqualification.

VIII. EXAMINATION TECHNIQUES

1) Read the general instructions carefully. These are usually printed on the first page of the exam booklet. As a rule, these instructions refer to the timing of the examination; the fact that you should not start work until the signal and must stop work at a signal, etc. If there are any *special* instructions, such as a choice of questions to be answered, make sure that you note this instruction carefully.

2) When you are ready to start work on the examination, that is as soon as the signal has been given, read the instructions to each question booklet, underline any key words or phrases, such as *least, best, outline, describe* and the like. In this way you will tend to answer as requested rather than discover on reviewing your paper that you *listed without describing*, that you selected the *worst* choice rather than the *best* choice, etc.

3) If the examination is of the objective or multiple-choice type – that is, each question will also give a series of possible answers: A, B, C or D, and you are called upon to select the best answer and write the letter next to that answer on your answer paper – it is advisable to start answering each question in turn. There may be anywhere from 50 to 100 such questions in the three or four hours allotted and you can see how much time would be taken if you read through all the questions before beginning to answer any. Furthermore, if you come across a question or group of questions which you know would be difficult to answer, it would undoubtedly affect your handling of all the other questions.

4) If the examination is of the essay type and contains but a few questions, it is a moot point as to whether you should read all the questions before starting to answer any one. Of course, if you are given a choice – say five out of seven and the like – then it is essential to read all the questions so you can eliminate the two that are most difficult. If, however, you are asked to answer all the questions, there may be danger in trying to answer the easiest one first because you may find that you will spend too much time on it. The best technique is to answer the first question, then proceed to the second, etc.

5) Time your answers. Before the exam begins, write down the time it started, then add the time allowed for the examination and write down the time it must be completed, then divide the time available somewhat as follows:

- If 3-1/2 hours are allowed, that would be 210 minutes. If you have 80 objective-type questions, that would be an average of 2-1/2 minutes per question. Allow yourself no more than 2 minutes per question, or a total of 160 minutes, which will permit about 50 minutes to review.
- If for the time allotment of 210 minutes there are 7 essay questions to answer, that would average about 30 minutes a question. Give yourself only 25 minutes per question so that you have about 35 minutes to review.

6) The most important instruction is to *read each question* and make sure you know what is wanted. The second most important instruction is to *time yourself properly* so that you answer every question. The third most important instruction is to *answer every question*. Guess if you have to but include something for each question. Remember that you will receive no credit for a blank and will probably receive some credit if you write something in answer to an essay question. If you guess a letter – say "B" for a multiple-choice question – you may have guessed right. If you leave a blank as an answer to a multiple-choice question, the examiners may respect your feelings but it will not add a point to your score. Some exams may penalize you for wrong answers, so in such cases *only*, you may not want to guess unless you have some basis for your answer.

7) Suggestions
   a. Objective-type questions
      1. Examine the question booklet for proper sequence of pages and questions
      2. Read all instructions carefully
      3. Skip any question which seems too difficult; return to it after all other questions have been answered
      4. Apportion your time properly; do not spend too much time on any single question or group of questions
      5. Note and underline key words – *all, most, fewest, least, best, worst, same, opposite,* etc.
      6. Pay particular attention to negatives
      7. Note unusual option, e.g., unduly long, short, complex, different or similar in content to the body of the question
      8. Observe the use of "hedging" words – *probably, may, most likely,* etc.
      9. Make sure that your answer is put next to the same number as the question
      10. Do not second-guess unless you have good reason to believe the second answer is definitely more correct
      11. Cross out original answer if you decide another answer is more accurate; do not erase until you are ready to hand your paper in
      12. Answer all questions; guess unless instructed otherwise
      13. Leave time for review

   b. Essay questions
      1. Read each question carefully
      2. Determine exactly what is wanted. Underline key words or phrases.
      3. Decide on outline or paragraph answer

4. Include many different points and elements unless asked to develop any one or two points or elements
5. Show impartiality by giving pros and cons unless directed to select one side only
6. Make and write down any assumptions you find necessary to answer the questions
7. Watch your English, grammar, punctuation and choice of words
8. Time your answers; don't crowd material

8) Answering the essay question

Most essay questions can be answered by framing the specific response around several key words or ideas. Here are a few such key words or ideas:

M's: manpower, materials, methods, money, management
P's: purpose, program, policy, plan, procedure, practice, problems, pitfalls, personnel, public relations
  a. Six basic steps in handling problems:
    1. Preliminary plan and background development
    2. Collect information, data and facts
    3. Analyze and interpret information, data and facts
    4. Analyze and develop solutions as well as make recommendations
    5. Prepare report and sell recommendations
    6. Install recommendations and follow up effectiveness

  b. Pitfalls to avoid
    1. *Taking things for granted* – A statement of the situation does not necessarily imply that each of the elements is necessarily true; for example, a complaint may be invalid and biased so that all that can be taken for granted is that a complaint has been registered
    2. *Considering only one side of a situation* – Wherever possible, indicate several alternatives and then point out the reasons you selected the best one
    3. *Failing to indicate follow up* – Whenever your answer indicates action on your part, make certain that you will take proper follow-up action to see how successful your recommendations, procedures or actions turn out to be
    4. *Taking too long in answering any single question* – Remember to time your answers properly

IX. AFTER THE TEST

Scoring procedures differ in detail among civil service jurisdictions although the general principles are the same. Whether the papers are hand-scored or graded by machine we have described, they are nearly always graded by number. That is, the person who marks the paper knows only the number – never the name – of the applicant. Not until all the papers have been graded will they be matched with names. If other tests, such as training and experience or oral interview ratings have been given, scores will be combined. Different parts of the examination usually have different weights. For example, the written test might count 60 percent of the final grade, and a rating of training and experience 40 percent. In many jurisdictions, veterans will have a certain number of points added to their grades.

After the final grade has been determined, the names are placed in grade order and an eligible list is established. There are various methods for resolving ties between those who get the same final grade – probably the most common is to place first the name of the person whose application was received first. Job offers are made from the eligible list in the order the names appear on it. You will be notified of your grade and your rank as soon as all these computations have been made. This will be done as rapidly as possible.

People who are found to meet the requirements in the announcement are called "eligibles." Their names are put on a list of eligible candidates. An eligible's chances of getting a job depend on how high he stands on this list and how fast agencies are filling jobs from the list.

When a job is to be filled from a list of eligibles, the agency asks for the names of people on the list of eligibles for that job. When the civil service commission receives this request, it sends to the agency the names of the three people highest on this list. Or, if the job to be filled has specialized requirements, the office sends the agency the names of the top three persons who meet these requirements from the general list.

The appointing officer makes a choice from among the three people whose names were sent to him. If the selected person accepts the appointment, the names of the others are put back on the list to be considered for future openings.

That is the rule in hiring from all kinds of eligible lists, whether they are for typist, carpenter, chemist, or something else. For every vacancy, the appointing officer has his choice of any one of the top three eligibles on the list. This explains why the person whose name is on top of the list sometimes does not get an appointment when some of the persons lower on the list do. If the appointing officer chooses the second or third eligible, the No. 1 eligible does not get a job at once, but stays on the list until he is appointed or the list is terminated.

X. HOW TO PASS THE INTERVIEW TEST

The examination for which you applied requires an oral interview test. You have already taken the written test and you are now being called for the interview test – the final part of the formal examination.

You may think that it is not possible to prepare for an interview test and that there are no procedures to follow during an interview. Our purpose is to point out some things you can do in advance that will help you and some good rules to follow and pitfalls to avoid while you are being interviewed.

What is an interview supposed to test?

The written examination is designed to test the technical knowledge and competence of the candidate; the oral is designed to evaluate intangible qualities, not readily measured otherwise, and to establish a list showing the relative fitness of each candidate – as measured against his competitors – for the position sought. Scoring is not on the basis of "right" and "wrong," but on a sliding scale of values ranging from "not passable" to "outstanding." As a matter of fact, it is possible to achieve a relatively low score without a single "incorrect" answer because of evident weakness in the qualities being measured.

Occasionally, an examination may consist entirely of an oral test – either an individual or a group oral. In such cases, information is sought concerning the technical knowledges and abilities of the candidate, since there has been no written examination for this purpose. More commonly, however, an oral test is used to supplement a written examination.

Who conducts interviews?

The composition of oral boards varies among different jurisdictions. In nearly all, a representative of the personnel department serves as chairman. One of the members of the board may be a representative of the department in which the candidate would work. In some cases, "outside experts" are used, and, frequently, a businessman or some other representative of the general public is asked to serve. Labor and management or other special groups may be represented. The aim is to secure the services of experts in the appropriate field.

However the board is composed, it is a good idea (and not at all improper or unethical) to ascertain in advance of the interview who the members are and what groups they represent. When you are introduced to them, you will have some idea of their backgrounds and interests, and at least you will not stutter and stammer over their names.

What should be done before the interview?

While knowledge about the board members is useful and takes some of the surprise element out of the interview, there is other preparation which is more substantive. It *is* possible to prepare for an oral interview – in several ways:

1) Keep a copy of your application and review it carefully before the interview

This may be the only document before the oral board, and the starting point of the interview. Know what education and experience you have listed there, and the sequence and dates of all of it. Sometimes the board will ask you to review the highlights of your experience for them; you should not have to hem and haw doing it.

2) Study the class specification and the examination announcement

Usually, the oral board has one or both of these to guide them. The qualities, characteristics or knowledges required by the position sought are stated in these documents. They offer valuable clues as to the nature of the oral interview. For example, if the job involves supervisory responsibilities, the announcement will usually indicate that knowledge of modern supervisory methods and the qualifications of the candidate as a supervisor will be tested. If so, you can expect such questions, frequently in the form of a hypothetical situation which you are expected to solve. NEVER go into an oral without knowledge of the duties and responsibilities of the job you seek.

3) Think through each qualification required

Try to visualize the kind of questions you would ask if you were a board member. How well could you answer them? Try especially to appraise your own knowledge and background in each area, *measured against the job sought*, and identify any areas in which you are weak. Be critical and realistic – do not flatter yourself.

4) Do some general reading in areas in which you feel you may be weak

For example, if the job involves supervision and your past experience has NOT, some general reading in supervisory methods and practices, particularly in the field of human relations, might be useful. Do NOT study agency procedures or detailed manuals. The oral board will be testing your understanding and capacity, not your memory.

5) Get a good night's sleep and watch your general health and mental attitude

You will want a clear head at the interview. Take care of a cold or any other minor ailment, and of course, no hangovers.

What should be done on the day of the interview?

Now comes the day of the interview itself. Give yourself plenty of time to get there. Plan to arrive somewhat ahead of the scheduled time, particularly if your appointment is in the fore part of the day. If a previous candidate fails to appear, the board might be ready for you a bit early. By early afternoon an oral board is almost invariably behind schedule if there are many candidates, and you may have to wait. Take along a book or magazine to read, or your application to review, but leave any extraneous material in the waiting room when you go in for your interview. In any event, relax and compose yourself.

The matter of dress is important. The board is forming impressions about you – from your experience, your manners, your attitude, and your appearance. Give your personal appearance careful attention. Dress your best, but not your flashiest. Choose conservative, appropriate clothing, and be sure it is immaculate. This is a business interview, and your appearance should indicate that you regard it as such. Besides, being well groomed and properly dressed will help boost your confidence.

Sooner or later, someone will call your name and escort you into the interview room. *This is it.* From here on you are on your own. It is too late for any more preparation. But remember, you asked for this opportunity to prove your fitness, and you are here because your request was granted.

What happens when you go in?

The usual sequence of events will be as follows: The clerk (who is often the board stenographer) will introduce you to the chairman of the oral board, who will introduce you to the other members of the board. Acknowledge the introductions before you sit down. Do not be surprised if you find a microphone facing you or a stenotypist sitting by. Oral interviews are usually recorded in the event of an appeal or other review.

Usually the chairman of the board will open the interview by reviewing the highlights of your education and work experience from your application – primarily for the benefit of the other members of the board, as well as to get the material into the record. Do not interrupt or comment unless there is an error or significant misinterpretation; if that is the case, do not hesitate. But do not quibble about insignificant matters. Also, he will usually ask you some question about your education, experience or your present job – partly to get you to start talking and to establish the interviewing "rapport." He may start the actual questioning, or turn it over to one of the other members. Frequently, each member undertakes the questioning on a particular area, one in which he is perhaps most competent, so you can expect each member to participate in the examination. Because time is limited, you may also expect some rather abrupt switches in the direction the questioning takes, so do not be upset by it. Normally, a board member will not pursue a single line of questioning unless he discovers a particular strength or weakness.

After each member has participated, the chairman will usually ask whether any member has any further questions, then will ask you if you have anything you wish to add. Unless you are expecting this question, it may floor you. Worse, it may start you off on an extended, extemporaneous speech. The board is not usually seeking more information. The question is principally to offer you a last opportunity to present further qualifications or to indicate that you have nothing to add. So, if you feel that a significant qualification or characteristic has been overlooked, it is proper to point it out in a sentence or so. Do not compliment the board on the thoroughness of their examination – they have been sketchy, and you know it. If you wish, merely say, "No thank you, I have nothing further to add." This is a point where you can "talk yourself out" of a good impression or fail to present an important bit of information. Remember, *you close the interview yourself.*

The chairman will then say, "That is all, Mr. _____, thank you." Do not be startled; the interview is over, and quicker than you think. Thank him, gather your belongings and take your leave. Save your sigh of relief for the other side of the door.

How to put your best foot forward

Throughout this entire process, you may feel that the board individually and collectively is trying to pierce your defenses, seek out your hidden weaknesses and embarrass and confuse you. Actually, this is not true. They are obliged to make an appraisal of your qualifications for the job you are seeking, and they want to see you in your best light. Remember, they must interview all candidates and a non-cooperative candidate may become a failure in spite of their best efforts to bring out his qualifications. Here are 15 suggestions that will help you:

1) Be natural – Keep your attitude confident, not cocky

If you are not confident that you can do the job, do not expect the board to be. Do not apologize for your weaknesses, try to bring out your strong points. The board is interested in a positive, not negative, presentation. Cockiness will antagonize any board member and make him wonder if you are covering up a weakness by a false show of strength.

2) Get comfortable, but don't lounge or sprawl

Sit erectly but not stiffly. A careless posture may lead the board to conclude that you are careless in other things, or at least that you are not impressed by the importance of the occasion. Either conclusion is natural, even if incorrect. Do not fuss with your clothing, a pencil or an ashtray. Your hands may occasionally be useful to emphasize a point; do not let them become a point of distraction.

3) Do not wisecrack or make small talk

This is a serious situation, and your attitude should show that you consider it as such. Further, the time of the board is limited – they do not want to waste it, and neither should you.

4) Do not exaggerate your experience or abilities

In the first place, from information in the application or other interviews and sources, the board may know more about you than you think. Secondly, you probably will not get away with it. An experienced board is rather adept at spotting such a situation, so do not take the chance.

5) If you know a board member, do not make a point of it, yet do not hide it

Certainly you are not fooling him, and probably not the other members of the board. Do not try to take advantage of your acquaintanceship – it will probably do you little good.

6) Do not dominate the interview

Let the board do that. They will give you the clues – do not assume that you have to do all the talking. Realize that the board has a number of questions to ask you, and do not try to take up all the interview time by showing off your extensive knowledge of the answer to the first one.

7) Be attentive

You only have 20 minutes or so, and you should keep your attention at its sharpest throughout. When a member is addressing a problem or question to you, give him your undivided attention. Address your reply principally to him, but do not exclude the other board members.

8) Do not interrupt

A board member may be stating a problem for you to analyze. He will ask you a question when the time comes. Let him state the problem, and wait for the question.

9) Make sure you understand the question

Do not try to answer until you are sure what the question is. If it is not clear, restate it in your own words or ask the board member to clarify it for you. However, do not haggle about minor elements.

10) Reply promptly but not hastily

A common entry on oral board rating sheets is "candidate responded readily," or "candidate hesitated in replies." Respond as promptly and quickly as you can, but do not jump to a hasty, ill-considered answer.

11) Do not be peremptory in your answers

A brief answer is proper – but do not fire your answer back. That is a losing game from your point of view. The board member can probably ask questions much faster than you can answer them.

12) Do not try to create the answer you think the board member wants

He is interested in what kind of mind you have and how it works – not in playing games. Furthermore, he can usually spot this practice and will actually grade you down on it.

13) Do not switch sides in your reply merely to agree with a board member

Frequently, a member will take a contrary position merely to draw you out and to see if you are willing and able to defend your point of view. Do not start a debate, yet do not surrender a good position. If a position is worth taking, it is worth defending.

14) Do not be afraid to admit an error in judgment if you are shown to be wrong

      The board knows that you are forced to reply without any opportunity for careful consideration. Your answer may be demonstrably wrong. If so, admit it and get on with the interview.

15) Do not dwell at length on your present job

      The opening question may relate to your present assignment. Answer the question but do not go into an extended discussion. You are being examined for a *new* job, not your present one. As a matter of fact, try to phrase ALL your answers in terms of the job for which you are being examined.

Basis of Rating

      Probably you will forget most of these "do's" and "don'ts" when you walk into the oral interview room. Even remembering them all will not ensure you a passing grade. Perhaps you did not have the qualifications in the first place. But remembering them will help you to put your best foot forward, without treading on the toes of the board members.

      Rumor and popular opinion to the contrary notwithstanding, an oral board wants you to make the best appearance possible. They know you are under pressure – but they also want to see how you respond to it as a guide to what your reaction would be under the pressures of the job you seek. They will be influenced by the degree of poise you display, the personal traits you show and the manner in which you respond.

ABOUT THIS BOOK

      This book contains tests divided into Examination Sections. Go through each test, answering every question in the margin. At the end of each test look at the answer key and check your answers. On the ones you got wrong, look at the right answer choice and learn. Do not fill in the answers first. Do not memorize the questions and answers, but understand the answer and principles involved. On your test, the questions will likely be different from the samples. Questions are changed and new ones added. If you understand these past questions you should have success with any changes that arise. Tests may consist of several types of questions. We have additional books on each subject should more study be advisable or necessary for you. Finally, the more you study, the better prepared you will be. This book is intended to be the last thing you study before you walk into the examination room. Prior study of relevant texts is also recommended. NLC publishes some of these in our Fundamental Series. Knowledge and good sense are important factors in passing your exam. Good luck also helps. So now study this Passbook, absorb the material contained within and take that knowledge into the examination. Then do your best to pass that exam.

———

EXAMINATION SECTION

EXAMINATION SECTION
TEST 1

DIRECTIONS: Each question or incomplete statement is followed by several suggested answers or completions. Select the one that BEST answers the question or completes the statement. *PRINT THE LETTER OF THE CORRECT ANSWER IN THE SPACE AT THE RIGHT.*

1. The cathode of a phototube is USUALLY coated with a thin layer of _____ oxide.   1._____

    A. magnesium   B. cesium   C. titanium   D. zinc

2. The capacitor on a capacitor motor is connected in _____ winding.   2._____

    A. parallel with the starting
    B. series with the running
    C. parallel with the running
    D. series with the starting

3. The refrigerant used in MOST modern home electric cooling appliances is   3._____

    A. neon   B. argon   C. zenon   D. freon

4. Splicing compound is USUALLY referred to as   4._____

    A. cable varnish   B. friction tape
    C. rubber tape   D. varnish cambric

5. The filament supports of an incandescent lamp are affixed to the   5._____

    A. button rod   B. lead-in wires
    C. steam seal   D. ceramic insulator

6. A non-tamperable fuse is known as a   6._____

    A. fusetron   B. fusetat
    C. circuit breaker   D. Kirkman tamp-lock

7. The wall plate used to cover two toggle switches mounted side by side in a wall box is known as a _____ plate.   7._____

    A. multiple toggle   B. duplex
    C. two gang   D. double

8. Building wire with a thermoplastic insulation is called type   8._____

    A. T.P.   B. R.H.   C. T.W.   D. RH-RW

9. A repulsion-start induction motor operates on   9._____

    A. 4 wire A.C.   B. single phase A.C.
    C. D.C. - 110V-220V   D. A.C. - D.C.

10. A *fish tape* is used to   10._____

    A. pull wires through a conduit   B. weatherproof a splice
    C. test a grounded circuit   D. support long cable runs

11. The color code of a 3 wire #12 cable is   11._____

    A. white black green   B. blue black red
    C. white black red   D. red white green

12. The motor that has no brushes or commutator is known as a _____ motor.   12._____

    A. split phase   B. capacitor
    C. compound   D. shunt

13. The temperature of a well-designed continuously run motor, delivering its full rated   13._____
horsepower, should NOT increase by more than _____ Fahrenheit.

    A. 40° B. 52° C. 60° D. 72°

14. A floodlight operating at a point 500 feet from the meter, wired with #14 wire whose resis-   14._____
tance is 2.575 ohms per 1000', has a voltage drop of *approximately* _____ volts.

    A. 5.7   B. 11.33   C. 12.74   D. 15.37

15. The grid in the vacuum tube was introduced by   15._____

    A. Fauere   B. Oersted   C. De Forest   D. Le Lanche

16. In an element for an electric range, the material that insulates the wire from the tube is   16._____

    A. magnesium oxide
    B. asbestos
    C. high temperature fibre glass
    D. titanium oxide

17. Most thermostats and relays that are used to activate and control a home heating system   17._____
operate on _____ volts.

    A. 6   B. 24   C. 32   D. 46

18. The revolutions per minute of an electric motor can be determined by using a(n)   18._____

    A. hydrometer   B. tachometer
    C. pulse indicator   D. prony brake

19. A record player pick-up arm, equipped with a phono cartridge that contains Rochelle-   19._____
Salts, will produce a voltage known as

    A. phono-electric   B. bio-electric
    C. piezoelectric   D. pyrometric

20. The device that controls the flow of electrons in a solid is the   20._____

    A. electron tube   B. transistor
    C. anode   D. cathode

21. Fluorescent lamps are designed to operate on   21._____

    A. the rated voltage that appears on the lamp
    B. a rectifier controlled voltage
    C. a 115 volt or 230 volt circuit
    D. a circuit where the voltage fluctuation does not exceed 5%

22. The efficiency of a 3 horsepower motor that requires 2.4 kilowatts to drive it is   22.____

    A. 74%   B. 82%   C. 90%   D. 94%

23. The magnetic resistance that opposes the flow of magnetic current is   23.____

    A. inductance   B. reluctance
    C. reactance   D. impedance

24. The output in lumens per watt for an incandescent lamp (filament type) is _____ to _____ lumens.   24.____

    A. 14; 23   B. 30; 55   C. 50; 57   D. 58; 75

25. The voltage of a battery cell depends upon   25.____

    A. the number of lines cut per second
    B. the size of the plates and the distance they are set apart
    C. material that the plate is made of and the electrolyte used
    D. area of the zinc container

26. Most window-type air conditioners, such as used in the home, are equipped with a(n) _____ motor.   26.____

    A. synchronous   B. R-I
    C. seal-vac   D. hermetically sealed

27. Light that contains only a single color and also a single wave length is known as the _____ light.   27.____

    A. spectrum   B. laser
    C. aurora   D. sodium vapor

28. The *Edison effect* led to the development of the   28.____

    A. mercury vapor lamp   B. radio tube
    C. phonograph   D. fluorescent lamp

29. A device for producing high tension induced current is the _____ coil.   29.____

    A. Ruhmkorff   B. Solenoid   C. Thury   D. Choke

30. In a triode tube, the element placed between the cathode and the plate is called   30.____

    A. rectifier   B. controlled grid
    C. S C C   D. D C C

———

KEY (CORRECT ANSWERS)

1.	B	11.	C	21.	C
2.	D	12.	A	22.	D
3.	D	13.	D	23.	B
4.	C	14.	C	24.	A
5.	A	15.	C	25.	C
6.	B	16.	A	26.	D
7.	C	17.	B	27.	B
8.	C	18.	B	28.	B
9.	B	19.	C	29.	A
10.	A	20.	B	30.	B

TEST 2

DIRECTIONS: Each question or incomplete statement is followed by several suggested answers or completions. Select the one that BEST answers the question or completes the statement. *PRINT THE LETTER OF THE CORRECT ANSWER IN THE SPACE AT THE RIGHT.*

1. A fixture hickey is used to

    A. bend pipe
    B. suspend a ceiling light
    C. make a 60° offset in BX
    D. ground a fixture

1.____

2. Nichrome wire is used in electrical heating devices because it

    A. is non-magnetic
    B. has a low melting point
    C. is cheaper than copper wire
    D. has a high resistance

2.____

3. The letters *E M T* in conduit work refer to

    A. underwriters approval
    B. thin wall conduit
    C. A.C. use only
    D. ready for first inspection

3.____

4. A 120 volt three-way incandescent lamp bulb has

    A. one filament
    B. two filaments
    C. three filaments
    D. a variable resistor

4.____

5. When an object to be copperplated is immersed in its electrolyte, it should be connected to the

    A. anode
    B. cathode
    C. right terminal
    D. electrolyte

5.____

6. A voltmeter consists of a milliammeter and a high resistance which are connected in

    A. multiple   B. parallel   C. series   D. shunt

6.____

7. A device for producing electricity directly from heat is called a

    A. turbine
    B. thermocouple
    C. transformer
    D. rheostat

7.____

8. The combined resistance of a circuit containing five 40 ohm resistances in parallel is _____ ohms.

    A. 8   B. 20   C. 40   D. 200

8.____

9. An alternator differs from a D.C. generator because it has no

    A. brushes
    B. commutator
    C. field poles
    D. rotor

9.____

10. The resistance of a wire 1/16 inch in diameter is one OHM. A wire of the same length, but twice the diameter, has a resistance of ohms.

    A. 1/4   B. 1/2   C. 1   D. 2

10.____

11. A device that measures energy consumption of electricity is called a 11.____

    A. wattmeter   B. kilowatthourmeter
    C. kilowatt meter   D. ammeter

12. A *universal* motor is a(n) _____motor. 12.____

    A. shunt   B. induction   C. series   D. synchronous

13. In a three phase, four wire, 208 volt distribution system, the voltage between any phase 13.____
wire and the neutral is _____ volts.

    A. 0   B. 120   C. 208   D. 240

14. Of the following, the motor that does NOT have a commutator is 14.____

    A. universal   B. series
    C. repulsion induction   D. split phase

15. An incandescent lamp rated at 130 volts-100 watts, and operated at 115 volts will 15.____

    A. consume more wattage and impair the life of the filament
    B. increase lamp life and reduce wattage consumed
    C. produce fewer lumens per watt and increase lamp efficiency
    D. have no effect on the lamp

16. A 2 horsepower 75% efficient D.C. motor operating at full load draws *approximately* 16.____
_____ watts.

    A. 1000   B. 1500   C. 2000   D. 3000

17. An insulating material that withstands heat better than wire with more ordinary insulation 17.____
is

    A. rubber   B. plastic
    C. rubber with cotton covering   D. varnished cambric

18. Electrical resistance can be measured with a(n) 18.____

    A. voltmeter and an ammeter   B. A.C. wattmeter
    C. thermocouple   D. induction coil

19. The property of a circuit that enables it to store electrical energy in the form of an electro- 19.____
static field is called

    A. inductance   B. reactance
    C. resistance   D. capacitance

20. If a 50 ohm resistance draws two amperes from a circuit, the power it uses is 20.____

    A. 0.2 KW   B. 25 watts
    C. 100 watts   D. none of the above

21. The world's FIRST central light and power plant was developed by   21.____

    A. Samuel F.B. Morse   B. Lee De Forest
    C. Edwin H. Armstrong   D. Thomas A. Edison

22. A *tuner* circuit consists of a   22.____

    A. zener diode and tunnel transistor
    B. capacitor and inductance coil
    C. resistor and R.F. amplifier tube
    D. resistor and capacitor

23. A hotplate having a resistance of 30 ohms, connected to a 120 volt outlet, would draw a   23.____
current of _____ amperes.

    A. 4   B. 90   C. 150   D. 3600

24. Of the following, the term that does NOT relate to magnetism is   24.____

    A. reluctance   B. oersted
    C. coulomb   D. magneto-motive force

25. A basic difference between radio waves and sound waves is that radio waves are   25.____

    A. of a different frequency   B. electrical currents
    C. molecules of air in motion   D. electromagnetic waves

26. An object that has a positive electrostatic charge would have an excess of   26.____

    A. electrons   B. protons
    C. neutrons   D. omega minus particles

27. Of the following, the statement that does NOT apply to a capacitor is that it can   27.____

    A. store electrons
    B. pass alternating current
    C. pass direct current
    D. be used to smooth out pulsating direct current

28. The section of a radio transmitter or receiver that causes a stream of electrons to vibrate   28.____
back and forth at high frequencies is known as a(n)

    A. modulator   B. oscillator   C. amplifier   D. detector

29. The separation of speech or music from a radio wave carrying music or speech is   29.____
referred to as

    A. audio filtration   B. separation
    C. demodulation   D. tracing

30. A circuit used to smooth out the surges of pulsating direct current from a rectifier is called   30.____
a

    A. filter   B. multiplexer
    C. demodulator   D. local oscillator

KEY (CORRECT ANSWERS)

1.	B	11.	B	21.	D
2.	D	12.	C	22.	B
3.	B	13.	B	23.	A
4.	B	14.	D	24.	C
5.	B	15.	B	25.	D
6.	C	16.	C	26.	B
7.	B	17.	D	27.	C
8.	A	18.	A	28.	B
9.	B	19.	D	29.	C
10.	A	20.	A	30.	A

———

TEST 3

DIRECTIONS: Each question or incomplete statement is followed by several suggested answers or completions. Select the one that BEST answers the question or completes the statement. *PRINT THE LETTER OF THE CORRECT ANSWER IN THE SPACE AT THE RIGHT.*

1. The simple motor found in an electric clock is called a(n) _____ motor.   1._____

   A. synchronous   B. induction
   C. rotor   D. D.C.

2. The amperage of a fully charged car storage battery is USUALLY near _____ amps.   2._____

   A. 10   B. 100   C. 1000   D. 10,000

3. To prevent the initial surge of current drawn by an electric motor from *burning out* the fuse in the circuit, one uses a   3._____

   A. cartridge fuse   B. circuit breaker
   C. plug fuse   D. fusetron

4. The many radio waves striking the antenna of a receiver are tuned-in with the   4._____

   A. transformer   B. choke coil
   C. variable condenser   D. diode detector

5. The starting motor of an automobile engine is shifted into mesh with the flywheel gear by a   5._____

   A. vibrator   B. solenoid
   C. bendix   D. starter button

6. The picture tube of a television set is also referred to as a _____ tube.   6._____

   A. cathode-ray   B. power beam
   C. oscilliscope   D. photo-electric

7. Generators that have two or more sets of field poles and require fewer revolutions to generate a 60-cycle-per second current are called   7._____

   A. duo-dynamos   B. vibrators
   C. poly-phase generators   D. alternators

8. A bar that has been artificially magnetized can be demagnetized by   8._____

   A. quenching it in hot oil
   B. pounding it with a heavy hammer
   C. bending it into a *U* shape
   D. wrapping it in insulating tape

9. The part of a generator which determines if it is a direct current generator is the   9._____

   A. stator   B. field   C. commutator   D. brush

10. The term which refers to pressure or force in electric current is   10._____

   A. amperage   B. voltage   C. ohms   D. electrons

11. Nichrome wire is MOST likely to be found in a(n) 11.____

    A. T.V. circuit   B. electric motor
    C. electric clock   D. electric heater

12. Electromagnetic waves are changed into pulses capable of producing sound waves in a 12.____
radio by means of a

    A. transformer   B. speaker
    C. detector   D. oscillator

13. The SIMPLEST form of electronic tube is called 13.____

    A. cathode   B. diode   C. plate   D. triode

14. Of the following, the one that is NOT a part of a radio tube is the 14.____

    A. envelope   B. plate   C. condenser   D. filament

15. The speed of a simple electric motor can be controlled with the use of a 15.____

    A. variable resistor   B. electrolytic condenser
    C. variable condenser   D. prony-brake

16. A single wet cell can be made from a copper penny and a *zinc* penny attached to two 16.____
copper leads immersed in

    A. mineral oil   B. salt-water solution
    C. distilled water   D. chromate of soda

17. The MINIMUM gauge wire for house circuits should be 17.____

    A. 10   B. 18   C. 14   D. 22

18. The safety device used in a house wiring circuit to protect against an overload is a 18.____

    A. circuit breaker   B. knife switch
    C. cut-off   D. mercury switch

19. To prevent the generator from burning out at high speeds, the battery circuit of the auto- 19.____
mobile employs a

    A. choke coil   B. variable resistor
    C. voltage regulator   D. current trap

20. An interrupted current of 6 volts flows in the primary circuit of an induction coil of 100 20.____
turns of wire. If the secondary coil has 1,000 turns, the theoretical voltage output is

    A. .6   B. 60   C. 600   D. .06

21. A 200 watt bulb in a 100 volt circuit uses _____ampere(s). 21.____

    A. .2   B. .02   C. 2   D. 20

22. A 220 volt air conditioner drawing 15 amperes of current operates 10 hours a day. The 22.____
total cost of operation for four weeks at the rate of 4 cents per kilowatt hour would be

    A. $18.48   B. $55.44   C. $26.40   D. $36.96

23. If a dry cell battery is capable of supplying a force of two volts and ten amperes of current, connecting five such batteries in parallel will result in a total capacity of _____ volts with _____ amperes.

    A. 2; 50   B. 20; 10   C. 10; 50   D. 10; 10

23.____

24. To calculate the number of turns of wire needed to make a step-up or step-down transformer when the voltages are known, and one set of windings is determined, we use the following formula:

    A. $\dfrac{\text{Primary turns}}{\text{Secondary turns}} = \dfrac{\text{Primary volts}}{\text{Secondary volts}}$

    B. $\dfrac{\text{Primary turns}}{\text{Primary volts}} = \dfrac{\text{Secondary volts}}{\text{Secondary turns}}$

    C. $\dfrac{\text{Primary turns}}{\text{Secondary volts}} = \dfrac{\text{Primary volts}}{\text{Secondary turns}}$

    D. $\dfrac{\text{Primary turns}}{\text{Secondary volts}} = \dfrac{\text{Primary volts}}{\text{Secondary turns}}$

24.____

25. To measure the specific gravity of the contents of a storage battery, one uses a

    A. hygrometer   B. galvanometer
    C. ammeter   D. hydrometer

25.____

26. Lightning is _____electricity.

    A. induced   B. ionized   C. static   D. magnetic

26.____

27. A lodestone is related to

    A. magnetism   B. resistance
    C. conductivity   D. reluctance

27.____

28. The term related to a storer of electricity is

    A. milliampere   B. microfarad
    C. megohm   D. microvolt

28.____

29. The thermostat as a switch employs the use of a

    A. diode tube   B. tungsten filament
    C. bimetallic strip   D. thermocouple

29.____

30. In servicing electrical apparatus, it is necessary to know the values of amperage, voltage, and resistance. When two of the factors are known, the third may be found by applying *Ohm's Law*.
    Of the following formulas, the one that does NOT apply is

    A. I = R/E   B. R = E/I   C. E = IR   D. I = E/R

30.____

─────────

KEY (CORRECT ANSWERS)

1.	A	11.	D	21.	C
2.	B	12.	C	22.	D
3.	D	13.	B	23.	A
4.	C	14.	C	24.	A
5.	B	15.	A	25.	D
6.	A	16.	B	26.	C
7.	D	17.	C	27.	A
8.	B	18.	A	28.	B
9.	C	19.	C	29.	C
10.	B	20.	B	30.	A

———

TEST 4

DIRECTIONS: Each question or incomplete statement is followed by several suggested answers or completions. Select the one that BEST answers the question or completes the statement. *PRINT THE LETTER OF THE CORRECT ANSWER IN THE SPACE AT THE RIGHT.*

1. The effect of a capacitor on direct current is to _____ it.   1._____

    A. modulate   B. block
    C. pass   D. demodulate

2. Factors which determine the resistance of a wire are: 2._____

    A. Diameter, insulating material, length, strands
    B. Length, diameter, material, temperature
    C. Material, light factor, pressure, circumference
    D. Pressure, magnetism, binding, length

3. Current flow in a triode vacuum tube may be controlled by the   3._____

    A. plate and the grid   B. filament and the plate
    C. grid and the heater   D. cathode and the filament

4. If the resistance in a parallel circuit is *increased,* the voltage drop across a resistor would   4._____

    A. *increase*   B. vary proportionally
    C. *decrease*   D. remain the same

5. In parallel and series circuits, current is   5._____

    A. inversely proportional to resistance and directly proportional to voltage
    B. directly proportional to resistance and inversely proportional to voltage
    C. not affected by voltage
    D. not affected by resistance

6. The process of mixing audio waves with radio waves is called   6._____

    A. rectification   B. attenuation
    C. modulation   D. superimposition

7. Transistors are made of three parts: a base, a collector, and an emitter. When compared to a vacuum tube, the collector is comparable to the   7._____

    A. grid   B. plate   C. cathode   D. filament

8. Resistance wire used in electrical appliances is *usually* an alloy of   8._____

    A. tungsten, chromium, brass
    B. nickel, chromium, iron
    C. copper, nickel, tungsten
    D. iron, copper, molybdenum

9. A meter with terminals connected in series and across the line is a   9._____

    A. voltmeter   B. ammeter   C. ohmmeter   D. wattmeter

10. One hundred volts will push _____milliamperes through 20k ohms of resistance.   10._____

    A. 2   B. 5   C. 50   D. 2000

11. A resistor having bands of orange, red, yellow, and silver would have a resistance value of _____ ohms.   11.____

    A. 32k   B. 320k   C. 2.3 meg   D. 43 meg

12. A flashbulb used for photographic purposes contains   12.____

    A. aluminum and oxygen   B. tungsten and helium
    C. aluminum and hydrogen   D. tungsten and argon

13. A generator having a cummutator produces _____ current.   13.____

    A. alternating   B. direct
    C. synchronous   D. modulating

14. A step-down transformer has 1,200 turns on the primary. 90 volts is applied to the primary, and the second is to produce 15 volts.   14.____
How many turns should be wound on the secondary?

    A. 200   B. 600   C. 7,200   D. 108,000

15. In a radio circuit, a transformer CANNOT be used to   15.____

    A. step-up a-c voltage
    B. isolate part of a circuit
    C. step-down d-c voltage
    D. couple part of a circuit to another

16. A transformer has 200 turns of #14 wire wound on primary and 1,000 turns of #14 wire wound on the secondary.   16.____
A voltmeter attached to the secondary terminals would indicate _____ volts if 50 volts were attached to the primary.

    A. 0   B. 10   C. 250   D. 600

17. Service entrance cable for the typical home is usually made up of three wires. The *hot* wires are usually No.   17.____

    A. 4 or No. 6   B. 8 or No. 10
    C. 12 or No. 14   D. 16 or No. 18

18. In the PNP type transistor, the collector is *normally*   18.____

    A. negative   B. positive
    C. shorted out   D. not needed

19. In a beam power tube, the screen grid is   19.____

    A. the plate   B. positive
    C. the suppressor   D. negative

20. A silicon controlled rectifier is   20.____

    A. a nuvistor   B. a CRT
    C. thermally operated   D. a semi-conductor

21. In copper plating a metallic object, it should be placed at the   21.____

     A.   anode   B.   switch   C.   cathode   D.   electrolyte

22. At five cents per kilowatt hour, a 100-watt lamp which is operated for one hundred (100)   22.____
     hours would use energy that would cost

     A.   5 cents   B.   less than 10 cents
     C.   50 cents   D.   5 dollars

23. A galvanometer may be converted to a voltmeter by adding a   23.____

     A.   shunt in series   B.   multiplier in series
     C.   multiplier in parallel   D.   shunt in parallel

24. The counter emf of an inductance coil is measured in   24.____

     A.   milliamperes   B.   microfarads
     C.   henrys   D.   millivolts

25. A fluorescent lamp lights when the   25.____

     A.   ballast coil produces a high-voltage charge
     B.   starter switch is placed in parallel with the filament
     C.   mercury forms minute droplets on the filament
     D.   ballast changes the A.C. to D.C. in the tube

26. The electrolyte used in a dry cell is composed of   26.____

     A.   carbon, magnesium oxide, ammonia, sodium chloride
     B.   sodium, manganese dioxide, alumina, zinc sulphate
     C.   carbon, manganese dioxide, sal ammoniac, zinc chloride
     D.   sodium, magnesium sulphate, arsenic, zinc oxide

27. A variable capacitor has its capacitance *increased* when the   27.____

     A.   plates are open
     B.   rotor is attached to the stator
     C.   plates are meshed
     D.   dielectric is given a full charge

28. The gas mixture commonly used in incandescent lamps is   28.____

     A.   nitrogen and argon   B.   nitrogen and helium
     C.   helium and argon   D.   hydrogen and oxygen

29. A motor with a high-starting torque and rapid acceleration is a(n) _____ motor.   29.____

     A.   D.C. shunt wound   B.   D.C. series wound
     C.   A.C. synchronous   D.   A.C. split phase

30. Bry cells used for powering cordless electric razors are usually _____ cells.   30.____

     A.   manganese alkaline   B.   nickel cadmium
     C.   nickel silver   D.   zinc carbon

KEY (CORRECT ANSWERS)

1.	B	11.	B	21.	C
2.	B	12.	A	22.	C
3.	A	13.	B	23.	B
4.	D	14.	A	24.	C
5.	A	15.	C	25.	A
6.	C	16.	A	26.	C
7.	B	17.	A	27.	C
8.	B	18.	A	28.	A
9.	D	19.	B	29.	B
10.	B	20.	D	30.	B

———

EXAMINATION SECTION
TEST 1

DIRECTIONS: Each question or incomplete statement is followed by several suggested answers or completions. Select the one that BEST answers the question or completes the statement. *PRINT THE LETTER OF THE CORRECT ANSWER IN THE SPACE AT THE RIGHT.*

1. A piece of No. 1/0 emery cloth should be used to sand the commutator of a D.C. dynamo   1._____

    A. when there is sparking at the brushes
    B. under no conditions
    C. when the commutator has a "chocolate" color
    D. only when the commutator has ridges

2. Compound D.C. generators connected in parallel are *generally* provided with   2._____

    A. 3 brushes   B. an equalizer
    C. no voltage relays   D. armature resistors

3. As compared with other types of A.C. motors, the advantage of the squirrel cage motor lies in its   3._____

    A. high starting torque   B. high power factor
    C. constant speed   D. simplicity

4. A counter E.M.F. starter is so named because   4._____

    A. the accelerating contactor has a high counter E.M.F.
    B. the accelerating relay depends upon the armature terminal voltage for operation
    C. it is used only on motors that build up a high C.E.M.F.
    D. it stops the motor by means of C.E.M.F.

5. There shall NOT be more than _____ quarter bends or their equivalent from outlet to outlet in rigid conduit.   5._____

    A. 3   B. 4   C. 5   D. 6

6. Armored cable may be imbedded in masonry in buildings under construction *provided*   6._____

    A. it is type AC   B. it is fastened securely
    C. it is type ACL   D. special permission is obtained

7. An armature core is laminated in order to reduce   7._____

    A. hysteresis loss   B. eddy current loss
    C. hysteresis and eddy current loss   D. impedance loss

8. The MOST efficient size of the "white" fluorescent lamps is   8._____

    A. 15 watts   B. 30 watts   C. 40 watts   D. 100 watts

9. Condensers are placed in parallel with fluorescent glow switches in order to   9._____

    A. reduce radio interference   B. reduce the arc
    C. compensate the power factor   D. increase the lamp life

10. The SMALLEST size wire that may be used on fire alarm systems is No. _____   10.____

    A. 18   B. 16   C. 14   D. 12

11. Under the National Electric Code, a 3-way switch is classified as a(n)   11.____

    A. single pole switch   B. double pole switch
    C. 3-way switch   D. electrolier switch

12. A capacitor start-and-run motor may be reversed by reversing the   12.____

    A. running and starting capacitor leads
    B. main winding leads
    C. line leads
    D. centrifugal switch leads

13. Opening a series field circuit while a compound motor is operating, will cause   13.____

    A. the motor to stop   B. no noticeable change
    C. the motor to race   D. the motor to slow down

14. Transformers for neon signs shall have a secondary voltage NOT exceeding   14.____

    A. 10,000 volts   B. 15,000 volts
    C. 20,000 volts   D. 25,000 volts

15. A capacitor of 10 ohms reactance and zero ohms resistance is connected in series with   15.____
an inductance of 7 ohms reactance and 4 ohms resistance. The total impedance is

    A. 5 ohms   B. 7 ohms   C. 17 ohms   D. 21 ohms

16. The BEST way to start a large shunt motor is with a   16.____

    A. strong field   B. weak field
    C. rheostat in series with the armature and the field
    D. starting compensator.

17. If an A.C. motor draws 50 amps., full load, the thermal cutout should be set at   17.____

    A. 75 amps.   B. 50 amps.   C. 62.5 amps.   D. 75 amps.

18. Using 1:1 ratio transformers at a given primary voltage, the HIGHEST secondary voltage   18.____
may be obtained by connecting them

    A. Wye primary and Delta secondary
    B. Delta primary and Delta secondary
    C. Wye primary and Wye secondary
    D. Delta primary and Wye secondary

19. In an A.C. fire alarm system, the number of gongs allowed on a circuit is   19.____

    A. 10   B. 12   C. 14   D. 20

20. Appliance branch circuit wires shall be NO smaller than No.   20.____

    A. 8   B. 10   C. 12   D. 14

21. A current of 2 amperes in a resistor of 10 ohms will use electrical energy at the rate of _____ watts.

    A. 10   B. 20   C. 40   D. 80

21.____

22. 20-, 40-, and 50-ohm resistances are connected in series across a 110-volt D.C. supply; the current through the 20-ohm resistance is

    A. 5.5 amperes   B. 1 ampere   C. 2.2 ampers   D. 2.75 amperes

22.____

23. An electric circuit has four resistances of 20,6,30, and 12 ohms in parallel with each other. The combined resistance, in ohms, is

    A. 300   B. 30   C. 3   D. .3

23.____

24. The load for general illumination in apartment and multifamily dwellings is based on

    A. 1 1/2 watts per square foot of floor area
    B. 2 watts per square foot of floor area
    C. 3 watts per square foot of floor area
    D. 4 watts per square foot of floor area

24.____

25. Ventilation of battery rooms is necessary to

    A. keep the batteries cool
    B. prevent accumulation of explosive gases
    C. prevent deterioration of insulation
    D. supply oxygen to the room

25.____

KEYS (CORRECT ANSWERS)

1. B	11. A
2. B	12. B
3. D	13. A
4. B	14. B
5. B	15. A
6. C	16. A
7. B	17. C
8. C	18. D
9. A	19. A
10. C	20. C

21. B
22. B
23. C
24. B
25. B

TEST 2

DIRECTIONS: Each question or incomplete statement is followed by several suggested answers or completions. Select the one that BEST answers the question or completes the statement. *PRINT THE LETTER OF THE CORRECT ANSWER IN THE SPACE AT THE RIGHT.*

1. Dynamic braking is obtained in a motor by means of   1._____

    A. a magnetic brake
    B. a resistance connected across the armature after the current is disconnected
    C. reversing the armature
    D. reversing the field

2. The reason for using flux when soldering splices is to   2._____

    A. lower the melting point of the solder
    B. cause the joint to heat rapidly
    C. reduce the oxide on the wires
    D. prevent corrosion of the wires after soldering

3. A good ammeter should have   3._____

    A. very high resistance   B. very low resistance
    C. low resistance   D. high resistance

4. A good voltmeter should have   4._____

    A. very high resistance   B. very low resistance
    C. low resistance   D. high resistance

5. The MOST efficient type of polyphase motor to install for a large, slow speed, direct con-   5._____
   nected machine would be a

    A. wound rotor induction motor
    B. squirrel cage induction motor
    C. synchronous motor
    D. high torque induction motor

6. Mercury is added to the gas in a neon tube in order to produce the color   6._____

    A. gold   B. blue   C. white   D. red

7. An electromotive force will be built up in a conductor if it is moving   7._____

    A. in the same direction as magnetic lines of force
    B. in the opposite direction
    C. at right angles to the lines of force
    D. in any direction

8. The BEST choice of an A.C. motor to produce a high starting torque would be a   8._____

    A. synchronous motor   B. split phase motor
    C. shaded pole motor   D. wound rotor induction motor

9. The speed of a squirrel cage motor may be reduced by   9.____

    A. inserting a line resistance
    B. inserting a line reactance
    C. increasing the number of poles
    D. decreasing the number of poles

10. Three-point starting boxes provide for   10.____

    A. speed regulation   B. no field release
    C. no voltage release   D. phase reversal

11. If the #10 wire feeding a circuit were replaced with a #7 wire, the voltage drop would be reduced, *approximately,*   11.____

    A. 100%   B. 33%   C. 66%   D. 50%

12. Theatre footlight and border light branch circuits shall be so wired that in NO case will they carry *more than* _____ amperes.   12.____

    A. 10   B. 14   C. 20   D. 25

13. Which of the following is the outstanding feature of the Edison storage battery?   13.____

    A. A continued short circuit will not ruin the battery
    B. The lead plates are smaller
    C. It has a greater voltage output per cell
    D. It is less expensive than the automobile lead storage battery

14. An impedance coil is connected into a telephone circuit in the   14.____

    A. ringing circuit   B. talking circuit
    C. ringing and talking circuit
    D. secondary side of the induction coil

15. An electro reset annunciator has   15.____

    A. two coils per figure   B. one coil per figure
    C. one coil and one permanent magnet   D. manual reset arrangement

16. Locking relays may be used in   16.____

    A. open circuit burglar alarm systems only
    B. closed circuit burglar alarm systems only
    C. any type of burglar alarm system
    D. no burglar alarm system

17. The unit or electrical inductance is the   17.____

    A. henry   B. farad   C. joule   D. mho

18. The method used in calculating the total of resistances in series is NEAREST to that used in calculating   18.____

    A. condensers in series   B. inductances in parallel
    C. condensers in parallel   D. impedances in parallel

19. If 36,000 joules of work produce 5 amperes of current between two points for 60 seconds, what is the difference of potential between the two points, in volts?

    A. 600   B. 400   C. 120   D. 100

19.____

20. To measure a circuit current of 300 amps with a 100 amp ammeter, the shunt MUST have a MINIMUM capacity of _____ amps.

    A. 100   B. 200   C. 300   D. 400

20.____

21. A D.C. motor field coil connected first across a D.C. line and then across an A.C. line of equal voltage, will draw

    A. more current on D.C. than A.C.
    B. less current on D.C. than A.C.
    C. the same current on D.C. as on A.C.
    D. no current on A.C.

21.____

22. The single phase A.C. motor that produces the WEAKEST starting torque is the

    A. series A.C. motor   B. repulsion motor
    C. split phase motor   D. shaded pole motor

22.____

23. The D.C. generator whose terminal voltage falls off MOST rapidly when loaded is the _____ type.

    A. shunt   B. flat-compounded
    C. over-compounded   D. series

23.____

24. The E.M.F. produced by a primary cell depends on the

    A. size of the elements   B. amount of electrolyte
    C. distance between the elements
    D. materials used for the elements

24.____

25. A D.C. circuit consisting of 5 lamps in parallel draws 5 amperes; the current in *each* lamp is

    A. 1 ampere   B. 5 amperes
    C. determined by the resistance of the lamp
    D. 1/5 of an ampere

25.____

KEY (CORRECT ANSWERS)

1.	B		11.	D
2.	C		12.	B
3.	B		13.	A
4.	A		14.	B
5.	C		15.	A
6.	B		16.	C
7.	C		17.	A
8.	D		18.	C
9.	C		19.	C
10.	B		20.	B

21.	A
22.	D
23.	A
24.	D
25.	C

———

TEST 3

DIRECTIONS: Each question or incomplete statement is followed by several suggested answers or completions. Select the one that BEST answers the question or completes the statement. *PRINT THE LETTER OF THE CORRECT ANSWER IN THE SPACE AT THE RIGHT.*

1. It is good practice to install a polarity reversing switch on a direct current fluorescent circuit to

    A. lessen ends blackening
    B. prevent one end from becoming dim
    C. ease starting
    D. prevent radio interference

1.____

2. A 40-watt fluorescent lamp with necessary equipment may be satisfactorily operated from a direct current source of

    A. 110 volts   B. 220 volts
    C. either voltage   D. corrected power factor

2.____

3. The National Electric Code provides that residential apartments be provided with receptacle outlets for *every* _____ feet of lineal wall space.

    A. 10   B. 15   C. 20   D. 25

3.____

4. If a person is rendered unconscious by an electric shock, one should break the electrical contact, call a physician, *and*

    A. make patient comfortable until physician arrives
    B. use prone-pressure method of resuscitation
    C. administer a stimulant
    D. rub patient's body to increase circulation

4.____

5. A 1 1/2" x 4" octagonal box may contain a MAXIMUM of

    A. 5 #14 conductors   B. 7 #14 conductors
    C. 8 #14 conductors   D. 11 #14 conductors

5.____

6. A 1 1/2" x 4" square box may contain a MAXIMUM of

    A. 5 #14 conductors   B. 7 #14 conductors
    C. 8 #14 conductors   D. 11 #14 conductors

6.____

7. Damaged cords for power tools should be

    A. coated with flux and covered with rubber tape
    B. repaired with insulating tape
    C. replaced
    D. shortened to remove the damaged section

7.____

8. A source of direct current connected to a vibrating bell in series with the primary of an induction coil, will cause the secondary coil to produce

    A. alternating current   B. direct current
    C. pulsating direct current   D. interrupted direct current

8.____

9. Switches and attachment plugs installed in garages shall be AT LEAST _____ above the floor.

    A. 1 foot   B. 2 feet   C. 3 feet, 6 inches   D. 4 feet

9.____

10. Rigid conduit used for electrical wiring is purchased in

    A. 10 feet lengths, including coupling
    B. 10 feet lengths
    C. 9'6" lengths
    D. no standard lengths

10.____

11. Switches controlling signs shall be placed

    A. at the service equipment
    B. in the office of the premises displaying the sign
    C. within sight of the sign
    D. at the main entrance to the building

11.____

12. A self-excited alternator has

    A. slip rings for the field excitation
    B. a storage battery for the field
    C. a winding connected to the commutator
    D. no coil for direct current

12.____

13. A copper wire twice the diameter of another has a carrying capacity of _____ as great.

    A. two times   B. one-half   C. four times   D. eight times

13.____

14. The resistance of a copper bus bar is

    A. directly proportional to its length
    B. inversely proportional to its length
    C. negligible
    D. higher than that of gold

14.____

15. The resistance of a conductor depends upon the material it is made of *and*

    A. its temperature   B. where it is used
    C. the ambient temperature   D. method of installation

15.____

16. The positive terminal of an unmarked lead storage battery can *often* be identified by

    A. being larger than the negative
    B. being smaller than the negative
    C. removing the filling caps and looking at the plates
    D. using a "Y" box

16.____

17. The discharge voltage of an Edison storage cell is _____ volt(s).   17.____

    A. 1   B. 1.2   C. 2   D. 6

18. Voltmeters *often* have   18.____

    A. external shunts in parallel   B. internal shunts
    C. internal resistance coils   D. low resistance shunts

19. Selsyn motors are used   19.____

    A. to operate clocks from a direct current source
    B. at repeater stations
    C. as a generator for cathode ray tubes
    D. to charge storage batteries

20. The secondary of a current transformer   20.____

    A. is always opened with a connected load
    B. is never used with meters
    C. cannot be used on alternating current
    D. should never be opened while primary is energized

21. Circline is a development in   21.____

    A. fluorescent lighting   B. raceways
    C. incandescent lighting   D. insulating material

22. Neon signs operate on   22.____

    A. low voltage-high current   B. high current-high voltage
    C. high voltage-low current   D. low voltage-low current

23. Thermo electricity can be generated by heat applied to   23.____

    A. glass between two layers of aluminum foil
    B. two dissimilar metals
    C. two similar metals
    D. two lead plates in an electrolyte

24. To determine the power in a two-phase lighting and power system, the proper formula to   24.____
use would be:

    A. $KW = \dfrac{E \times I \times PF}{1000}$ B. $KW = 1.73 \times E \times I \times PF \times 1000$

    C. $KW = \dfrac{\sqrt{2} \times E \times I \times PF}{1000}$ D. $KW = \dfrac{1.42 \times E \times W \times PF}{1000}$

25. An electric toaster operating on 120 volts has a resistance (hot) of 15 ohms. The wattage   25.____
of the toaster is

    A. 1200   B. 1140   C. 1080   D. 960

KEY (CORRECT ANSWERS)

1.	B	11.	C
2.	B	12.	C
3.	C	13.	C
4.	B	14.	A
5.	C	15.	A
6.	C	16.	A
7.	C	17.	B
8.	A	18.	C
9.	D	19.	B
10.	A	20.	D

21.	A
22.	C
23.	B
24.	C
25.	D

TEST 4

DIRECTIONS: Each question or incomplete statement is followed by several suggested answers or completions. Select the one that BEST answers the question or completes the statement. *PRINT THE LETTER OF THE CORRECT ANSWER IN THE SPACE AT THE RIGHT.*

1. When using lead cable, the inner radius of the bend shall be *no less than* _____ times the internal diameter of the conduit.

    A. four   B. six   C. eight   D. ten

    1._____

2. A telephone hook switch is similar in operation to a

    A. strop key   B. locking type push button
    C. locking type relay   D. two circuit electrolier switch

    2._____

3. The "dielectric" of a condenser is the

    A. air surrounding the condenser
    B. material separating the plates
    C. voltage impressed on the condenser
    D. lines of force established by the current

    3._____

4. The depolarizing substance in the dry cell is

    A. manganese dioxide   B. ammonium chloride
    C. zinc chloride   D. lead oxide

    4._____

5. The SMALLEST wattage fluorescent lamp manufactured for home use is

    A. 6   B. 8   C. 9   D. 15

    5._____

6. The Carter system of connecting three-way switches for lighting

    A. will not operate lamps in parallel
    B. is not permitted under the National Electric Code
    C. will not operate when used in conjunction with a pilot light
    D. will not operate lamps in series

    6._____

7. The material offering the LEAST resistance to the flow of an electric current is

    A. iron   B. aluminum   C. German silver   D. zinc

    7._____

8. To replace a four-way switch, we may use the following type:

    A. Double pole snap   B. Double pole, double throw
    C. Three-circuit electrolier   D. Three-way switch

    8._____

9. The LARGEST size conductor permitted in surface metal raceways is No.

    A. 10   B. 8   C. 6   D. 4

    9._____

10. The energy accumulated in a storage battery is

    A. electrical   B. chemical   C. kinetic   D. mechanical

    10._____

11. A strop key is MOST similar in operation to the following switch: 11.____

    A. Double pole   B. Three-way
    C. Four-way   D. Two circuit electrolier

12. Compensators are used to start motors at 12.____

    A. reduced voltage   B. reduced speed
    C. reduced load   D. increased voltage

13. A self-excited D.C. shunt generator is operating properly in clockwise rotation. If the direction of rotation is reversed, the 13.____

    A. brush polarity will reverse
    B. field polarity will reverse
    C. generator will fail to build up voltage
    D. output voltage will be the same in magnitude

14. If the intake port on an oil burner blower were closed, the motor would 14.____

    A. slow down   B. require more current
    C. heat up   D. require less current

15. In the event of a burnout of one single-phase transformer on a 3-phase, Wye-connected system, you can 15.____

    A. connect the remaining two in "delta"
    B. connect the remaining two "Scott"
    C. connect the remaining two "Open Wye"
    D. not connect them to obtain 3-phase with same voltage

16. The short circuited coil imbedded in the pole face of an A.C. contactor is used to 16.____

    A. blow out the arc   B. reduce residual magnetism
    C. close the contactor   D. reduce noise and vibration

17. A motor that is built for plugging service 17.____

    A. has a built-in brake
    B. helps to compensate power factor
    C. may be connected in reverse from full speed forward
    D. has built-in reduction gears

18. Eleven #14 conductors are permitted in a 1" conduit 18.____

    A. in apartment house risers   B. under all conditions
    C. at no time
    D. for conductors between a motor and its controller

19. The number of mogul sockets on a two-wire branch circuit shall NOT exceed 19.____

    A. 8   B. 7   C. 6   D. 5

20. A 1 1/2" x 3 1/4" octagonal box may contain a MAXIMUM of 20.____

    A. 5 #14 conductors   B. 7 #14 conductors
    C. 8 #14 conductors   D. 11 #14 conductors

21. The average value of an alternating current is equal to its MAXIMUM value *times*   21.____

    A. 1.7232   B. .707   C. .636   D. 1.41

22. In a D.C. fire alarm system, the number of gongs allowed on a circuit is   22.____

    A. 10   B. 12   C. 13   D. 20

23. If the total resistance of the wire wound on a bipolar armature is 2 ohms, the armature   23.____
resistance is _____ ohm(s).

    A. 1   B. 2   C. 1/2   D. 4

24. Increasing the field excitation of a synchronous motor will cause the   24.____

    A. motor to speed up   B. motor to slow down
    C. current to lead   D. voltage to lead

25. Mercury rectifiers have   25.____

    A. mercury anodes   B. the positive terminal at the cathode
    C. high tank pressure   D. one anode always

KEY (CORRECT ANSWERS)

1. D		11. B	
2. A		12. A	
3. B		13. C	
4. A		14. C	
5. A		15. C	
6. B		16. B	
7. B		17. C	
8. B		18. D	
9. C		19. B	
10. B		20. C	

21. C
22. C
23. C
24. B
25. C

EXAMINATION SECTION
TEST 1

DIRECTIONS: Each question or incomplete statement is followed by several suggested answers or completions. Select the one that BEST answers the question or completes the statement. *PRINT THE LETTER OF THE CORRECT ANSWER IN THE SPACE AT THE RIGHT.*

Questions 1-8.

DIRECTIONS: Questions 1 through 8 involve tests on the fuse box arrangement shown below. All tests are to be performed with a neon tester or a lamp test bank consisting of two 6-watt, 120-volt lamps connected in series. Do not make any assumptions about the conditions of the circuits. Draw your conclusions only from the information obtained with the neon tester or the two-lamp test bank, applied to the circuits as called for.

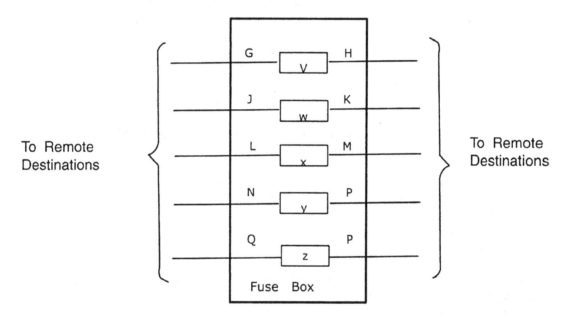

1. The two lamp test bank is placed from point G to joint J, and both lamps light. One of the lamps is momentarily removed from its socket; during that instant, the other lamp in the series-connected test bank should

    A. go dark
    B. get dimmer
    C. remain at same brightness
    D. get brighter

1.____

2. The test bank with two 60-watt, 120-volt lamps in series should be used on circuits with

    A. wattages only from 60 to 120 watts
    B. wattages only from 0 to 120 watts
    C. voltages only from 120 to 240 volts
    D. voltages only from 0 to 240 volts

2.____

3. The neon tester is placed from point G to point J and only one-half of the neon tester lights.   3.____
 It should be concluded that

     A. half of the tester has gone bad
     B. a wire has become disconnected in the circuit
     C. the voltage is AC
     D. the voltage is DC

4. If both lamps in the test bank light when placed directly across one of the above fuses, it should be concluded that   4.____

     A. the fuse is good
     B. the fuse is blown
     C. the fuse is overrated
     D. further tests have to be made to determine the condition of the fuse

5. If the lamp test bank does not light when placed directly across one of the above fuses, it should be concluded that   5.____

     A. the fuse is good
     B. the fuse is blown
     C. the fuse is overrated
     D. further tests have to be made to determine the condition of the fuse

6. The lamp test bank lights when placed from point G to point J but does not light when placed from point H to point J.   6.____
 It should be concluded that

     A. the wire to point H has become disconnected
     B. the wire to point J has become disconnected
     C. fuse v is bad
     D. fuse w is bad

7. The lamp test bank lights when placed from point L to point N but does not light when placed from point M to point P.   7.____
 It should be concluded that

     A. both fuses x and y are bad
     B. either fuse x or fuse y is bad or both are bad
     C. both fuses x and y are good
     D. these tests do not indicate the condition of any fuse

8. The lamp test bank is placed from point L to point N, then from N to point Q, and finally from point L to point Q. In each case, both lamps light to full brightness.   8.____
 It should be concluded that points L, N, and Q have

     A. three-phase, 120 volts, AC, line-to-line
     B. plus and minus 120 volts, DC
     C. three-phase, 208 volts, AC
     D. plus and minus 240 volts, DC

9. The resistance of a copper wire to the flow of electricity _____ as the _____ of the wire _____.   9.____

    A. increases; diameter; increases
    B. decreases; diameter; decreases
    C. decreases; length; increases
    D. increases; length; increases

10. Where galvanized steel conduit is used, the PRIMARY purpose of the galvanizing is to   10.____

    A. increase mechanical strength
    B. retard rusting
    C. provide a good surface for painting
    D. provide good electrical contact for grounding

11. The lamps used for station and tunnel lighting in subways are generally operated at slightly less than their rated voltage.
The LOGICAL reason for this is to   11.____

    A. prevent overloading of circuits
    B. increase the life of the lamps
    C. decrease glare
    D. obtain a more even distribution of light

12. The CORRECT method of measuring the power taken by an AC electric motor is to use a   12.____

    A. wattmeter   B. voltmeter and an ammeter
    C. power factor meter   D. tachometer

13. Wood ladders should NOT be painted because the paint may   13.____

    A. deteriorate the wood   B. make ladders slippery
    C. be inflammable   D. cover cracks or defects

14. Goggles would be LEAST necessary when   14.____

    A. recharging soda-acid fire extinguishers
    B. chipping stone
    C. putting electrolyte into an Edison battery
    D. scraping rubber insulation from a wire

15. The number and type of precautions to be taken on a job generally depend LEAST on the   15.____

    A. nature of the job
    B. length of time the job is expected to last
    C. kind of tools and materials being used
    D. location of the work

16. When training workers in the use of tools and equipment, safety precautions related to their use should be FIRST mentioned   16.____

    A. in the introductory training session before the workers begin to use the equipment or tools
    B. during training sessions when workers practice operating the tools or equipment

C. after the workers are qualified to use the equipment in their daily tasks
D. when an agency safety bulletin related to the tools and equipment is received

17. Artificial respiration should be started immediately on a man who has suffered an electric shock if he is   17.____

A. *unconscious* and breathing
B. *unconscious* and not breathing
C. *conscious* and in a daze
D. *conscious* and badly burned

18. The fuse of a certain circuit has blown and is replaced with a fuse of the same rating which also blows when the switch is closed.
In this case,   18.____

A. a fuse of higher current rating should be used
B. a fuse of higher voltage rating should be used
C. the fuse should be temporarily replaced by a heavy piece of wire
D. the circuit should be checked

19. Operating an incandescent electric light bulb at less than its rated voltage will result in   19.____

A. shorter life and brighter light
B. longer life and dimmer light
C. brighter light and longer life
D. dimmer light and shorter life

20. In order to control a lamp from two different positions, it is necessary to use   20.____

A. two single pole switches
B. one single pole switch and one four-way switch
C. two three-way switches
D. one single pole switch and one four-way switch

21. One method of testing fuses is to connect a pair of test lamps in the circuit in
such a manner that the test lamp will light
up if the fuse is good and will remain dark
if the fuse is bad. In the illustration at the
right, 1 and 2 are fuses.
In order to test if fuse 1 is bad, test
lamps should be connected between   21.____

A. A and B
B. B and D
C. A and D
D. C and B

22. The PRINCIPAL reason for the grounding of electrical equipment and circuits is to   22.____

A. prevent short circuits   B. insure safety from shock
C. save power   D. increase voltage

23. An interlock is generally installed on electronic equipment to   23.____

    A. prevent loss of power
    B. maintain VHF frequencies
    C. keep the vacuum tubes lit
    D. prevent electric shock during maintenance operations

24. A flame should not be used to inspect the electrolyte level in a lead-acid battery because   24.____
the battery cells give off highly flammable

    A. hydrogen   B. lead oxide
    C. lithium   D. xenon

25. The purpose of the third prong in a three-prong male electric plug used in a 120 volt cir-   25.____
cuit is to

    A. make a firm connection   B. strengthen the plug
    C. ground to prevent shock   D. act as a transducer

—————

KEY (CORRECT ANSWERS)

1.	A		11.	B
2.	D		12.	A
3.	D		13.	D
4.	B		14.	D
5.	D		15.	B
6.	C		16.	A
7.	B		17.	B
8.	C		18.	D
9.	D		19.	B
10.	B		20.	C

21.	C
22.	B
23.	D
24.	A
25.	C

—————

TEST 2

DIRECTIONS: Each question or incomplete statement is followed by several suggested answers or completions. Select the one that BEST answers the question or completes the statement. *PRINT THE LETTER OF THE CORRECT ANSWER IN THE SPACE AT THE RIGHT.*

1. The BEST procedure to follow when replacing a blown fuse is to

    A. immediately replace it with the same size fuse
    B. immediately replace it with a larger size fuse
    C. immediately replace it with a smaller size fuse
    D. correct the cause of the fuse failure and replace it with the correct size

    1.____

2. The amperage rating of the fuse to be used in an electrical circuit is determined by the

    A. size of the connected load
    B. size of the wire in the circuit
    C. voltage of the circuit
    D. ambient temperature

    2.____

3. In a 208 volt, three-phase, 4 wire circuit, the voltage, in volts, from any line to the grounded neutral is APPROXIMATELY

    A. 208   B. 150   C. 120   D. zero

    3.____

4. The device commonly used to change an AC voltage to a DC voltage is called a

    A. transformer   B. rectifier
    C. relay   D. capacitor or condenser

    4.____

5. Where conduit enters a knock-out in an outlet box, it should be provided with a

    A. bushing on the inside and locknut on the outside
    B. locknut on the inside and bushing on the outside
    C. union on the outside and a nipple on the inside
    D. nipple on the outside and a union on the inside

    5.____

6. The electric circuit to a ten kilowatt electric hot water heater which is automatically controlled by an aquastat will also require a

    A. transistor   B. choke coil
    C. magnetic contactor   D. limit switch

    6.____

7. An electric power consumption meter USUALLY indicates the power used in

    A. watts   B. volt-hours
    C. amperes   D. kilowatt-hours

    7.____

8. Of the following sizes of copper wire, the one which can SAFELY carry the greatest amount of amperes is

    A. 14 ga. stranded   B. 12 ga. stranded
    C. 12 ga. solid   D. 10 ga. solid

    8.____

9. If a 110 volt lamp were used on a 220 volt circuit, the 9.____

    A. fuse would burn out   B. lamp would burn out
    C. line would overheat   D. lamp would flicker

10. The material which is LEAST likely to be found in use as the outer covering of rubber insulated wires or cables is 10.____

    A. cotton   B. varnished cambric
    C. lead   D. neoprene

11. In measuring to determine the size of a stranded insulated conductor, the PROPER place to use the wire gauge is on 11.____

    A. the insulation
    B. the outer covering
    C. the stranded conductor
    D. one strand of the conductor

12. Rubber insulation on an electrical conductor would MOST quickly be damaged by continuous contact with 12.____

    A. acid   B. water   C. oil   D. alkali

13. If a fuse clip becomes hot under normal circuit load, the MOST probable cause is that the 13.____

    A. clip makes poor contact with the fuse ferrule
    B. circuit wires are too small
    C. current rating of the fuse is too high
    D. voltage rating of the fuse is too low

14. If the input to a 10 to 1 step-down transformer is 15 amperes at 2400 volts, the secondary output would be NEAREST to _____ amperes at _____ volts. 14.____

    A. 1.5; 24,000   B. 150; 240
    C. 1.5; 240   D. 150; 24,000

15. In a two-wire electrical system, the color of the wire which is grounded is USUALLY 15.____

    A. white   B. red   C. black   D. green

16. It is generally recommended that wooden ladders be kept coated with a suitable protective coating.
The one of the following which is NOT a suitable protective coating is 16.____

    A. clear lacquer   B. clear varnish
    C. linseed oil   D. paint

17. The tool you should use to mend metal by soldering is 17.____

A.

B.

C.

D.

18. The one of the following that is NOT part of an electric motor is a   18.____

    A. brush   B. rheostat   C. pole   D. commutator

19. An electrical transformer would be used to   19.____

    A. change current from AC to DC
    B. raise or lower the power
    C. raise or lower the voltage
    D. change the frequency

20. The piece of equipment that would be rated in ampere hours is a   20.____

    A. storage battery   B. bus bar
    C. rectifier   D. capacitor

21. A ballast is a necessity in a(n)   21.____

    A. motor generator set
    B. fluorescent lighting system
    C. oil circuit breaker
    D. synchronous converter

22. The power factor in an AC circuit is on when

    A. no current is flowing
    B. the voltage at the source is a minimum
    C. the voltage and current are in phase
    D. there is no load

22.____

23. Neglecting the internal resistance in the battery, the current flowing through the battery shown at the right is _____ amp.
    A. 3
    B. 6
    C. 9
    D. 12

23.____

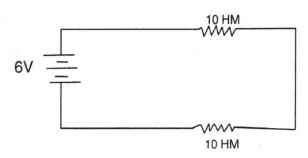

6V

10 HM

10 HM

24. Using a fuse with a LARGER rated capacity than that of the circuit is

    A. *advisable;* such use prevents the fuse from blowing
    B. *advisable;* larger capacity fuses last longer than smaller capacity fuses
    C. *inadvisable;* larger capacity fuses are more expensive than smaller capacity fuses
    D. *inadvisable;* such use may cause a fire

24.____

25. You can MOST easily tell when a screw-in type fuse has blown because the center of the strip of metal in the fuse is

    A. broken   B. visible
    C. nicked   D. cool to the touch

25.____

KEY (CORRECT ANSWERS)

1.	D		11.	D
2.	B		12.	C
3.	C		13.	A
4.	B		14.	B
5.	A		15.	A
6.	C		16.	D
7.	D		17.	B
8.	D		18.	B
9.	B		19.	C
10.	B		20.	A

21.	B
22.	C
23.	A
24.	D
25.	A

TEST 3

DIRECTIONS: Each question or incomplete statement is followed by several suggested answers or completions. Select the one that BEST answers the question or completes the statement. *PRINT THE LETTER OF THE CORRECT ANSWER IN THE SPACE AT THE RIGHT.*

1. The ordinary single-pole flush wall type switch must be connected   1.____

    A. across the line
    B. in the hot conductor
    C. in the grounded conductor
    D. in the white conductor

2. A DC shunt motor runs in the wrong direction.   2.____
   This fault can be CORRECTED by

    A. reversing the connections of both the field and the armature
    B. interchanging the connections of either main or auxiliary windings
    C. interchanging the connections to either the field or the armature windings
    D. interchanging the connections to the line of the power leads

3. The MOST common type of motor that can be used with both AC and DC sources is the   3.____
   _____ motor.

    A. compound   B. repulsion   C. series   D. shunt

4. A fluorescent fixture in a new building has been in use for several months without trouble.   4.____
   Recently, the ends of the fluorescent lamp have remained lighted when the light was
   switched off.
   The BEST way to clear up this trouble is to replace the

    A. lamp   B. ballast   C. starter   D. sockets

5. A ballast is a part of a(n)   5.____

    A. fluorescent light fixture
    B. electric motor
    C. doorbell circuit
    D. incandescent light fixture

6. Most of the lighting circuits in buildings operate on _____ volts.   6.____
    A. 6   B. 12   C. 120   D. 208

7. An ordinary wall switch called a *silent switch* contains a liquid called   7.____
    A. water   B. mercury   C. oil   D. naptha

8. The rating of the circuit breaker in a lighting circuit is determined by the   8.____

    A. load connected to the circuit
    B. current carrying capacity of the wire
    C. ambient temperature
    D. length of the wire

9. One ADVANTAGE of rubber insulation is that it   9.____

    A. does not deteriorate with age
    B. is able to withstand high temperatures
    C. does not absorb much moisture
    D. is not damaged by oil

10. The SIMPLEST device for interrupting an overloaded electrical circuit is a   10.____

    A. fuse   B. relay
    C. capacitor   D. choke coil

11. Electric service meters are read in   11.____

    A. kilowatt hours   B. electrons
    C. amperes   D. volts

12. The device used to reduce the voltage of an electric circuit is the   12.____

    A. voltmeter   B. fuse
    C. circuit breaker   D. transformer

13. Ordinary light bulbs are USUALLY rated in   13.____

    A. watts   B. ohms   C. amperes   D. filaments

14. The electric plug on a scrubbing machine should be plugged into a   14.____

    A. light socket   B. wall outlet
    C. fuse receptacle   D. dimmer switch

15. The device which should be used to connect the output shaft of an electric motor to the input shaft of a centrifugal pump is the   15.____

    A. flexible coupling   B. petcock
    C. alemite fitting   D. clutch

16. When comparing a 60 watt yellow bulb with a 60 watt clear bulb, it can be said that they BOTH   16.____

    A. give the same amount of light
    B. use the same amount of power
    C. will burn for at least 60 hours
    D. will burn for at least 60 days

17. The output capacity of an electric motor is USUALLY rated in   17.____

    A. kilowatts   B. horsepower
    C. percent   D. cubic feet

18. A fuse will burn out whenever it is subjected to excessive   18.____

    A. resistance   B. voltage
    C. current   D. capacitance

19. The one of the following that is BEST to use to smooth a commutator is   19.____

    A. Number 1/0 emery cloth   B. Number 00 sandpaper
    C. Number 2 steel wool   D. a safe edge file

20. The electric service that is provided to MOST schools in the city is NOMINALLY _____ 20.____
volt- _____ phase - _____ wire - _____ volts to ground.

    A. 208; 3; 4; 120   B. 208; 3; 3; 208
    C. 220; 2; 3; 110   D. 440; 3; 4; 240

21. All the fuses in an electrical panel are good but the clips on the fuse in circuit No. 1 are 21.____
much hotter than the clips of the other fuses.
Of the following, the MOST likely cause of this condition is that

    A. circuit No. 1 is greatly overloaded
    B. circuit No. 1 is carrying much less than rated load
    C. the room temperature is abnormally high
    D. the fuse in circuit No. 1 is very loose in its clips

22. Before putting two DC engine generators on the line in parallel, it is USUALLY necessary 22.____
to

    A. adjust the speeds so that both are running at exactly the same speed
    B. adjust the loads so that each machine will take its proportionate share
    C. adjust the field of the incoming unit
    D. lower the line voltage

23. Of the following, the BEST type of AC motor to use for direct connection to a timing 23.____
device which must be very accurate is a _____ motor.

    A. synchronous   B. squirrel cage
    C. wound rotor   D. single phase capacitor

24. In running temporary electric wiring for a display requiring the use of 30 incandescent 50- 24.____
watt lamps at the usual lighting voltage, the two main 120V loads supplying this load
would carry MOST NEARLY _____ amps.

    A. 23.9   B. 12.5   C. 17.8   D. 9.5

25. The BEST of the following tools to use for cutting off a piece of single conductor #6 rub- 25.____
ber insulated lead covered cable is a

    A. pair of electrician's pliers
    B. hacksaw
    C. hammer and cold chisel
    D. lead knife

KEY (CORRECT ANSWERS)

1.	B		11.	A
2.	C		12.	D
3.	C		13.	A
4.	C		14.	B
5.	A		15.	A
6.	C		16.	B
7.	B		17.	B
8.	B		18.	C
9.	C		19.	B
10.	A		20.	A

21.	D
22.	C
23.	A
24.	B
25.	B

———

TEST 4

DIRECTIONS: Each question or incomplete statement is followed by several suggested answers or completions. Select the one that BEST answers the question or completes the statement. *PRINT THE LETTER OF THE CORRECT ANSWER IN THE SPACE AT THE RIGHT.*

1. An indication that a fluorescent lamp in a fixture should be replaced is   1._____

   A. humming in the fixture
   B. the ends of the lamp remain black when the lamp is lit
   C. poor or slow starting
   D. the lamp does not shut off each time the OFF button is pressed

2. Asbestos is used as a covering on electrical wires to provide protection from   2._____

   A. high voltage   B. high temperatures
   C. water damage   D. electrolysis

3. Many electric power tools, such as drills, have a third conductor in the line cord which   3._____
   should be connected to a grounded part of the power receptacle.
   The reason for this is to

   A. have a spare wire in case one power wire should break
   B. strengthen the power lead so that it cannot be easily damaged
   C. protect the user of the tool from electrical shocks
   D. allow use of the tool for extended periods of time without overheating

4. A riser diagram is an electrical drawing which would give information about the   4._____

   A. voltage drop in feeders
   B. size of feeders and panel loads
   C. external connections to equipment
   D. sequence of operation of devices and equipment

5. An electric motor driven air compressor is automatically started and stopped by a   5._____

   A. thermostat   B. line air valve
   C. pressure switch   D. float trap

6. The term *kilowatt hours* describes the consumption of   6._____

   A. energy   B. radiation
   C. cooling capacity   D. conductance

7. AC voltage may be converted to DC voltage by means of a   7._____

   A. magnet   B. rectifier
   C. voltage regulator   D. transducer

8. The metal which has the GREATEST resistance to the flow of electricity is   8._____

   A. steel   B. copper   C. silver   D. gold

44

9. Tinning a soldering iron means

    A. applying flux to the tip
    B. cleaning the tip to make it bright
    C. applying a coat of solder to the tip
    D. heating the iron to the proper temperature

9.____

10. Electricians working around *live wires* should wear gloves made of

    A. asbestos   B. metal mesh
    C. leather   D. rubber

10.____

11.

METER READING AT BEGENNING OF PERIOD

METER READING AT END OF PERIOD

The above are the readings on the electric meter at the beginning and end of a period. The TOTAL kilowatt hour consumption is

    A. 264   B. 570   C. 61   D. 175

11.____

12. The modern multiple-circuit program instrument which automatically controls bell signals in a school USUALLY includes

    A. automatic resetting of electric clocks throughout the school
    B. automatic ringing of room bells when the fire bell switch is closed
    C. prevention of manual control of schedules by eliminating manual control switches
    D. provision for automatic cutout of the schedule for any 24-hour day desired

12.____

13. Of the following, the device which uses the GREATEST amount of electric power is the

    A. electric typewriter

    B. $\frac{1}{4}$ inch electric drill

    C. floor scrubbing machine
    D. oil burner ignition transformer

13.____

14. Meters which indicate the electric power consumed in a public building are read in

    A. kilowatt-hours   B. volts
    C. cubic feet   D. degree days

14.____

15. The MAIN reason for grounding the outer shell of an electric fixture is to 15.____

    A. provide additional support for the fixture
    B. reduce the cost of installation of the fixture
    C. provide a terminal to which the wires can be attached
    D. reduce the chance of electric shock

16. The BEST way to determine whether the locknuts on terminals in an electrical terminal box have become loose is to 16.____

    A. use an electric tester
    B. try to tighten the nuts with an appropriate wrench
    C. tap the nuts with an insulated handle
    D. try to loosen the nuts with a pair of pliers

17. The PROPER flux to use for soldering electric wire connections is 17.____

    A. rosin   B. killed acid
    C. borax   D. zinc chloride

18. A fusestat differs from an ordinary plug fuse in that a fusestat has 18.____

    A. less current carrying capacity
    B. different size threads
    C. an aluminum shell instead of a copper shell
    D. no threads

19. A grounding type 120-volt receptacle differs from an ordinary electric receptacle MAINLY in that a grounding receptacle 19.____

    A. is larger than the ordinary receptacle
    B. has openings for a three prong plug
    C. can be used for larger machinery
    D. has a built-in circuit breaker

20. In a 110-220 volt three-wire circuit, the neutral wire is USUALLY 20.____

    A. black   B. red   C. white   D. green

21. Brushes on fractional horsepower universal motors are MOST often made of 21.____

    A. flexible copper strands   B. rigid carbon blocks
    C. thin wire strips   D. collector rings

22. A ground wire that is too small is dangerous because it will 22.____

    A. generate heat   B. blow a fuse
    C. increase the voltage   D. increase the current

23. A 115-volt hot water heater has a resistance of 5.75 ohms. The current it will take at rated voltage is 23.____

    A. 15   B. 20   C. 13   D. 23

24. If a 30 ampere fuse is placed in a fuse box for a circuit requiring a 15 ampere fuse,   24.____

    A. serious damage to the circuit may result from an overload
    B. better protection will be provided for the circuit
    C. the larger fuse will tend to blow more often since it carries more current
    D. it will eliminate maintenance problems

25. Metal tubing through which electric wires of buildings are run is called   25.____

    A. insulation   B. conduit
    C. duct   D. sleeve

KEY (CORRECT ANSWERS)

1.	B		11.	D
2.	B		12.	A
3.	C		13.	C
4.	B		14.	A
5.	C		15.	D
6.	A		16.	B
7.	B		17.	A
8.	A		18.	B
9.	C		19.	B
10.	D		20.	C

21.	B
22.	A
23.	B
24.	A
25.	B

47

TEST 5

DIRECTIONS: Each question or incomplete statement is followed by several suggested answers or completions. Select the one that BEST answers the question or completes the statement. *PRINT THE LETTER OF THE CORRECT ANSWER IN THE SPACE AT THE RIGHT.*

1. *Found reading* and *left reading* are terms associated with   1.____

     A. petrometers   B. electric meters
     C. gas meters   D. water meters

2. When lamps are wired in parallel, the failure of one lamp will   2.____

     A. break the electric circuit to the other lamps
     B. have no effect on the power supply to the other lamps
     C. increase noticeably the light production of the other lamps
     D. cause excessive current to flow through the other lamps

3. The MAIN objection to using a copper penny in place of a blown fuse is that   3.____

     A. the penny will conduct electric current
     B. the penny will reduce the current flowing in the line
     C. melting of the penny will probably occur
     D. the line will not be protected against excessive current

4. The term *mogul base* is GENERALLY associated with   4.____

     A. boiler compound   B. stock cleaning solution
     C. insecticide   D. lamps

5. When connecting lamp sockets to a lighting circuit, the shell should ALWAYS be connected to the white wire of the circuit to   5.____

     A. balance the load on the system
     B. reduce the possibility of accidental shock
     C. eliminate blowing the fuse in case the socket becomes grounded
     D. protect the circuit against reverse current

6. The MAIN purpose of periodic inspections and tests of electrical equipment is to   6.____

     A. encourage the workers to take better care of the equipment
     B. familiarize the workers with the equipment
     C. keep the workers busy during otherwise slack periods
     D. discover minor faults before they develop into major faults

7. The current rating of the fuse to use in a lighting circuit is determined by the   7.____

     A. connected load   B. line voltage
     C. capacity of the wiring   D. rating of the switch

8. Artificial respiration after a severe electric shock is ALWAYS necessary when the shock results in   8.____

     A. unconsciousness   B. stoppage of breathing
     C. bleeding   D. a burn

9. If you find a co-worker lying unconscious across an electric wire, the FIRST thing you should do is

    A. get him off the wire
    C. get a doctor
    B. call the foreman
    D. shut off the power

9.____

10. A solenoid valve is actuated by

    A. air pressure
    C. temperature change
    B. electric current
    D. light rays

10.____

11.

The electrician's bit is indicated by the number

    A. 1   B. 2   C. 3   D. 4

11.____

12. BX is a designation for a type of

    A. flexible armored electric cable
    B. flexible gas line
    C. rigid conduit
    D. electrical insulation

12.____

13. *WYE-WYE* and *DELTA-WYE* are two

    A. types of DC motor windings
    B. arrangements of 3-phase transformer connections
    C. types of electrical splices
    D. shapes of commutator bars

13.____

14. When joining electric wires together in a fixture box, the BEST thing to use are wire

    A. connectors
    C. clamps
    B. couplings
    D. bolts

14.____

15. If the name plate of a motor indicates that it is a split phase motor, it is LIKELY that this   15.____
    motor

    A. is a universal motor
    B. operates on DC only
    C. operates on AC only
    D. operates either on DC at full power or on AC at reduced power

16. Rigid steel conduit used for the protection of electrical wiring is GENERALLY either gal-   16.____
    vanized or enameled both inside and out in order to

    A. prevent damage to the wire insulation
    B. make threading of the conduit easier
    C. prevent corrosion of the conduit
    D. make the conduit easier to handle

17. If a test lamp does not light when placed in series with a fuse and an appropriate battery,   17.____
    it is a GOOD indication that the fuse

    A. is open-circuited
    B. is short-circuited
    C. is in operating condition
    D. has zero resistance

18. The process of removing the insulation from a wire is called   18.____

    A. braiding   B. skinning   C. sweating   D. tinning

19. A 10-to-1 step-down transformer has an input of 1 ampere at 120 volts AC.   19.____
    If the losses are negligible, the output of the transformer is _____ volts.

    A. 1 ampere at 12   B. .1 ampere at 1200
    C. 10 amperes at 12   D. 10 amperes at 120

20. In city schools, wiring for motors or lighting is _____ volt, _____.   20.____

    A. 208-220; 4 wire, 60 cycle
    B. 240-110; 3 wire, 4 phase
    C. 120-208; 3 phase, 4 wire
    D. 160-210; 4 phase, 3 wire

21. When using a voltmeter in testing an electric circuit, the voltmeter should be connected   21.____

    A. across the circuit
    B. in series with the circuit
    C. in parallel or series with the circuit
    D. in series with the active element

22. A kilowatt is _____ watts.   22.____

    A. 500   B. 2,000   C. 1,500   D. 1,000

23. Of the following classifications, the one which pertains to fires in electrical equipment is   23.____
    Class

    A. A   B. B   C. C   D. D

24. The lighting systems in public buildings usually operate MOST NEARLY on _____ volts.   24.____

    A. 6   B. 24   C. 115   D. 220

25. A type of portable tool used to bend electrical conduit is called a   25.____

    A. helve   B. newel   C. spandrel   D. hickey

KEY (CORRECT ANSWERS)

1. B	11. C		
2. B	12. A		
3. D	13. B		
4. D	14. A		
5. B	15. C		
6. D	16. C		
7. C	17. A		
8. B	18. B		
9. D	19. C		
10. B	20. B		

21. A
22. D
23. C
24. C
25. D

TEST 6

DIRECTIONS: Each question or incomplete statement is followed by several suggested answers or completions. Select the one that BEST answers the question or completes the statement. *PRINT THE LETTER OF THE CORRECT ANSWER IN THE SPACE AT THE RIGHT.*

1. In a 4-wire, 3-phase electrical supply system, the voltage between one phase and ground used for the lighting load is MOST NEARLY

   A. 440   B. 230   C. 208   D. 115

   1._____

2. Of the following, the one that takes the place of a fuse in an electrical circuit is a

   A. transformer   B. circuit breaker
   C. condenser   D. knife switch

   2._____

3. Escutcheons are USUALLY located

   A. on switch plates
   B. on electrical outlets
   C. around pipes, to cover pipe sleeve openings
   D. around armored electric cable going into a gem box

   3._____

4. It is ADVISABLE to remove broken bulbs from light sockets with

   A. a wooden or hard rubber wedge
   B. pliers
   C. a hammer and chisel
   D. a fuse puller

   4._____

5. A 3-ohm resistor placed across a 12-volt battery will dissipate _____ watts.

   A. 3   B. 4   C. 12   D. 48

   5._____

6. Instead of using fuses, modern electric wiring uses

   A. quick switches   B. circuit breakers
   C. fusible links   D. lag blocks

   6._____

7. In order to reverse the direction of rotation of a series motor, the

   A. connections to the armature should be reversed
   B. connections to both the armature and the series field should be reversed
   C. connections of the motor to the power lines should be reversed
   D. series field should be placed in shunt with the armature

   7._____

8. The BEST flux to use when soldering copper wires in an electric circuit is

   A. sal ammoniac   B. zinc chloride
   C. rosin   D. borax

   8._____

9. A megger is an instrument used to measure

   A. capacitance   B. insulation resistance
   C. power   D. illumination levels

   9._____

10. An electrical drawing is drawn to a scale of 1/4" = 1'.   10.____
    If a length of conduit on the drawing measures 7 3/8", the actual length of the conduit,
    in feet, is MOST NEARLY

    A. 7.5'   B. 15.5'   C. 22.5'   D. 29.5'

11. Standard 120-volt plug-type fuses are GENERALLY rated in   11.____

    A. farads   B. ohms   C. watts   D. amperes

12. Standard 120-volt electric light bulbs are GENERALLY rated in   12.____

    A. farads   B. ohms   C. watts   D. amperes

13. Of the following colors of electrical conductor coverings, the one which indicates a con-   13.____
    ductor used SOLELY for grounding portable or fixed electrical equipment is

    A. blue   B. green   C. red   D. black

14. A device that operates to vary the resistance of an electrical circuit is USUALLY part of a   14.____
    _____ pressuretrol.

    A. high-limit   B. low-limit
    C. manual-reset   D. modulating

15. The type of screwdriver SPECIALLY made to be used in tight spots is the   15.____

    A. Phillips   B. offset
    C. square shank   D. truss

16. On a plan, the symbol shown at the right USUALLY represents a(n)   16.____
    A. duplex receptacle
    B. electric switch
    C. ceiling outlet
    D. pull box

17. Electric power is measured in   17.____

    A. volts   B. amperes   C. watts   D. ohms

18. Of the following sizes of copper conductors, the one which has the LEAST current-carry-   18.____
    ing capacity is _____ AWG.

    A. 000   B. 0   C. 8   D. 12

19. When excess current flows, a circuit breaker is opened directly by the action of a   19.____

    A. condenser   B. transistor
    C. relay   D. solenoid

20. Conduit is used in electrical wiring in order to the wires.   20.____

    A. waterproof   B. color code
    C. protect   D. insulate

KEY (CORRECT ANSWERS)

1.	D	11.	D
2.	B	12.	C
3.	D	13.	B
4.	A	14.	D
5.	B	15.	B
6.	B	16.	C
7.	A	17.	C
8.	C	18.	D
9.	B	19.	D
10.	D	20.	C

EXAMINATION SECTION
TEST 1

DIRECTIONS: Each question or incomplete statement is followed by several suggested answers or completions. Select the one that BEST answers the question or completes the statement. *PRINT THE LETTER OF THE CORRECT ANSWER IN THE SPACE AT THE RIGHT.*

1. The one of the following which is a unit of inductance is the   1._____

    A. millihenry   B. microfarad   C. kilohm   D. weber

2. Of the following, the BEST conductor of electricity is   2._____

    A. aluminum   B. copper   C. silver   D. iron

3. A voltage of 1000 microvolts is the SAME as   3._____

    A. 1,000 volts   B. 0.100 volts
    C. 0.010 volts   D. 0.001 volts

4. The function of a rectifier is SIMILAR to that of a(n)   4._____

    A. inverter   B. relay   C. commutator   D. transformer

5. A 9-ohm resistor rated at 225 watts is used in a 120-volt circuit. In order not to exceed the rating of the resistor, the MAXIMUM current, in amperes, which can flow through the circuit is   5._____

    A. 2   B. 3   C. 4   D. 5

6. The number of circular mils in a conductor 0.036 inch in diameter is   6._____

    A. 6   B. 36   C. 72   D. 1296

7. The color of the label on most commercially available 250-volt cartridge fuses of 15-amperes or less capacity is   7._____

    A. green   B. blue   C. red   D. yellow

8. Assume that a two-microfarad capacitor is connected in parallel with a three-microfarad capacitor. The resulting capacity, in microfarads, is   8._____

    A. 2/3   B. 6/5   C. 3/2   D. 5

9. The speed of the rotating magnetic field in a 12-pole 60-cycle stator is   9._____

    A. 1800 rpm   B. 1200 rpm   C. 720 rpm   D. D 600 rpm

10. The transformer connection *generally* used to convert from three-phase to two-phase by means of two transformers is the   10._____

    A. Scott or T   B. V or Open delta
    C. Wye-Delta   D. Delta-Wye

11. The conductance, in mhos, of a circuit whose resistance is one ohm is 11.____

    A. 1/10   B. 1   C. 10   D. 100

12. Assume that a 220-volt, 25 cycle, A.C., e.m.f. is impressed across a circuit consisting of a 25-ohm resistor in series with a 30-microfarad capacitor. The current in this circuit, in amperes, is, *most nearly,* 12.____

    A. 0.5   B. 0.8   C. 1.0   D. 1.5

13. An ammeter has a full scale deflection with a current of 0.010 amperes and an internal resistance of 20 ohms.
In order for the ammeter to have a full scale deflection with a current of 10 amperes and not damage its movement, a shunt should be used having a value of 13.____

    A. 10 ohms   B. 0.2 ohms   C. 0.02 ohms   D. 0.01 ohms

14. American Wire Gage (A.W.G.) wire size numbers are set so that the resistance of wire per 1,000 ft. doubles with every increase of 14.____

    A. one gage number   B. two gage numbers
    C. three gage numbers   D. four gage numbers

15. In an ideal transformer for transforming or "stepping down" the voltage from 1200 volts to 120 volts, the turns ratio is 15.____

    A. 10:1   B. 12:1   C. 1:12   D. 1:10

16. When a lead-acid battery is fully charged, the negative plate consists of lead 16.____

    A. peroxide   B. sponge   C. sulfate   D. dioxide

17. Improving the commutation of a D.C. generator is MOST often done by using 17.____

    A. a rheostat in series with the equalizer
    B. an equalizer alone
    C. a compensator
    D. interpoles

18. In a wave-wound armature, the MINIMUM number of commutator brushes necessary is 18.____

    A. two times the number of poles
    B. two, regardless of the number of poles
    C. one-half times the number of poles
    D. four, regardless of the number of poles

19. A three-phase induction motor runs hot with all stator coils at the same temperature. The trouble which would cause this condition is that 19.____

    A. the motor is running single phase
    B. the motor is overloaded
    C. a part of the motor windings is inoperative
    D. the rotor bars are loose

20. Where constant speed is required, the one of the following motors that should be used is   20.____
a

    A. wound-rotor motor   B. series motor
    C. compound motor   D. shunt motor

21. To reverse the direction of rotation of a 3-phase induction motor,   21.____

    A. the field connections should be reversed
    B. the armature connections should be reversed
    C. any two line leads should be interchanged
    D. the brushes should be shifted in the direction opposite to that of the armature rotation

22. The speed of a wound-rotor motor may be increased by   22.____

    A. *decreasing* the resistance in the secondary circuit
    B. *increasing* the resistance in the secondary circuit
    C. *decreasing* the shunt field current
    D. *increasing* the series field resistance

23. The one of the following methods which can be used to increase the slip of the rotor in a   23.____
single-phase shaded-pole motor, is the

    A. reversal of the leads of the field winding
    B. addition of capacitors in series with the starting winding
    C. reduction of the impressed voltage
    D. addition of more capacitors in parallel with the starting winding

24. The direction of rotation of a single-phase A.C. repulsion motor may be reversed by   24.____

    A. interchanging the two line leads to the motor
    B. interchanging the leads to the main winding
    C. interchanging the leads to the starting winding
    D. moving the brushes to the other side of the neutral position

25. The torque developed by a D.C. series motor is   25.____

    A. *inversely proportional* to the square of the armature current
    B. *proportional* to the square of the armature current
    C. *proportional* to the armature current
    D. *inversely proportional* to the armature current

———

KEY (CORRECT ANSWERS)

1.	A		11.	B
2.	C		12.	C
3.	D		13.	C
4.	C		14.	C
5.	D		15.	A
6.	D		16.	B
7.	B		17.	D
8.	D		18.	B
9.	D		19.	B
10.	A		20.	D

21.	C
22.	A
23.	C
24.	D
25.	B

TEST 2

DIRECTIONS: Each question or incomplete statement is followed by several suggested answers or completions. Select the one that BEST answers the question or completes the statement. *PRINT THE LETTER OF THE CORRECT ANSWER IN THE SPACE AT THE RIGHT.*

1. The one of the following which is MOST commonly used to clean a commutator is

    A. emery cloth   B. graphite
    C. a smooth file   D. fine-grit sandpaper

1.____

2. The type of motor which requires BOTH A.C. and D.C. for operation is the

    A. compound motor   B. universal motor
    C. synchronous motor   D. squirrel-cage motor

2.____

3. Compensators are used for starting large

    A. shunt motors   B. series motors
    C. induction motors   D. compound motors

3.____

4. The device MOST frequently used to correct low lagging power factor is a(n)

    A. solenoid   B. induction regulator
    C. induction motor   D. synchronous motor

4.____

5. Of the following motors, the one with the HIGHEST starting torque is the

    A. compound motor   B. series motor
    C. shunt motor   D. split phase motor

5.____

6. The approximate efficiency of a 60-cycle, 6-pole induction motor running at 1050 rpm and having a synchronous speed of 1200 rpm, is

    A. 67.0%   B. 78.5%   C. 87.5%   D. 90.0%

6.____

7. The MAIN contributing factor to motor starter failures *usually* is

    A. overloading   B. dirt
    C. bearing trouble   D. friction

7.____

8. The neutral or grounded conductors in branch circuit wiring must be identified by being colored

    A. black or brown   B. black with white traces
    C. white with black traces   D. white or natural gray

8.____

9. The SMALLEST radius for the inner edge of any field bend in a 1-inch rigid or flexible conduit when type R wire is being used, is

    A. 3 inches   B. 5 inches   C. 6 inches   D. 10 inches

9.____

10. Thermal cutouts used to protect a motor against overloads may have a current rating of not more than

    A. the starting current of the motor
    B. 125% of the full-load current rating of the motor

10.____

C. the full-load current of the motor

D. the current-carrying capacity of the branch circuit conductors

11. The MAXIMUM size of EMT permitted is   11._____

    A. 4 inches   B. 3 1/2 inches   C. 3 inches   D. 2 inches

12. The type of equipment which is defined as a set of conductors originating at the load side   12._____
    of the service equipment and supplying the main and/or one or more secondary distribu-
    tion centers, is a

    A. sub-feeder   B. feeder   C. main   D. service cable

13. The SMALLEST size rigid conduit that may be used in wiring is   13._____

    A. 3/8 inch   B. 1/2 inch   C. 3/4 inch   D. 1 inch

14. An enclosed 600-volt cartridge fuse must be of the knife-blade contact type if its ampere   14._____
    rating is

    A. 20   B. 40   C. 60   D. 80

15. An insulated ground for fixed equipment should be color coded   15._____

    A. yellow
    B. green or green with a yellow stripe
    C. blue or blue with a yellow stripe
    D. black

16. Of the following, the meter that CANNOT be used to measure A.C. voltage is the   16._____

    A. electrodynamic voltmeter   B. electrostatic voltmeter
    C. D'Arsonval voltmeter   D. thermocouple voltmeter

17. Of the following, an instrument frequently used to measure high insulation resistance is   17._____
    a(n)

    A. tong-test ammeter   B. megger
    C. ohmmeter   D. electrostatic voltmeter

18. When using a voltmeter in testing an electric circuit, the voltmeter should be placed in   18._____

    A. *series* with the circuit
    B. *parallel* with the circuit
    C. *parallel* or in *series* with a current transformer, depending on the current
    D. *series* with the active element

19. The MINIMUM number of wattmeters necessary to measure the power in the load of a   19._____
    balanced 3-phase, 4-wire system, is

    A. 1   B. 2   C. 3   D. 4

20. An instrument that measures electrical energy is the   20._____

    A. current transformer   B. watthour meter
    C. dynamometer   D. wattmeter

21. The one of the following items which can be used to *properly* test an armature for a shorted coil is a   21._____

    A. neon light   B. megger
    C. growler   D. pair of series test lamps

22. The instrument that measures loads at the load terminals, averaged over specified time periods, is the   22._____

    A. coulomb meter   B. wattmeter
    C. demand meter   D. var-hour meter

23. A multiplier is usually used to increase the range of   23._____

    A. voltmeter   B. watthour meter
    C. wheatstont bridge   D. Nernst bridge

24. The instrument used to indicate the phase relation between the voltage and the current of an A.C. circuit is called a   24._____

    A. power factor meter   B. synchroscope
    C. phase indicator   D. var-hour meter

25. Except where busways are entering or leaving service or distribution equipment, the bottom of the busway enclosure for all horizontal busway runs should be kept at a MINIMUM height above the floor of   25._____

    A. 4 feet   B. 6 feet   C. 8 feet   D. 10 feet

KEY (CORRECT ANSWERS)

1.	D		11.	D
2.	C		12.	B
3.	C		13.	B
4.	D		14.	D
5.	B		15.	B
6.	C		16.	C
7.	B		17.	B
8.	D		18.	B
9.	C		19.	A
10.	B		20.	B

21.	C
22.	C
23.	A
24.	A
25.	C

TEST 3

DIRECTIONS: Each question or incomplete statement is followed by several suggested answers or completions. Select the one that BEST answers the question or completes the statement. *PRINT THE LETTER OF THE CORRECT ANSWER IN THE SPACE AT THE RIGHT.*

1. The lubricant *commonly* used to make it easier to pull braid-covered cable into a duct is   1.____

    A. soapstone   B. soft soap
    C. heavy grease   D. light oil

2. Of the following, the conductor insulation which may be used in wet locations is type   2.____

    A. RH   B. RHH   C. RHW   D. RUH

3. Assume that at a certain distribution point you notice that among several of the conductors entering the same raceway, some have a half-inch band of yellow tape, while the others do not. The conductors with the yellow tape are all   3.____

    A. grounded   B. ungrounded   C. A.C.   D. D.C.

4. Conductors of the same length, same circular mil area and type of insulation, may be run in multiple   4.____

    A. under no circumstances
    B. if each conductor is #4 or larger
    C. if each conductor is #2 or larger
    D. if each conductor is #1/0 or larger

5. In order to keep conduits parallel where several parallel runs of conduit of varying size are installed through 45 or 90 degree bends, it is BEST to   5.____

    A. bend conduit on the job
    B. use standard factory-made elbows
    C. use flexible connectors to adjust runs
    D. bend conduit at the factory

6. The BEST way to join two lengths of conduit which cannot be turned is to   6.____

    A. use a split adapter
    B. use a conduit union ("Erickson")
    C. cut running threads on one end of one length of the conduit
    D. cut running threads on the ends of both lengths of conduit

7. When an electrical splice is wrapped with both rubber tape and friction tape, the MAIN purpose of the friction tape is to   7.____

    A. protect the rubber tape
    B. provide additional insulation
    C. build up the insulation to the required thickness
    D. increase the strength of the splice

8. Assume that explosion-proof wiring is required in a certain area. Conduits entering an enclosure in this area which contains apparatus that may produce arcs, sparks or high temperature, should be provided with   8.____

    A. a cable terminator
    B. an approved sealing compound
    C. couplings with three full threads engaged
    D. insulated bushings

9. If installed in dry locations, wireways may be used for circuits of not more than   9.____

    A. 208 volts   B. 440 volts   C. 600 volts   D. 1100 volts

10. An interior wiring circuit has two conductors, one white and one black. Assume that it becomes necessary to add a third conductor as a switch leg. The color of the THIRD conductor should be   10.____

    A. blue   B. red   C. green   D. natural gray

11. Keyless lampholders rated at 1500 watts have bases which are classed as   11.____

    A. Intermediate   B. Medium   C. Mogul   D. Admedium

12. In precast cellular concrete floor raceways, the LARGEST conductor which may be installed, except by special permission, is   12.____

    A. No. 2   B. No. 0   C. No. 00   D. No. 000

13. The conductor insulation which may be used for fixture wire is type   13.____

    A. TF   B. TW   C. TA   D. RW

14. Multiple fuses are permissible   14.____

    A. under no circumstances
    B. for conductors longer than 1/0
    C. for conductors larger than 2/0
    D. for conductors larger than 4/0

15. In loosening a nut, a socket wrench with a ratchet handle should be used in preference to other types of wrenches if   15.____

    A. the nut is out of reach
    B. the turning space for the handle is limited
    C. the nut is worn
    D. greater leverage is required

16. Solders used for electrical connections are alloys of   16.____

    A. tin and lead   B. tin and zinc
    C. lead and zinc   D. tin and copper

17. Another name for a pipe wrench is a   17.____

    A. crescent wrench   B. torque wrench
    C. Stillson wrench   D. monkey wrench

18. The tool used to cut raceways is a hacksaw with fine teeth, *commonly* called a   18.____

    A. crosscut saw   B. keyhole saw
    C. rip saw   D. tube saw

19. Lead expansion anchors are MOST commonly used to fasten conduit to a   19.____

    A. wooden partition wall   B. plaster wall
    C. solid concrete wall   D. gypsum wall

20. The use of "running" threads when coupling two sections of conduit is   20.____

    A. always good practice
    B. good practice only when installing enameled conduit
    C. good practice only if it is impossible to turn one of the conduits
    D. always poor practice

21. A quick-break knifeswitch is often used rather than a standard knifeswitch of the same   21.____
rating because the quick-break knife switch

    A. resists burning due to arcing at the contact points
    B. is easier to install and align
    C. is simpler in construction
    D. can carry a higher current without over-heating

22. The tip of a soldering iron is made of copper because   22.____

    A. copper is a very good conductor of heat
    B. solder will not stick to other metals
    C. it is the cheapest metal available
    D. the melting point of copper is very high

23. Good practice requires that cartridge fuses be removed from their clips by using a fuse   23.____
puller rather than the bare hand. The **reason** for using the fuse puller is that the

    A. bare hand may be burned or otherwise injured
    B. fuse is less likely to break
    C. fuse clips may be damaged when pulled
    D. use of the bare hands slows down removal of fuse and causes arcing

24. The frame of a portable electric tool should be **grounded** in order to   24.____

    A. reduce leakage from the winding
    B. prevent short circuits
    C. reduce the danger of overheating
    D. prevent the frame from becoming alive to ground

25. The LEAST desirable device for measuring the dimensions of an electrical equipment   25.____
cabinet containing live equipment, is a

    A. wooden yardstick
    B. six-foot folding wooden ruler
    C. twelve-inch plastic ruler
    D. six-foot steel tape

KEY (CORRECT ANSWERS)

1.	A		11.	C
2.	C		12.	B
3.	D		13.	A
4.	D		14.	A
5.	A		15.	B
6.	B		16.	A
7.	A		17.	C
8.	B		18.	D
9.	C		19.	C
10.	B		20.	D

21. A
22. A
23. A
24. D
25. D

———

TEST 4

DIRECTIONS: Each question or incomplete statement is followed by several suggested answers or completions. Select the one that BEST answers the question or completes the statement. *PRINT THE LETTER OF THE CORRECT ANSWER IN THE SPACE AT THE RIGHT.*

1. If three equal resistance coils are connected in parallel, the resistance of this combination is **equal to**   1._____

    A. one-third the resistance of one coil
    B. the resistance of one coil
    C. three times the resistance of one coil
    D. nine times the resistance of one coil

2. The voltage to neutral of a 3-phase, 4-wire system, is 120 volts. The line-to-line voltage is   2._____

    A. 208 volts   B. 220 volts   C. 230 volts   D. 240 volts

3. Three 6-ohm resistances are connected in Y across a 3-phase circuit. If a current of 10 amperes flows through each resistance, the TOTAL power in watts drawn by this load is, *most nearly,*   3._____

    A. 600   B. 1200   C. 1800   D. 2400

4. A conduit in an outlet box should be provided with a locknut   4._____

    A. on the outside and bushing on the inside
    B. and bushing on the inside
    C. on the inside and bushing on the outside
    D. and bushing on the inside

5. If the current in a single-phase, 120-volt circuit is 10 amperes and a wattmeter in this circuit reads 1080 watts, the power factor is, *most nearly,*   5._____

    A. 1.11   B. .9   C. .8   D. .7

6. It is poor practice to use a file without a handle because the   6._____

    A. file may be dropped and damaged
    B. unprotected end may mar the surface being filed
    C. user may be injured
    D. file marks will be too deep

7. If a 60-cycle, 4-pole squirrel-cage, induction motor has a slip of 5%, its speed is, *most nearly,*   7._____

    A. 1800 rpm   B. 1795 rpm   C. 1750 rpm   D. 1710 rpm

8. The PROPER way to reverse the direction of rotation of a 3-phase wound rotor induction motor is to   8._____

    A. reverse two leads between the rotor and the control resistances
    B. shift the brushes
    C. reverse two supply leads
    D. open one rotor lead

9. Sulphuric acid should **always** be poured into the water when new electrolyte for a lead-acid battery is prepared. The reason for this precaution is to

    A. *avoid* splattering of the acid
    B. *avoid* explosive fumes
    C. *prevent* corrosion of the mixing vessel
    D. *prevent* clotting of the acid

9.____

10. The direction of rotation of a d.c. shunt motor can be reversed PROPERLY by

    A. reversing the two supply leads
    B. shifting the position of the brushes
    C. reversing the connections to both the armature and the field
    D. reversing the connections to the field

10.____

Questions 11-13.

DIRECTIONS: Questions 11 to 13, inclusive, refer to this excerpt from the electrical code on the subject of grounding electrodes.

Each buried plate electrode shall present not less than two square feet of surface to the exterior soil. Electrodes of plate copper shall be at least .06 inch in thickness. Electrodes of iron or steel plate shall be at least one-quarter inch in thickness. Electrodes of iron or steel pipe shall be galvanized and not less than three-quarter inch in internal diameter. Electrodes of rods of steel or iron shall be at least three-quarter inch minimum cross-section dimension... Driven electrodes of pipes or rods... shall be driven to a depth of at least eight feet regardless of the size or number of electrodes used... Each electrode used shall be separated at least six feet from any other electrode including those used for signal circuits, radio, lightning rods or any other purposes.

11. According to the above paragraph, all grounding electrodes MUST be

    A. of plate copper
    B. of iron pipe
    C. at least three-quarter inch minimum cross-section dimension
    D. separated at least six feet from any other electrode

11.____

12. According to the above paragraph, the one of the following electrodes which meets the code requirements is a(n)

    A. copper plate 12" X 18" X .06"
    B. steel plate 14" X 24" X .06"
    C. copper plate 12" X 24" X .06"
    D. iron plate 12" X 18" X .25'"

12.____

13. According to the above paragraph, the one of the following electrodes which meets the code requirements is

    A. plain iron pipe, 1" in internal diameter, driven to a depth of 10 feet
    B. galvanized iron pipe, 3/4" in internal diameter, driven to a depth of 6 feet
    C. plain steel pipe, 1" in internal diameter, driven to a depth of 7 feet
    D. galvanized steel pipe, 3/4" in internal diameter, driven to a depth of 9 feet

13.____

14. With reference to armature windings, lap windings are often called   14.____

    A. ring windings   B. multiple windings
    C. series windings   D. toroidal windings

15. The question refers to the diagram below.   15.____

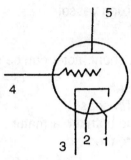

    The element numbered 4 is usually called the

    A. plate   B. grid   C. filament   D. cathode

16. To properly mount an outlet box on a concrete ceiling, it is BEST to use   16.____

    A. expansion screw anchors   B. wooden plugs
    C. wood screws   D. masonry nails

17. A d.c. motor takes 30 amps, at 110 volts and has an efficiency of 90%. The horsepower   17.____
available at the pulley is, *approximately*,

    A. 5   B. 4   C. 3   D. 2

18. If the armature current drawn by a series motor doubles, the torque   18.____

    A. remains the same   B. doubles
    C. becomes 4 times as great   D. becomes 8 times as great

19. The full load current, in amperes, of a 110-volt, 10 H.P., d.c. motor having an efficiency of   19.____
80% is, *approximately*,

    A. 62   B. 85   C. 99   D. 133

Questions 20-21.

DIRECTIONS: Questions 21 and 22 are to be answered in accordance with the diagram
below.

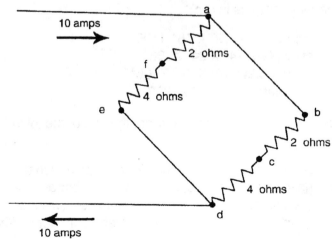

20. With reference to the above diagram, the voltage difference between points c and f is, *most nearly,*   20.____

    A. 40 volts   B. 20 volts   C. 10 volts   D. 0 volts

21. With reference to the above diagram, the current flowing through the resistance c d is, *most nearly,*   21.____

    A. 10 amperes   B. 5 amperes   C. 4 amperes   D. 2 amperes

Questions 22-25.

DIRECTIONS: Questions 22 through 25, inclusive, refer to the diagram below

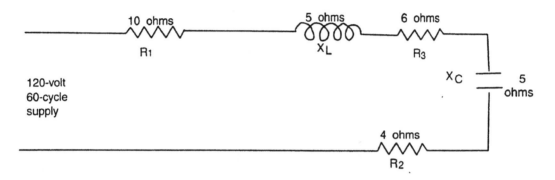

22. The value of the impedance in ohms of the above circuit is, *most nearly,*   22.____

    A. 60   B. 30   C. 25   D. 20

23. The current, in amperes, flowing in the above circuit is, *most nearly,*   23.____

    A. 2   B. 3   C. 6   D. 8

24. The potential drop, in volts, across R_3 is, *most nearly,*   24.____

    A. 12   B. 18   C. 36   D. 48

25. The power, in watts, consumed in the above circuit is, *most nearly,*   25.____

    A. 1080   B. 720   C. 180   D. 80

KEY (CORRECT ANSWERS)

1.	A		11.	D
2.	A		12.	C
3.	C		13.	D
4.	A		14.	B
5.	B		15.	B
6.	C		16.	A
7.	D		17.	B
8.	C		18.	C
9.	A		19.	B
10.	D		20.	D

21.	B
22.	D
23.	C
24.	C
25.	B

TEST 5

DIRECTIONS: Each question or incomplete statement is followed by several suggested answers or completions. Select the one that BEST answers the question or completes the statement. *PRINT THE LETTER OF THE CORRECT ANSWER IN THE SPACE AT THE RIGHT.*

1. The heat dissipation, W, in a resistor having a resistance of R ohms connected across a supply of E volts, is proportional to E^2/R.
    If R is reduced to one-half of its former value and E is doubled, the heat dissipation in this resistor is *now*   1.____

    A. 8W   B. 2W   C. 4W   D. 1/2W

2. Solder commonly used for electrical work is composed, *most likely*, of   2.____

    A. lead and tin   B. antimony and zinc
    C. lead and zinc   D. silver and antimony

3. A condenser having a capacitance of 3 microfarads is connected in parallel with a condenser having a capacitance of 2 microfarads. The combination is equal to a single condenser having a capacitance, in microfarads, of, *most nearly*,   3.____

    A. 5/6   B. 6/5   C. 5   D. 6

4. Of the following units, the one which is a unit of inductance is the   4.____

    A. maxwell   B. henry   C. weber   D. oersted

5. The tool *commonly* used for bending conduit of small sizes is called a   5.____

    A. mandrel   B. bending wrench C. hickey   D. kinker

6. If a cartridge fuse clip makes contact with its fuse with much less than normal spring tension, the result would MOST likely be that the   6.____

    A. fuse will immediately burn out
    B. voltage at the supply will be high
    C. voltage at the load will be high
    D. clips will become warm

7. Of the following units, the one which is a unit of work or energy is the   7.____

    A. joule   B. faraday   C. coulomb   D. farad

8. The one of the following substances which is the BEST conductor of electricity is   8.____

    A. iron   B. aluminum   C. tin   D. copper

9. The formula for the resistance of one branch of a wye which is equivalent to a given delta is $R_a = \dfrac{A}{A+B+C}$.   9.____
    If A = B = C = 3, the value of R_a is, *most nearly*,

    A. 1   B. 3   C. 6   D. 9

10. When a splice is soldered, flux is used to   10._____

    A. act as a binder   B. lubricate the surfaces
    C. keep the surfaces clean   D. prevent rapid loss of heat

11. A 2000 ft. cable which has an insulation resistance of 180 megohms is cut in half. The   11._____
insulation resistance of one of the 1000-ft. lengths will be, *most nearly,*

    A. 720 megohms   B. 360 megohms
    C. 90 megohms   D. 45 megohms

12. The area in circular mils of a piece of bare copper wire whose diameter is 0.1" is, *most*   12._____
nearly,

    A. 780   B. 1,000   C. 7,800   D. 10,000

13. The resistance of a piece of copper wire is   13._____

    A. *directly* proportional to its diameter
    B. *inversely* proportional to its length
    C. *directly* proportional to the square of its diameter
    D. *inversely* proportional to its cross-sectional area

14. If an incandescent lamp is operated at a voltage which is higher than its rated voltage,   14._____
the

    A. lumens output will be less than rated value
    B. current drawn will be less than rated value
    C. power consumed will be less than rated value
    D. life of the lamp will be less than rated value

15. The one of the following that is BEST suited to fight electrical fires is a   15._____

    A. CO_2 fire extinguisher   B. soda-acid fire extinguisher
    C. foam fire extinguisher   D. very fine spray of water

16. In order to get MAXIMUM power output from a battery, the external resistance should   16._____
equal

    A. zero
    B. one-half of the internal resistance of the battery
    C. the internal resistance of the battery
    D. twice the internal resistance of the battery

17. A voltmeter with a scale range of 0-5 has a resistance of 500 ohms. The resistance, in   17._____
ohms, of a multiplier for this instrument which will give it a range of 0 to 150 volts is, *most*
nearly,

    A. 750   B. 2,500   C. 14,500   D. 75,000

18. The one of the following items which is *commonly* used to increase the range of a d.c.   18._____
ammeter is a

    A. ceramicon   B. shunt
    C. current transformer   D. bridging transformer

19. Continuity of the conductors in an electrical circuit can be determined *conveniently* in the field by means of a(n)　　19.＿＿＿

    A. bell and battery set   B. Maxwell bridge
    C. Preece test   D. ammeter

Questions 20-25.

DIRECTIONS: Questions 20 to 25, inclusive, refer to the symbols of the A.S.A. which are listed below.

20. A push button is designated by the symbol numbered　　20.＿＿＿

    A. 4   B. 7   C. 13   D. 15

21. A fire alarm station is designated by the symbol numbered　　21.＿＿＿

    A. 3   B. 6   C. 9   D. 10

22. A duplex convenience outlet is designated by the symbol numbered　　22.＿＿＿

    A. 1   B. 2   C. 5   D. 17

23. A battery is designated by the symbol numbered　　23.＿＿＿

    A. 10   B. 13   C. 16   D. 18

24. A double pole switch is designated by the symbol numbered　　24.＿＿＿

    A. 1   B. 2   C. 8   D. 15

25. The designation for a 3-wire circuit is numbered　　25.＿＿＿

    A. 3   B. 5   C. 11   D. 14

KEY (CORRECT ANSWERS)

1.	A		11.	B
2.	A		12.	D
3.	C		13.	D
4.	B		14.	D
5.	C		15.	A
6.	D		16.	C
7.	A		17.	C
8.	D		18.	B
9.	A		19.	A
10.	C		20.	B

21.	C
22.	B
23.	C
24.	C
25.	D

TEST 6

DIRECTIONS: Each question or incomplete statement is followed by several suggested answers or completions. Select the one that BEST answers the question or completes the statement. *PRINT THE LETTER OF THE CORRECT ANSWER IN THE SPACE AT THE RIGHT.*

1. A good magnetic material is   1.____

    A.   aluminum   B.   iron   C.   brass   D.   carbon

2. A thermo-couple is a device for   2.____

    A.   changing frequency   B.   changing d.c. to a.c.
    C.   measuring temperature   D.   heat insulation

3. It is desired to operate a 6-volt lamp from a 120-volt a.c source. This can be done with   3.____
    the LEAST waste of power by using a

    A.   series resistor   B.   rectifier
    C.   step-down transformer   D.   rheostat

4. Rosin is a material *generally* used   4.____

    A.   in batteries   B.   as a dielectric
    C.   as a soldering flux   D.   for high voltage insulation

5. A milliampere is   5.____

    A.   1000 amperes   B.   100 amperes
    C.   .01 ampere   D.   .001 ampere

6. A compound motor usually has   6.____

    A.   only a shunt field   B.   only a series field
    C.   no brushes   D.   both a shunt and a series field

7. To connect a d.c. voltmeter to measure a voltage higher than the scale maximum, use a   7.____

    A.   series resistance   B.   shunt
    C.   current transformer   D.   voltage transformer

8. The voltage applied to the terminals of a storage battery to charge it CANNOT be   8.____

    A.   rectified a.c.   B.   straight d.c.
    C.   pulsating d.c.   D.   ordinary a.c.

9. When two unequal condensers are connected in parallel, the   9.____

    A.   total capacity is decreased
    B.   total capacity is increased
    C.   result will be a short-circuit
    D.   smaller one will break down

10. A megohm is   10.____

    A.   10 ohms   B.   100 ohms
    C.   1000 ohms   D.   1,000,000 ohms

11. Of the following, the poorest conductor of electricity is   11.____

    A. brass   B. lead   C. an acid solution D. slate

12. A flashlight battery, a condenser, and a flashlight bulb are connected in series with each   12.____
other. If the bulb burns brightly and steadily, then the condenser is

    A. open-circuited   B. short-circuited
    C. good   D. fully charged

13. A kilowatt of power will be taken from a 500-volt d.c. supply by a load of   13.____

    A. 200 amperes   B. 20 amperes   C. 2 amperes   D. 0.2 ampere

14. A commutator is used on a shunt generator in order to   14.____

    A. step-up voltage   B. step-up current
    C. change a.c. to d.c.   D. control generator speed

15. The number of cells connected in series in a 6-volt storage battery of the lead-acid type   15.____
is

    A. 2   B. 3   C. 4   D. 5

16. A 15-ampere circuit breaker as compared to a 15-ampere plug fuse   16.____

    A. can be reclosed   B. is cheaper
    C. is safer   D. is smaller

17. Lengths of rigid conduit are connected together to make up a long run by means of   17.____

    A. couplings   B. bushings   C. hickeys   D. lock nuts

18. BX is *commonly* used to indicate   18.____

    A. rigid conduit without wires
    B. flexible conduit without wires
    C. insulated wires covered with flexible steel armor
    D. insulated wires covered with a non-metallic covering

19. Good practice is to cut BX with a   19.____

    A. hacksaw   B. 3-wheel pipe cutter
    C. bolt cutter   D. heavy pliers

20. Silver is used for relay contacts in order to   20.____

    A. improve conductivity   B. avoid burning
    C. reduce costs   D. avoid arcing

21. Rigid conduit is fastened on the inside of the junction box by means of   21.____

    A. a bushing   B. a locknut
    C. a coupling   D. set-screw clamps

22. Of the following, the material which can BEST withstand high temperature is   22.____

    A. plastic   B. enamel   C. fiber   D. mica

23. A lead-acid type of storage battery exposed to freezing weather is *most likely* to freeze   23.____
when the

    A. battery is fully charged   B. battery is complete discharged
    C. water level is low   D. cap vent holes are plugged

24. An important reason making it poor practice to put telephone wires in the same conduit   24.____
with a.c. power lines is that

    A. power will be lost from the a.c. line
    B. the conduit will overheat
    C. the wires may be confused
    D. the telephone circuits will be noisy

25. In a loaded power circuit, it is MOST dangerous to   25.____

    A. *close* the circuit with a circuit breaker
    B. *close* the circuit with a knife switch
    C. *open* the circuit with a knife switch
    D. *open* the circuit with a circuit breaker

KEY (CORRECT ANSWERS)

1.	B	11.	D
2.	C	12.	B
3.	C	13.	C
4.	C	14.	C
5.	D	15.	B
6.	D	16.	A
7.	A	17.	A
8.	D	18.	C
9.	B	19.	A
10.	D	20.	A

21.	A
22.	D
23.	B
24.	D
25.	C

TEST 7

DIRECTIONS: Each question or incomplete statement is followed by several suggested answers or completions. Select the one that BEST answers the question or completes the statement. *PRINT THE LETTER OF THE CORRECT ANSWER IN THE SPACE AT THE RIGHT.*

1. When fastening electrical equipment to a hollow tile wall, it is good practice to use   1._____

    A. toggle bolts
    C. nails
    B. wood screws
    D. ordinary bolts and nuts

2. Of the following, the MOST important reason for keeping the oil in a transformer tank moisture-free is to prevent   2._____

    A. rusting
    C. freezing of the oil
    B. voltage breakdown
    D. overheating

3. A voltmeter is generally connected to a high potential a.c. bus through a(n)   3._____

    A. auto-transformer
    C. resistor
    B. potential transformer
    D. relay

4. The HIGHEST total voltage which can be measured by using two identical 0-300 volt range d.c. meters connected in series would be   4._____

    A. 150 volts   B. 300 volts   C. 450 volts   D. 600 volts

5. Transistors are MAINLY employed in electrical circuits to take the place of   5._____

    A. resistors   B. condensers   C. inductances   D. vacuum tubes

6. The MINIMUM number of 10-ohm, 1-ampere resistors which would be required to give an equivalent resistance of 10 ohms capable of carrying a 2-ampere load is   6._____

    A. 2   B. 3   C. 4   D. 5

7. To increase the current measuring range of an ammeter, the equipment *commonly* employed is a   7._____

    A. series resistor
    C. short-circuiting switch
    B. shunt
    D. choke

8. If a 10-watt lamp and a 100-watt lamp, each rated at 120 volts, are connected in series to a 240-volt source, then the voltage *across* the 10-watt lamp will be   8._____

    A. zero
    C. exactly 120 volts
    B. about 24 volts
    D. much more than 120 volts

9. If the load on the secondary of a small 10 to 1 step-up transformer is 100 watts, then the power being taken by the *primary* from the power line   9._____

    A. is less than 100 watts
    B. is exactly 100 watts
    C. is more than 100 watts
    D. may be more or less than 100 watts depending on the nature of the load

10. A 1/2-ohm, a 2-ohm, a 5-ohm, and a 25-ohm resistor are connected in series to a power source. The resistor which will consume the MOST power is the 10.____

    A. 1/2-ohm   B. 2-ohm   C. 5-ohm   D. 25-ohm

11. With respect to 60-cycle current, it is CORRECT to say that one cycle takes 11.____

    A. 1/60th of a second   B. 1/30th of a second
    C. 1/60th of a minute   D. 1/30th of a minute

12. A rheostat is used in the field circuit of a shunt generator to control the 12.____

    A. generator speed   B. load
    C. generator voltage   D. power factor

13. If a condenser has a safe working voltage of 250 volts d.c. then it would be *most likely* to break down if used across a 13.____

    A. 250-volt,60-cycle a.c. line   B. 250-volt d.c. line
    C. 240-volt battery   D. 120-volt, 25-cycle a.c. line

14. Transformer cores are generally made up of thin steel lamin-ations. The MAIN purpose of this is to 14.____

    A. reduce the transformer losses
    B. reduce the initial cost of the transformer
    C. increase the weight of the transformer
    D. prevent voltage breakdown in the transformer

15. The MAIN reason for using copper tips in soldering irons is that copper 15.____

    A. is a good heat conductor   B. is a good electrical conductor
    C. has a low melting point   D. is very soft

16. Five identical electric fans, each rated at 120-volts d.c., are connected in series with each other on a 600-volt circuit. If one fan develops an open circuit, then . 16.____

    A. the remaining fans will run, but at slow speed
    B. the remaining fans will run, but at above normal speed
    C. only one fan will run
    D. none of the fans will run

17. The pressure of a carbon brush on a commutator is measured with a 17.____

    A. spring balance   B. feeler gage   C. taper gage   D. wire gage

18. A non-inductive carbon resistor consumes 50 watts when connect ted across a 120-volt d.c.source. If it is connected across a 120-volt a.c. source, the power consumed by the resistor will be nearest to 18.____

    A. 30 watts   B. 40 watts   C. 50 watts   D. 60 watts

19. Of the following, the combination of lamps which will draw the MOST current from a stan-dard 120-volt branch circuit is one with 19.____

    A. three 150-watt lamps   B. one 300-watt lamp
    C. four 100-watt lamps   D. six 50-watt lamps

20. A condenser is sometimes connected across contact points which make and break a d.c.   20.____
    circuit in order to reduce arcing of the points. The condenser produces this effect
    because it

    A. discharges when the contacts open
    B. charges when the contacts open
    C. charges while the contacts are closed
    D. discharges when the contacts are closed

KEY (CORRECT ANSWERS)

1.	A	11.	A
2.	B	12.	C
3.	B	13.	A
4.	D	14.	A
5.	D	15.	A
6.	C	16.	D
7.	B	17.	A
8.	D	18.	C
9.	C	19.	A
10.	D	20.	B

EXAMINATION SECTION
TEST 1

DIRECTIONS: Each question or incomplete statement is followed by several suggested answers or completions. Select the one that BEST answers the question or completes the statement. *PRINT THE LETTER OF THE CORRECT ANSWER IN THE SPACE AT THE RIGHT.*

1. The one of the following items which is used to test the electrolyte of a battery is a(n)   1.____

    A. manometer   B. hydrometer   C. electrometer   D. hygrometer

2. The one of the following instruments which CANNOT be used to measure the current in both a.c. circuits and d.c. circuits *without* additional equipment is a(n)   2.____

    A. D'Arsonval galvanometer
    B. hot wire ammeter
    C. iron vane ammeter
    D. electro-dynamometer type ammeter

3. A growler is *commonly* used to test   3.____

    A. relays   B. armatures   C. cable joints   D. rectifiers

4. In cutting a large stranded copper cable with a hacksaw, the PRIMARY reason for using a blade with fine teeth rather than one with coarse teeth is   4.____

    A. that using a coarse blade overheats the copper
    B. to avoid making too wide a cut
    C. that the coarse blade bends too easily
    D. to avoid snagging or pulling the strands

5. Toggle bolts are MOST commonly used to fasten an outlet box to a   5.____

    A. solid brick wall   B. solid concrete wall
    C. plaster or tile wall   D. wooden partition wall

6. Laminated sheet steel is *usually* used to make up transformer cores in order to minimize   6.____

    A. copper loss   B. weight
    C. hysterisis loss   D. eddy current loss

Questions 7-9.

DIRECTIONS: Questions 7 to 9, inclusive, refer to the diagram below.

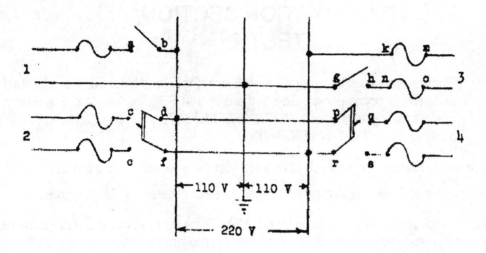

7. Circuit No. 3 in the above diagram

    A. supplies 220 volts to the load
    B. would be correctly wired if there were a direct connection instead of a fuse between points k and m
    C. would be correctly wired if there were a direct connection instead of a fuse between points n and o
    D. would be correctly wired if the switch and fuse were eliminated and replaced by a direct connection between g and o

7.____

8. Circuit No. 4 in the above diagram

    A. is not properly fused as it should have only one fuse in the hot leg
    B. supplies 220 volts to the load
    C. is grounded if, with the switch open, test lamps light when placed between points p and r
    D. is shorted if, with the switch open, test lamps light when placed between points p and r

8.____

9. Circuit No. 1 in the above diagram

    A. supplies 220 volts to the load
    B. is grounded if a pair of test lamps light when placed between point b and ground
    C. is not properly fused as it should have a fuse in each leg
    D. is shorted if, with the switch open, a pair of test lamps light when placed between points a and b

9.____

10. An ideal transformer which has 1 ampere in the primary and 10 amperes in the secondary MUST have

    A. 10 volt amperes in the primary
    B. a ratio of primary turns to secondary turns of 1 to 10
    C. 10 volt amperes in the secondary
    D. a ratio of primary turns to secondary turns of 10 to 1

10.____

11. In soldering electric wires, rosin is used in preference to acid as a flux PRIMARILY because rosin is   11.____

    A. a dry powder   B. non-conducting
    C. non-corrosive   D. a strong electrolyte

12. The one of the following items which should be used to test whether a circuit is a.c. or d.c. is a   12.____

    A. pair of test lamps   B. hot wire ammeter
    C. psychrometer   D. neon light

13. An ideal transformer has 200 volts impressed across its primary. If the primary current is 10 amperes,   13.____

    A. the ratio of primary turns to secondary turns is 20 to 1
    B. the ratio of primary turns to secondary turns is 1 to 20
    C. there are approximately 2 KVA in the secondary
    D. the secondary voltage is 20 volts

14. To control a lamp independently from five locations, the one of the following groups of switches which is required is: 14.____

    A. Four 3-way switches and one 4-way switch
    B. Three 3-way and two 4-way switches
    C. Two 3-way and three 4-way switches
    D. Two single-pole, single throw switches and three 4-way switches

Questions 15-20.

DIRECTIONS: Questions 15 to 20, inclusive, refer to the terms listed below which are defined in the electrical code.

1. Appliance	9. Periodic duty	17. Service
2. Branch Circuit	10. Short time duty	18. Service cable
3. Connected load	11. Varying duty	19. Service conductor
4. Concealed	12. Enclosed	20. Service drop
5. Computed load	13. Equipment	21. Service Entrance conductors
6. Device	14. Feeder	22. Sub-feeder
7. Demand factor	15. Isolated	23. Scalable
8. Intermittent duty	16. Mains	24. Rating

15. The one term in the above which is defined as a unit of an electrical system, other than a conductor, which is intended to carry but not consume electrical energy, is numbered   15.____

    A. 1   B. 6   C. 13   D. 19

16. The one term in the above which is defined as that portion of the wiring system extending beyond the final overcurrent device protecting the circuit, is numbered   16.____

    A. 2   B. 14   C. 16   D. 22

17. The one term in the above which is defined as that portion of the overhead service con-   17.____
    ductors between the last pole and the first point of attachment to the building, is num-
    bered

    A. 17   B. 18   C. 20   D. 21

18. The one term in the above which is defined as rendered inaccessible by the structure or   18.____
    finish of the building, is numbered

    A. 4   B. 12   C. 15   D. 23

19. The one term in the above which is defined as a requirement of service that demands   19.____
    operation at loads, and for intervals of time, both of which may be subject to wide varia-
    tion, is numbered

    A. 8   B. 9   C. 10   D. 11

20. The one term in the above which is defined as the sum of the continuous ratings of the   20.____
    load consuming apparatus connected to the system or part of the system under con-
    sideration, is numbered

    A. 3   B. 5   C. 7   D. 24

21. In electrical tests, a megger is calibrated to read   21.____

    A. amperes   B. ohms   C. volts   D. watts

22. Metal cabinets for lighting circuits are grounded in order to   22.____

    A. save insulating material
    B. provide a return for the netural current
    C. eliminate short circuits
    D. minimize the possibility of shock

23. In an a.c. circuit containing only resistance, the power factor will be   23.____

    A. zero   B. 50% lagging   C. 50% leading   D. 100%

24. The size of fuse for a two-wire lighting circuit using No. 14 wire should NOT exceed   24.____

    A. 15 amperes   B. 20 amperes
    C. 25 amperes   D. 30 amperes

25. When working near acid storage batteries, extreme care should be taken to guard   25.____
    against sparks MAINLY because a spark may

    A. cause an explosion
    B. set fire to the electrolyte
    C. short-circuit a ceil
    D. ignite the battery case

────────

KEY (CORRECT ANSWERS)

1.	B		11.	C
2.	A		12.	D
3.	B		13.	C
4.	D		14.	C
5.	C		15.	B
6.	D		16.	A
7.	D		17.	C
8.	B		18.	A
9.	D		19.	D
10.	D		20.	A

21.	B
22.	D
23.	D
24.	A
25.	A

———

TEST 2

DIRECTIONS: Each question or incomplete statement is followed by several suggested answers or completions. Select the one that BEST answers the question or completes the statement. *PRINT THE LETTER OF THE CORRECT ANSWER IN THE SPACE AT THE RIGHT.*

1. If a blown fuse in an existing lighting circuit is replaced by another of the same rating which also blows, the PROPER maintenance procedure is to

    A. use a higher rating fuse
    B. cut out some of the outlets in the circuit
    C. check the circuit for grounds or shorts
    D. install a renewable fuse

1.____

2. The number of fuses required in a three-phase, four-wire branch circuit with grounded neutral is

    A. one   B. two   C. three   D. four

2.____

3. The electrodes of the common dry cell are carbon *and*

    A. zinc   B. lead   C. steel   D. tin

3.____

4. An electrician's hickey is used to

    A. strip insulation off wire   B. pull cable through conduits
    C. thread metallic conduit   D. bend metallic conduit

4.____

5. A group of wire sizes that is CORRECTLY arranged in the order of increasing current-carrying capacity is:

    A. 6; 12; 3/0   B. 12; 6; 3/0   C. 3/0; 12; 6   D. 3/0; 6; 12

5.____

6. The metal which is the BEST conductor of electricity is

    A. silver   B. copper   C. aluminum   D. nickel

6.____

7. If the two supply wires to a d.c. series motor are reversed, the motor will

    A. run in the opposite direction   B. not run
    C. run in the same direction   D. become a generator

7.____

8. Before doing work on a motor, to prevent accidental starting, you should

    A. short-circuit the motor leads   B. remove the fuses
    C. block the rotor   D. ground the frame

8.____

9. The material *commonly* used for brushes on d.c. motors is

    A. copper   B. carbon   C. brass   D. aluminum

9.____

10. The conductors of a two-wire No. 12 armored cable used in an ordinary lighting circuit are _____ insulated.

    A. stranded and rubber   B. solid and rubber
    C. stranded and cotton   D. solid and cotton

10.____

11. The rating, 125V.-10A.; 250V.-5A., *commonly* applies to a   11._____

    A. snap switch   B. lamp   C. conductor   D. fuse

12. Commutators are found on   12._____

    A. alternators   B. d.c. motors
    C. transformers   D. circuit breakers

13. A proper *use* for an electrician's knife is to   13._____

    A. cut wires
    B. pry out a small cartridge fuse
    C. mark the place where a conduit is to be cut
    D. skin wires

14. A d.c. device taking one milliampere at one kilovolt takes a *total* power of one   14._____

    A. milliwatt   B. watt   C. kilowatt   D. megawatt

15. In connection with electrical work, it is GOOD practice to   15._____

    A. scrape the silvery coating from a wire before soldering
    B. nick a wire in several places before bending it around a terminal
    C. assume that a circuit is alive
    D. open a switch to check the load

16. Mica is *commonly* used as an insulation   16._____

    A. for cartridge fuse cases
    B. between commutator bars
    C. between lead acid battery plates
    D. between transformer steel laminations

17. The function of a step-down transformer is to *decrease* the   17._____

    A. voltage   B. current   C. power   D. frequency

18. A conduit run is MOST often terminated in a(n)   18._____

    A. coupling   B. elbow   C. bushing   D. outlet box

19. In long conduit runs, pull boxes are *sometimes* installed at intermediate points to   19._____

    A. avoid using couplings
    B. support the conduit
    C. make use of short lengths of conduit
    D. facilitate pulling wire

20. A rheostat would LEAST likely be used in connection with the operation of   20._____

    A. transformers   B. motors
    C. generators   D. battery charging M.G. sets

21. The fiber bushing inserted at the end of a piece of flexible metallic conduit prevents   21.____

    A. moisture from entering the cable
    B. the rough edges from cutting the insulation
    C. the wires from touching each other
    D. the wires from slipping back into the armor

22. Portable lamp cord is MOST likely to have   22.____

    A. paper insulation   B. solid wire
    C. armored wire   D. stranded wire

23. Thermal relays are used in motor circuits to protect a-gainst   23.____

    A. reverse current   B. overspeed
    C. overvoltage   D. overload

24. It is GOOD practice to connect the ground wire for a building electrical system to a   24.____

    A. vent pipe   B. steam pipe
    C. cold water pipe   D. gas pipe

25. The MOST practical way to determine in the field the *approximate* length of insulated   25.____
wire in a large coil is to

    A. unreel the wire and measure it with a 6-foot rule
    B. find another coil with the length marked on it and compare
    C. count the turns and multiply by the average circumference
    D. weigh the coil and compare it with a 1000-ft. coil

———————

KEY (CORRECT ANSWERS)

1.	C		11.	A
2.	C		12.	B
3.	A		13.	D
4.	D		14.	B
5.	B		15.	C
6.	A		16.	B
7.	C		17.	A
8.	B		18.	D
9.	B		19.	D
10.	B		20.	A

21.	B
22.	D
23.	D
24.	C
25.	C

TEST 3

DIRECTIONS: Each question or incomplete statement is followed by several suggested answers or completions. Select the one that BEST answers the question or completes the statement. *PRINT THE LETTER OF THE CORRECT ANSWER IN THE SPACE AT THE RIGHT.*

1. The property of an electric circuit tending to prevent the flow of current and, at the same time, causing electric energy to be converted into heat energy, is called   1.____

    A. conductance   B. inductance
    C. resistance   D. reluctance

2. If a certain length of copper wire is elongated by stretching and its volume does not change, it then can be said that, for a fixed volume, the resistance of this conductor varies *directly* as   2.____

    A. the square of its length
    B. its length
    C. the cube of its length
    D. the square root of its length

3. The property of a circuit or of a material which tends to permit the flow of an electric current is called   3.____

    A. conductance   B. inductance
    C. resistance   D. reluctance

4. The equivalent resistance in ohms of a circuit having four resistances, respectively, 1, 2, 3, and 4 ohms in parallel, is   4.____

    A. 14.8   B. 10   C. 4.8   D. .48

5. The area in square inches of one circular mil is   5.____

    A. $(\pi/4)(0.001)^2$ B. $4\pi(.01)$
    C. $(0.001)^2$ D. $(0.01)^2$

6. The current through a field rheostat is 5 amperes and its resistance is 10 ohms. The power lost as heat in the rheostat is, *approximately,*   6.____

    A. 500 watts   B. 250 watts   C. 125 watts   D. 50 watts

7. A d.c. motor takes 30 amps at 220 volts and has an efficiency of 80%. The horsepower available at the pulley is, *approximately,*   7.____

    A. 10   B. 7   C. 5   D. 2

8. A tap is a tool *commonly* used to   8.____

    A. remove broken screws   B. cut internal threads
    C. cut external threads   D. smooth the ends of conduit

9. Lead covering is used on conductors for   9.____

    A. heat prevention   B. explosion protection
    C. grounding   D. moisture proofing

10. The one of the following tools which is run through a conduit to clear it before wire is pulled through is a(n)   10.____

    A. auger   B. borer   C. stop   D. mandrel

11. A pothead as used in the trade is a   11.____

    A. pot to heat solder
    B. cable terminal
    C. protective device used for cable splicing
    D. type of fuse

12. Resistance measurements show that an electro-magnet coil consisting of 90 turns of wire having an average diameter of 8 inches is shorted. The length of wire, in feet, required to rewind this coil is, *approximately,*   12.____

    A. 110   B. 190   C. 550   D. 2280

13. An inexpensive and portable instrument *commonly* used for detecting the presence of static electricity is the   13.____

    A. neon-tube electrical circuit tester   B. gauss meter
    C. photo-electric cell   D. startometer

14. A coil of wire is connected to an a.c. source of supply. If an iron bar is placed in the center of this coil, it will affect the magnetic circuit in such a way that the   14.____

    A. inductance of the coil will increase
    B. power taken by the coil will increase
    C. coil will draw more current
    D. impedance of the coil will decrease

15. The electrolyte used with the Edison nickel-iron-alkaline cell is   15.____

    A. sulphuric acid   B. nitric acid
    C. potassium hydroxide   D. lead peroxide

16. The D'Arsonval galvanometer principle used in sensitive current-measuring instruments is *nothing more than*   16.____

    A. the elongation of a wire- due to the flow of current
    B. two coils carrying current reacting from one another
    C. the dynamic reaction of an aluminum disc due to eddy currents
    D. a coil turning in a magnetic field

17. With reference to armature windings, lap windings are *often* called   17.____

    A. series windings   B. cascade windings
    C. multiple or parallel windings   D. ring windings

18. With reference to armature windings, wave windings are *often* called   18.____

    A. series windings   B. cascade windings
    C. multiple or parallel windings   D. ring windings

19. Polarization in a dry cell causes the reduction in the current capacity of the cell after it has delivered current for some time. A remedy for polarization is to bring oxidizing agents into intimate contact with the cell cathode. A chemical agent *commonly* used for this purpose is   19.____

    A. potash
    C. lead carbonate
    B. manganese dioxide
    D. acetylene

20. The e.m.f. inducted in a coil is GREATEST where the magnetic field within the coil is   20.____

    A. constant
    C. decreasing
    B. increasing
    D. changing most rapidly

21. The BRIGHTNESS of incandescent lamps is *commonly* rated in   21.____

    A. foot candles   B. kilowatts   C. lumens   D. watts

22. The effect of eddy currents in a.c. magnetic circuits may be *reduced* by   22.____

    A. laminating the iron used
    B. making the magnet core of solid steel
    C. making the magnet core of solid cast iron
    D. inserting brass rings around the magnet core

23. The direction of rotation of a single-phase repulsion induction motor can be *reversed* by   23.____

    A. reversing two supply leads
    B. shifting the position of the brushes
    C. changing the connections to the field
    D. changing the connections to the armature

24. Underexciting the d.c. field of a synchronous motor will cause it to   24.____

    A. slow down
    B. speed up
    C. draw lagging current
    D. be unable to carry full normal load

25. A certain 6-pole 60-cycle induction motor has a slip of 5% when operating at a certain load. The *actual* speed of this motor under these conditions is, *most nearly,*   25.____

    A. 1200 rpm   B. 1140 rpm   C. 570 rpm   D. 120 rpm

KEY (CORRECT ANSWERS)

1.	C		11.	B
2.	A		12.	B
3.	A		13.	A
4.	D		14.	A
5.	A		15.	C
6.	B		16.	D
7.	B		17.	C
8.	B		18.	A
9.	D		19.	B
10.	D		20.	D

21.	C
22.	A
23.	B
24.	C
25.	B

———

TEST 4

Questions 1-4.

DIRECTIONS: Questions 1 to 4, inclusive, refer to the diagram below.

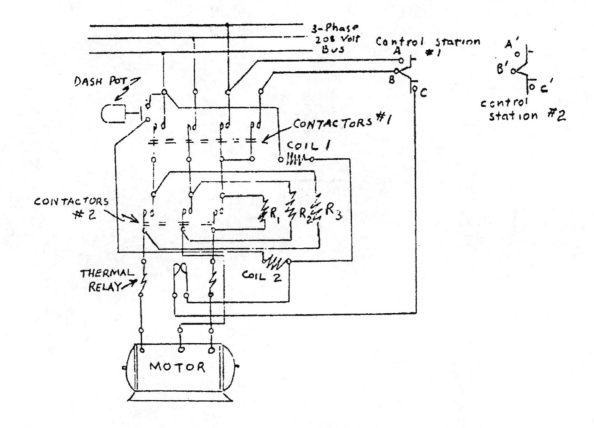

The above is a wiring diagram of a resistance starting controller for a.c. motors. This type of starter limits the starting current by means of equal resistances in each line wire leading to the motor. These resistances are automatically shunted out after the motor has gained full speed connecting the motor directly across the lines.

Station #2 may be added to Station #1 by connecting the start buttons in parallel and the stop buttons in series.

1. When the starting button is pressed,   1.____

   A. contactor coil #1 is immediately energized, causing contactors #1 to close
   B. contactor coil #2 is immediately energized, causing contactors #2 to close

    C.   contactor coil #1 is energized, but contactors #1 close only after contactors #2 close

    D.   both contactors #1 and contactors #2 close at the same time

2.   The motor shown in the above diagram is a 3-phase   2.____

    A.   wound rotor induction motor
    B.   squirrel-cage induction motor
    C.   capacitator-type induction motor
    D.   synchronous motor

3.   When the motor current becomes excessive, the thermal relay will actuate and cause   3.____

    A.   contactors #1 to open first
    B.   contactors #2 to open first
    C.   contactors #1 and contactors #2 to open simultaneously
    D.   the dash pot to energize coil #2

4.   To add control station #2 to the circuit,   4.____

    A.   A is connected to A^1, lead to C is disconnected and connected to C^1, and C is connected to B^1

    B.   A is connected to A^1, C to C, and B to B^1

    C.   lead to B is disconnected and connected to B^1, A^1 to B, and C to C^1

    D.   A is connected to B^1, A^1 to B, and C to C^1

Questions 5-12.

DIRECTIONS: Questions 5 to 12, inclusive, refer to the electric wiring plan below.

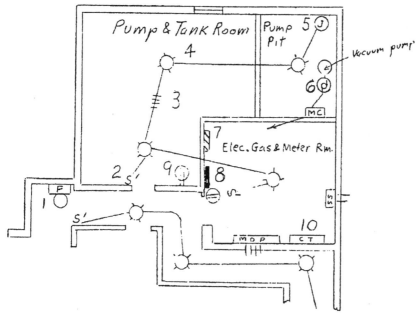

PART OF BUILDING CELLAR PLAN

5. Symbol numbered 1 represents a   5.____

    A. local fire alarm gong   B. bell
    C. buzzer   D. local fire alarm station

6. Symbol numbered 2 represents a   6.____

    A. 3-way switch   B. 2-way switch
    C. single pole switch   D. push button switch and pilot

7. Symbol numbered 3 represents a   7.____

    A. flexible conduit
    B. the number of phases
    C. the number of conductors in the conduit
    D. the size of wire in the conduit

8. Symbol numbered 4 represents a   8.____

    A. drop cord   B. lamp holder
    C. floor outlet   D. ceiling outlet

9. Symbol numbered 5 represents a   9.____

    A. telephone jack   B. junction box
    C. Jandus fixture   D. convenience outlet

10. Symbol numbered 6 represents a   10.____

    A. doorbell   B. drop cord   C. transformer   D. motor

11. Symbol numbered 7 represents a(n)   11.____

    A. power panel   B. telephone box
    C. interconnection cabinet   D. voltmeter

12. Symbol numbered 8 represents a(n)   12.____

    A. meter panel   B. interconnection cabinet
    C. lighting panel   D. underfloor duct

Questions 13-16.

DIRECTIONS: Questions 13 to 16, inclusive, refer to the diagram below.

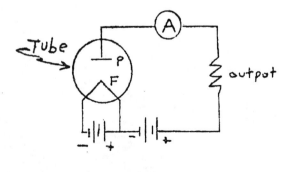

Figure I

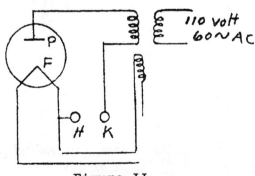

Figure II

13. With reference to Figure I, the flow of electrons is

    A. blocked by the negative filament
    B. blocked by the negative plate
    C. from F to P
    D. from P to F

13.____

14. Figure II represents the diagram of a(n)

    A. rectifier   B. amplifier
    C. oscillator   D. voltage doubler

14.____

15. With reference to Figure II, under normal operating conditions, terminal

    A. H is negative
    B. H is alternately plus or minus
    C. K is positive
    D. H is positive

15.____

16. The tube in the above diagram (Figure I) is a *commonly* used symbol for a

    A. tetrode   B. heptode   C. pentode   D. diode

16.____

17. A 10" pulley revolving at 950 rpm is belted to a 20" pulley. The rpm of the 20" pulley is, *most nearly,*

    A. 1900   B. 1425   C. 950   D. 475

17.____

18. A battery composed of 5 cells, each having an e.m.f. of 1.5 volts and an internal resistance of .1 ohm, is connected to a .5 ohm resistance. If the cells are all in parallel, the current in amperes drawn from the battery is, *most nearly,*

    A. 2.88   B. 3.00   C. 12.50   D. 14.50

18.____

19. The MAXIMUM power delivered by a battery is obtained when the external resistance of the battery is made

    A. two times as large as its internal resistance
    B. one-half as large as its internal resistance
    C. one-quarter as large as its internal resistance
    D. equal to its internal resistance

19.____

20. A voltmeter is connected across the terminals of a certain battery. The difference between the open-circuit voltage and the voltage when current is taken from the battery is the

    A. internal voltage drop in the battery
    B. external voltage drop of the battery
    C. emf of the battery
    D. drop in voltage across the load resistance

20.____

Questions 21-22.

DIRECTIONS: According to the electrical code, the number of wires, running through or terminating in an outlet or junction box, shall be limited according to the free space within the box and the size of the wires. For combinations NOT found in a table provided for the selection of junction boxes, the code gives the following table:

Size of Conductor	Free Space Within Box for Each Conductor
No . 14	2 cubic inches
No . 12	2.25 cubic inches
No . 10	2.5 cubic inches
No . 8	3 cubic inches

21.   In accordance with the above information, the MINIMUM size of box, in inches, for nine No. 12 wires is   21.____

    A.   1 1/2 X 4 square   B.   1 1/2 X 3 square
    C.   2 X 3 square   D.   2 X 4 square

22.   With reference to the above information, the MINIMUM size of box, in inches, for four No. 8 wires and four No. 10 wires is   22.____

    A.   1 1/2 X 4 square   B.   1 1/2 X 3 square
    C.   2 X 3 square   D.   2 X 4 square

23.   The current, in amperes, drawn from a battery cell having an e.m.f. of 3 volts and an internal resistance of 0.02 ohm when connected to an external resistance of 0.28 ohm is, *most nearly,*   23.____

    A. 5   B. 10   C. 15   D. 20

24.   The term OPEN CIRCUIT means that   24.____

    A.   the wiring is exposed
    B.   the fuse is located outdoors
    C.   the circuit has one end exposed
    D.   all parts of the circuit (or path) are not in contact

25.   The direction of rotation of a 3-phase wound rotor induction motor can be *reversed* by   25.____

    A.   interchanging the connections to any two rotor terminals
    B.   interchanging the connections to any two stator terminals
    C.   interchanging the connections to the field
    D.   shifting the position of the brushes

KEY (CORRECT ANSWERS)

1.	A		11.	A
2.	B		12.	C
3.	C		13.	C
4.	A		14.	A
5.	A		15.	D
6.	C		16.	D
7.	C		17.	D
8.	D		18.	A
9.	B		19.	D
10.	D		20.	A

21.	A
22.	A
23.	B
24.	D
25.	B

———

TEST 5

DIRECTIONS: Each question or incomplete statement is followed by several suggested answers or completions. Select the one that BEST answers the question or completes the statement. *PRINT THE LETTER OF THE CORRECT ANSWER IN THE SPACE AT THE RIGHT.*

Questions 1-4.

DIRECTIONS: Questions 1 through 4, inclusive, refer to the diagram below.

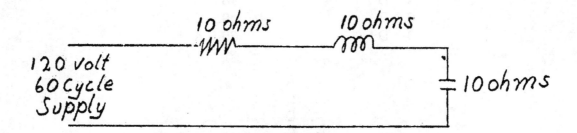

1. The value of the impedance, in ohms, of the above circuit is, *most nearly,*   1.____

    A. 30   B. 10   C. 3.33   D. 1.73

2. The current, in amperes, flowing in the above circuit is, *most nearly,*   2.____

    A. 4   B. 6   C. 12   D. 18

3. The power, in watts, consumed in the above circuit is, *most nearly,*   3.____

    A. 480   B. 635   C. 720   D. 1440

4. The voltage drop across the 10-ohm resistance is, *most nearly,*   4.____

    A. 10V   B. 40V   C. 60V   D. 120V

Questions 5-6.

DIRECTIONS: Questions 5 and 6 are to be answered in accordance with the information in the paragraph below.

    In the year 1914, a circuit was produced in which an electric current showed no diminution in strength 5 hours after the e.m.f. was removed. The current was induced magnetically in a short-circuited coil of lead wire at -270°C, produced by liquid helium, and the inducing source was removed. This experiment indicates that the resistance of lead was practically zero at this extremely low temperature.

5. In accordance with the above paragraph, the current in the short-circuited lead wire MUST have been   5.____

    A. electro-static current   B. induced current
    C. leading current   D. lagging current

6. According to the above paragraph, the resistance of lead   6._____

    A. is practically zero at -270°C
    B. is practically infinity at -270°C

7. A form of metal *suitable* for carrying electrical current, such as a wire or cable, is called   7._____
a(n)

    A. raceway   B. trough   C. conductor   D. appliance

8. In accordance with the electrical code, the MINIMUM size of the wire used on a 15-   8._____
ampere circuit is

    A. No. 16   B. No. 14   C. No. 12   D. No. 10

9. In cutting conduit, the pressure applied on a hacksaw should be on   9._____

    A. the forward stroke only
    B. the return stroke only
    C. the forward and return strokes equally
    D. either the forward or return stroke, depending on the material

10. To measure the diameter of wire *most* accurately, it is BEST to use a   10._____

    A. wire gauge   B. depth gauge
    C. micrometer   D. microtome

11. To measure the speed of an armature directly in rpm, it is BEST to use a   11._____

    A. tachometer   B. chronometer
    C. bolometer   D. manometer

12. The PRIMARY purpose for the use of oil in certain transformers is   12._____

    A. for lubrication
    B. to reduce the permeability
    C. to provide insulation and aid in cooling
    D. as a rust inhibitor

13. A single-throw switch should be mounted in such a way that, to,open the switch,the blade   13._____
MUST move

    A. to the right   B. upward
    C. to the left   D. downward

14. Of the following, the metal MOST commonly used as a filament in electric lamps is   14._____

    A. platinum   B. tungsten   C. manganin   D. constantin

15. Of the following tools, the one MOST commonly used to cut holes in masonry is the   15._____

    A. star drill   B. auger   C. router   D. reamer

16. Resistance coils having a small resistance temperature coefficient, are made with a wire   16._____
of a metal alloy called

    A. mallacca   B. massicot   C. manganin   D. malachite

17. For lead-acid type storage batteries, the *normal* battery potential is calculated on the basis of   17.____

    A. 12 volts per cell   B. 6 volts per cell
    C. 3 volts per cell   D. 2 volts per cell

18. Fluorescent lamps, while designed for alternating-current operation, can be used on a direct-current circuit if a specially designed d.c. auxiliary *and*   18.____

    A. parallel condenser of currect value are employed
    B. series condenser of correct value are employed
    C. parallel resistance of correct value are employed
    D. series resistance of correct value are employed

19. A transformer bank composed of three single-phase transformers is to be connected delta-delta. The primary side is first connected, but, before making the last secondary connection, the transformer should be tested for   19.____

    A. an open-circuit   B. a grounded-circuit
    C. a cross-circuit   D. the proper phase relation

20. As a safety measure, water should not be used to extinguish fires involving electrical equipment. The MAIN reason is that water   20.____

    A. is ineffective on electrical fires
    B. may transmit current and shock to the user
    C. may destroy the insulation property of wire
    D. may short-circuit the equipment

21. The SMALLEST number of wires necessary to carry 3-phase current is   21.____

    A. 2 wires   B. 3 wires   C. 4 wires   D. 5 wires

22. A 5-ampere d.c. ammeter may be *safely* used on a 50-ampere circuit provided the   22.____

    A. correct size current transformer is used
    B. proper size shunt is used
    C. proper circuit series resistance is used
    D. proper size multiplier is used

23. As used in the electrical code, the term "device" refers to   23.____

    A. an electrical appliance which does not have moving parts
    B. a unit of an electrical system other than a conductor which is intended to carry but not consume electrical energy
    C. current consuming equipment
    D. an accessory which is intended primarily to perform a mechanical rather than an electrical function

24. The difference of electrical potential between two wires of a circuit is its   24.____

    A. voltage   B. resistance   C. amperage   D. wattage

25. On long straight horizontal conduit runs, it is GOOD practice to use   25.____

    A. expansion joints   B. universal joints
    C. isolation joints   D. insulation joints

KEY (CORRECT ANSWERS)

1.	B	11.	A
2.	C	12.	C
3.	D	13.	D
4.	D	14.	B
5.	B	15.	A
6.	A	16.	C
7.	C	17.	D
8.	C	18.	D
9.	A	19.	D
10.	C	20.	B

21.	B
22.	B
23.	B
24.	A
25.	A

———

TEST 6

DIRECTIONS: Each question or incomplete statement is followed by several suggested answers or completions. Select the one that BEST answers the question or completes the statement. *PRINT THE LETTER OF THE CORRECT ANSWER IN THE SPACE AT THE RIGHT.*

1. A circular mil is a measure of   1.____

    A. area   B. length   C. volume   D. weight

2. In electrical tests, a megger is calibrated to read   2.____

    A. amperes   B. ohms   C. volts   D. watts

3. Metal cabinets for lighting circuits are grounded in order to   3.____

    A. save insulating material
    B. provide a return for the neutral current
    C. eliminate short circuits
    D. minimize the possibility of shock

4. In an a.c. circuit containing only resistance, the power factor will be   4.____

    A. zero   B. 50% lagging   C. 50% leading   D. 100%

5. The size of fuse for a two-wire lighting circuit using No. 14 wire should NOT exceed   5.____

    A. 15 amperes   B. 20 amperes
    C. 25 amperes   D. 30 amperes

6. When working near acid storage batteries, extreme care should be taken to guard against   6.____
sparks MAINLY because a spark may

    A. cause an explosion
    B. set fire to the electrolyte
    C. short-circuit a cell
    D. ignite the battery case

7. If a blown fuse in an existing lighting circuit is replaced by another of the same rating   7.____
which also blows, the PROPER maintenance procedure is to

    A. use a higher rating fuse
    B. cut out some of the outlets in the circuit
    C. check the circuit for grounds or shorts
    D. install a renewable fuse

8. The number of fuses required in a three-phase, four-wire, branch circuit, with grounded   8.____
neutral, is

    A. one   B. two   C. three   D. four

9. The electrodes of the common dry cell are carbon *and*   9.____

    A. zinc   B. lead   C. steel   D. tin

10. An electrician's hickey is used to   10.____

    A. strip insulation off wire
    B. pull cable through conduits
    C. thread metallic conduit
    D. bend metallic conduit

11. A group of wire sizes that is *correctly* arranged in the order of INCREASING current-car-   11.____
rying capacity is:

    A. 6;12;3/0   B. 12;6;3/0   C. 3/0;12;6   D. 3/0;6;12

Questions 12-19.

DIRECTIONS: Questions 12 to 19 inclusive refer to the figures below. Each question gives the proper figure to use with that question.

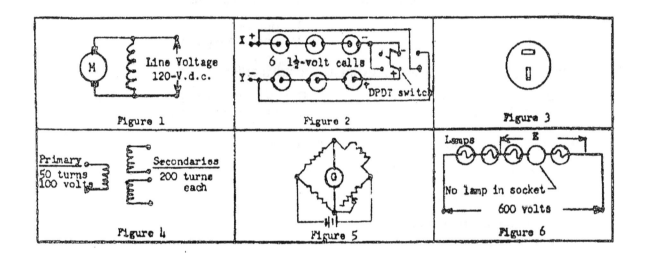

12. Figure 1 shows the standard diagram for a(n)   12.____

    A. synchronous motor   B. shunt motor
    C. series motor   D. induction motor

13. In Figure 1, if the line current is 5 amperes, the energy consumed by the motor if in con-   13.____
tinuous operation for 3 hours, is _____ watthours.

    A. 200   B. 600   C. 1800   D. 9000

14. In Figure 2, with the DPDT switch closed to the right, the voltage between X and Y is   14.____

    A. 0   B. 1 1/2   C. 4 1/2   D. 9

15. In Figure 2, with the DPDT closed to the left, the voltage between X and Y is   15.____

    A. 9   B. 4 1/2   C. 1 1/2   D. 0

16. The convenience outlet shown in Figure 3 is used, particularly, for a device which   16.____

    A. is polarized   B. is often disconnected
    C. takes a heavy current   D. vibrates

17. In Figure 4,the MAXIMUM secondary voltage possible by the interconnecting the secondaries is _____ volts.

    A. 50   B. 200   C. 400   D. 800

17.____

18. Figure 5 shows a Wheatstone bridge which is used to measure

    A. voltage   B. resistance   C. current   D. power

18.____

19. In Figure 6,with one of the five good lamps removed from its socket as indicated, the voltage E is *nearest* to

    A. 240   B. 0   C. 600   D. 360

19.____

20. The metal which is the BEST conductor of electricity is

    A. silver   B. copper   C. aluminum   D. nickel

20.____

21. If the two supply wires to a d.c.series motor are reversed, the motor will

    A. run in the opposite direction   B. not run
    C. run in the same direction   D. become a generator

21.____

22. Before doing work on a motor,to prevent accidental starting you *should*

    A. short circuit the motor leads   B. remove the fuses
    C. block the rotor   D. ground the frame

22.____

23. The material *commonly* used for brushes on d.c. motors is

    A. copper   B. carbon   C. brass   D. aluminum

23.____

24. The conductors of a two-wire,No.12,armored cable used in an ordinary lighting circuit are

    A. stranded and rubber insulated
    B. solid and rubber insulated
    C. stranded and cotton insulated
    D. solid and cotton insulated

24.____

25. The rating,125C.-10A,; 250V.-5A., *commonly* applies to a

    A. snap switch   B. lamp   C. conductor   D. fuse

25.____

KEY (CORRECT ANSWERS)

1.	A		11.	B
2.	B		12.	B
3.	D		13.	C
4.	D		14.	C
5.	A		15.	A
6.	A		16.	A
7.	C		17.	D
8.	C		18.	B
9.	A		19.	C
10.	D		20.	A

21.	C
22.	B
23.	B
24.	B
25.	A

———

EXAMINATION SECTION
TEST 1

DIRECTIONS: Each question or incomplete statement is followed by several suggested answers or completions. Select the one that BEST answers the question or completes the statement. *PRINT THE LETTER OF THE CORRECT ANSWER IN THE SPACE AT THE RIGHT.*

1.   A set of conductors originating at the load side of the service equipment and supplying the main and/or one or more secondary distribution centers is commonly called a   1._____
    A. circuit   B. line   C. cable   D. feeder

2.   A 5-microfarad condenser is charged by putting 100 volts d.c. across its terminals. If this condenser is now placed across another condenser which has the same capacity rating and is identical in every other respect, the NEW voltage across these two condensers is *most nearly*   2._____
    A. 100   B. 75   C. 50   D. 25

3.   A synchronous condenser, so far as construction and appearance is concerned, *closely* resembles a(n)   3._____
    A. electrolytic condenser   B.   synchronous motor
    C. synchroscope   D. wound rotor induction motor

4.   In an electric spot welding machine, the primary winding contains 200 turns of #10 wire and the secondary contains one turn made up of laminated copper sheeting.
When the primary current is 5 amperes, the current, in amperes, passing through the metal to be welded is *approximately*   4._____
    A. 100   B. 200   C. 500   D. 1000

5.   With reference to an electric spot welding machine, the metal BEST suited to be united by spot welding is   5._____
    A. copper   B. zinc   C. lead   D. iron

6.   Two steel bars "G" and "H" have equal dimensions but one of them is a magnet and the other an ordinary piece of soft steel. In order to find out which one of the two bars is the magnet, you would touch the point midway between the ends of bar "G" with one end of bar "H". Then, if bar "H" tends to   6._____
    A. *pull* bar "G," bar "H" is not the magnet
    B. *pull* bar "G," bar "H" is the magnet
    C. *repel* bar "G," bar "H" is the magnet
    D. *repel* bar "G," bar "H" is not the magnet

7. The MAIN purpose of a cutting fluid used in threading electrical conduits is to
   A. prevent the formation of electrolytic pockets
   B. improve the finish of the thread
   C. wash away the chips
   D. prevent the eventual formation of rust

7.____

8. If a certain electrical job requires 212 feet of ½" rigid conduit, the number of lengths that you should requisition is
   A. 16   B. 18   C. 20   D. 22

8.____

9. The number of threads per inch *commonly* used for ½" electrical conduit is
   A. 15   B. 14   C. 13   D. 12

9.____

10. For mounting a heavy pull box on a hollow tile wall, it is BEST to use
    A. lag screws   B. masonry nails
    C. toggle bolts   D. expansion shields

10.____

11. For mounting an outlet box on a concrete ceiling, it is BEST to use
    A. ordinary wood screws   B. masonry nails
    C. expansion screw anchors   D. toggle bolts

11.____

12. The electrical code states that incandescent lamps shall not be equipped with medium bases if above 1500 watts; special approved bases or other devices shall be used.
    In accordance with the above statement, the lamp base that you should use for a 750 watt incandescent lamp is the _____ base.
    A. medium   B. candelabra   C. intermediate   D. mogul

12.____

13. In order to remove rough edges after cutting, all ends of conduit should be
    A. filed   B. sanded   C. reamed   D. honed

13.____

14. Where a conduit enters a box, in order to protect the wire from abrasion, you should use an approved
    A. coupling   B. close nipple   C. locknut   D. bushing

14.____

15. The MAXIMUM number of No. 10 type R conductors permitted in a ¾" conduit is
    A. 8   B. 6   C. 4   D. 2

15.____

16. A large switch which opens automatically when the current *exceeds* a predetermined limit is called a
    A. disconnect   B. contactor
    C. circuit breaker   D. limit switch

16.____

17. The flux *commonly* used for soldering electrical wires is
    A. rosin   B. borax   C. zinc chloride   D. tallow

17.____

18. The cost of the electrical energy consumed by a 50-watt lamp burning for 100 hours as compared to that consumed by a 100-watt lamp burning for 50 hours is   18.____
    A. four times as much   B. three times as much
    C. twice as much   D. the same

19. Pneumatic tools are run by   19.____
    A. electricity   B. steam
    C. compressed air   D. oil

20. It is required to make a right angle turn in a conduit run in which there are already 3 quarter bends following the last pull box. The fitting BEST suited to *properly* do this is a(n)   20.____
    A. cross   B. tee   C. union   D. ell

21. A 10,000 ohms resistance in an electronic timing switch burned out and must be replaced. The service manual states that this resistance should have an accuracy of 5%. This means that the value of the new resistance should differ from 10,000 ohms by NOT more than ____ ohms.   21.____
    A. 50   B. 150   C. 300   D. 500

22. Of the following, the A.W.G. size of single conductor bare copper wire which has the LOWEST resistance per foot is   22.____
    A. #40   B. #10   C. #00   D. #0

23. The voltage output of 6 ordinary flashlight dry cells of the zinc-carbon type, when connected in parallel with each other, will be *approximately* _____ volts.   23.____
    A. 1.5   B. 3   C. 9   D. 12

24. Full load current for a 5-ohm, 20-watt resistor is   24.____
    A. 4   B. 3   C. 2   D. 1

25. An auto-transformer could NOT be used to   25.____
    A. step-up voltage   B. step-down voltage
    C. act as a choke cell   D. change a.c. frequency

KEY (CORRECT ANSWERS)

1.	D		11.	C
2.	C		12.	D
3.	B		13.	C
4.	D		14.	D
5.	D		15.	C
6.	B		16.	C
7.	B		17.	A
8.	D		18.	D
9.	B		19.	C
10.	C		20.	D

21.	D
22.	C
23.	A
24.	C
25.	D

TEST 2

DIRECTIONS: Each question or incomplete statement is followed by several suggested answers or completions. Select the one that BEST answers the question or completes the statement. *PRINT THE LETTER OF THE CORRECT ANSWER IN THE SPACE AT THE RIGHT.*

1. A resistor is connected across a supply of "E" volts. The heat produced in this resistor is proportion to I^2R. If R is reduced in value, the heat produced in this resistor now

    A. increases   B. decreases
    C. remains the same   D. is indeterminate

1.____

2. A d.c. shunt generator has developed some trouble. You find that there is an open armature coil. As a *temporary* measure, you should

    A. use new brushes having a thickness of at least 3 commutator segments
    B. bridge the two commutator bars across which the open coil is connected
    C. use new brushes having a thickness of at least 4 commutator segments
    D. disconnect the open coil from the commutator

2.____

3. A cable composed of two insulated stranded conductors laid parallel, having a common cover is called a _____ cable.

    A. twin   B. duplex   C. concentric   D. sector

3.____

4. If two equal resistance coils are connected in parallel, the resistance of this combination is *equal* to

    A. the resistance of one coil   B. ½ the resistance of one coil
    C. twice the resistance of one coil   D. ¼ the resistance of one coil

4.____

5. A condenser whose capacity is one microfarad is connected in parallel with a condenser whose capacity is 2 microfarads. This combination is equal to a single condenser having a capacity, in microfarads, of *approximately*

    A. 2/3   B. 1   C. 3   D. 3/2

5.____

Questions 6-7.

DIRECTIONS: Questions 6 and 7 are to be answered on the basis of the diagram sketched below.

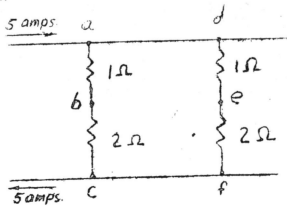

6. With reference to the diagram above, the current flowing through resistance ab is _____ amperes.
   A. 5   B. 4   C. 2½   D. 1½   6._____

7. With reference to the diagram above, the voltage difference between points b and e is _____ volt(s).
   A. 1   B. 10   C. 5   D. 0   7._____

8. The resistance of copper wire is _____ proportional to its _____.   8._____
   A. directly; cross-sectional area   B. directly; length
   C. inversely; length   D. inversely; diameter

9. The insulation resistance of 50 ft. of #12 BS rubber-covered wire, as compared to the insulation resistance of 100 ft. of this wire, is   9._____
   A. one-half as much   B. the same
   C. four times as much   D. twice as much

10. The resistance of a 150-scale voltmeter is 10,000 ohms. The power, in watts, consumed by this voltmeter when it is connected across a 100-volt circuit is   10._____
    A. 10   B. 5   C. 2.5   D. 1

11. A battery cell having an e.m.f. of 2.2 volts and an internal resistance of 0.2 ohm is connected to an external resistance 0.2 ohm. The current, in amperes, of the battery under this condition is *approximately*   11._____
    A. 15   B. 10   C. 2.5   D. 1

12. In reference to the preceding question, the efficiency, in percent, of the battery under this condition is *most nearly*   12._____
    A. 70   B. 80   C. 90   D. 100

13. During discharge, the internal resistance of a storage battery   13._____
    A. increases   B. remains the same
    C. decreases   D. is negative

14. The weight of a round copper bar is given by the formula, 3.14 R^2LK, where R is the radius, L is the length, and K for copper is .32 lbs. per cubic inch. The weight of a round copper bar 8'4" long and 2" in diameter is *approximately*   14._____
    A. 400 lbs.   B. 300 lbs.   C. 100 lbs.   D. 50 lbs.

15. Compound d.c. generators are usually wound so as to be somewhat over-compounded. The degree of compounding is *usually* regulated by   15._____
    A. shunting more or less current from the series field
    B. shunting more or less current from the shunt field
    C. connecting it short-shunt
    D. connecting it long-shunt

16. With reference to a shunt wound d.c. generator, if the resistance of the field   16.____
    is increased to a value exceeding its critical field resistance, the generator
        A. output may exceed its name plate rating
        B. may burn out when loaded to its name plate rating
        C. output voltage will be less than its name plate rating
        D. cannot build up

17. The PROPER way to reverse the direction of rotation of a compound motor   17.____
    is to interchange the
        A. line leads   B. armature connections
        C. shunt-field connections   D. series field connections

18. In the d.c. series motor, the field   18.____
        A. has comparatively few turns of wire
        B. has comparatively many turns of wire
        C. is connected across the armature
        D. current is less than the line current

19. In the d.c. series motor, when the load torque is *decreased*, the   19.____
        A. armature rotates at a lower speed
        B. armature rotates at a higher speed
        C. current through the field is increased
        D. current through the armature is increased

20. To fasten an outlet box to a concrete ceiling, you should use   20.____
        A. wooden plugs   B. toggle bolts
        C. mollys   D. expansion bolts

21. To fasten an outlet box to a finished hollow tile wall, it is BEST to use   21.____
        A. wooden plugs   B. toggle bolts
        C. through bolts and fishplates   D. expansion bolts

Questions 22-23.

DIRECTIONS: Questions 22 and 23 are to be answered in keeping with the statement below
                   and Figure I, which is an incomplete diagram of the connections of a
                   fluorescent lamp. The ballast and starter are not shown.

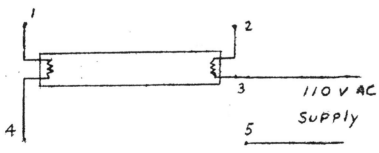

Figure I

The glow type starter used to operate a fluorescent lamp is designed to act as a time switch which will connect the two filament type electrodes in each end of the lamp in series with the ballast during the short preheating period when the lamp is first turned on. The starter will then open the circuit to establish the arc.

22. From the above statement, the competent electrician should know that the starter should be shown connected between points
    A. 4 and 3   B. 1 and 2   C. 4 and 5   D. 3 and 5

    22._____

23. From the above statement, the competent electrician should know that the choke of the ballast should be shown connected between points
    A. 4 and 3   B. 1 and 2   C. 4 and 5   D. 3 and 5

    23._____

24. A 6000-watt 3-phase heater composed of three resistance units in delta is connected to a 3-phase, 208-volt supply. The resistance, in ohms, of each resistance unit is *most nearly*
    A. 20.8   B. 41.6   C. 83.2   D. 208

    24._____

25. Based upon the data given in the preceding question, if the 3-heater resistance units are now connected in star (or wye) to a 3-phase, 208-volt supply, the power, in watts, consumed by this heater is *most nearly*
    A. 10,400   B. 6,000   C. 3,500   D. 2,000

    25._____

KEY (CORRECT ANSWERS)

1.	A		11.	B
2.	B		12.	C
3.	A		13.	A
4.	B		14.	C
5.	C		15.	A
6.	C		16.	D
7.	D		17.	B
8.	B		18.	A
9.	D		19.	B
10.	D		20.	D

21.	B
22.	B
23.	C
24.	A
25.	D

TEST 3

DIRECTIONS: Each question or incomplete statement is followed by several suggested answers or completions. Select the one that BEST answers the question or completes the statement. *PRINT THE LETTER OF THE CORRECT ANSWER IN THE SPACE AT THE RIGHT.*

Questions 1-3.

DIRECTIONS: Questions 1 through 3 are to be answered on the basis of the diagram below. The sketch is a lamp independently controlled from 3 points.

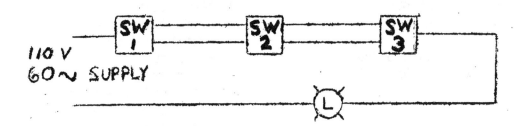

1.   The conductor running from the supply to switch No. 1 should be the _____ wire.   1.____
     A. blue   B. white   C. black   D. ground

2.   Switch No. 1 should be a _____ switch.   2.____
     A. single-pole   B. four-way   C. two-way   D. three-way

3.   Switch No. 2 should be a _____ switch.   3.____
     A. single-pole   B. two-way   C. four-way   D. three-way

Questions 4-15.

DIRECTIONS: Questions 4 through 15 refer to the material given on the next page. Column I lists descriptions of work to be done. Column II lists a tool or instrument for each description listed in Column I. For each description in Column I, select the instrument or tool from Column II which is used for the particular job and write the letter which appears in front of the name of the tool or instrument.

Column I	Column II	
4. Testing an armature for a shorted coil	A. Neon light	4._____
	B. Growler	
5. Measure of electrical pressure	C. Iron-vane Voltmeter	5._____
	D. Ohmmeter	
6. Measurement of electrical energy	E. Wattmeter	6._____
	F. Hot-wire Ammeter	
7. Measurement of electrical power	G. Megger	7._____
	H. Watthour Meter	
8. Direct measurement of electrical insulation resistance	J. Manometer	8._____
	K. Cable clamp pliers	
	L. Pair of test lamps	
9. Direct measurement of electrical resistance (1 ohm to 10,000 ohms)	M. Hack Saw	9._____
	N. Hydrometer	
	O. Electrician's blow torch	
10. Direct measurement of electrical current	P. American wire gage	10._____
	Q. Micrometer	
	R. Hygrometer	
11. Testing to find if supply is d.c. or a.c.	S. Rip Saw	11._____

12. Testing the electrolyte of battery   12._____

13. Cutting an iron bar   13._____

14. Soldering a rat-tail splice   14._____

15. A standard for checking the size of wire   15._____

16. To transmit power economically over considerable distances, it is necessary that the voltage be high. High voltages are *readily* obtainable with _____ current.   16._____

    A. d.c.   B. a.c.   C. rectified   D. carrier

17. With reference to the preceding question, the one *favorable* economic factor in the transmission of power by using high voltages is the   17._____.
    A. reduction of conductor cross section
    B. decreased amount of insulation required by the line
    C. increased I^2R loss
    D. decreased size of generating stations

18. The electric meter NOT in itself capable of measuring both d.c. and a.c. voltages is the _____ voltmeter.   18._____
    A. D'Arsonval   B. electrodynamometer
    C. iron vane   D. inclined-coil

19. The hot wire voltmeter   19.____
    A. is a high precision instrument
    B. is used only for d.c. circuits
    C. reads equally well on d.c. and/or a.c. circuits
    D. is used only for a.c. circuits

Questions 20-22.

DIRECTIONS: Questions 20 through 22 are to be answered on the basis of the diagram
              below.

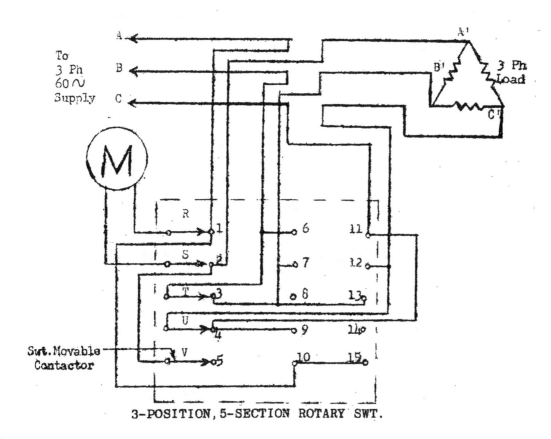

3-POSITION, 5-SECTION ROTARY SWT.

20. With switch movable contacts R, S, T, U and V in position 1, 2, 3, 4, and 5 as   20.____
    shown, Meter M is connected between points _____ and load is _____
    connected to supply.
    A. A-A'; improperly   B. A-A'; properly
    C. C-C'; improperly   D. C-C'; properly

21. With switch movable contactors R, S, T, U and V in position 6, 7, 8, 9 and 10,   21.____
    the function of Meter M is to measure the
    A. current in line B-B'   B. voltage in line B-B'
    C. power drawn by the load   D. power factor of the load

22. With switch movable contactors R, S, T, U and V in position 11, 12, 13, 14 and 15, Meter M is connected between points _____ and load is _____ connected to supply.
    A. A-A'; improperly
    B. A-A'; properly
    C. C-C'; improperly
    D. C-C'; properly

22.____

23. To increase the range of d.c. ammeters, you would use a(n)
    A. current transformer
    B. inductance
    C. condenser
    D. shunt

23.____

24. To increase the range of an a.c. ammeter, the one of the following which is MOST commonly used is a(n)
    A. current transformer
    B. inductance
    C. condenser
    D. straight shunt (not U-shaped)

24.____

25. In order to properly connect a single-phase wattmeter to a circuit, you should use two
    A. current and two potential leads
    B. current leads only
    C. potential leads only
    D. current leads and two power leads

25.____

KEY (CORRECT ANSWERS)

1.	C		11.	A
2.	D		12.	N
3.	C		13.	M
4.	B		14.	O
5.	C		15.	P
6.	H		16.	B
7.	E		17.	A
8.	G		18.	A
9.	D		19.	C
10.	F		20.	B

21.	A
22.	D
23.	D
24.	A
25.	A

120

TEST 4

DIRECTIONS: Each question or incomplete statement is followed by several suggested answers or completions. Select the one that BEST answers the question or completes the statement. *PRINT THE LETTER OF THE CORRECT ANSWER IN THE SPACE AT THE RIGHT.*

Questions 1-2.

DIRECTIONS: Questions 1 and 2 are to be answered on the basis of the following diagram.

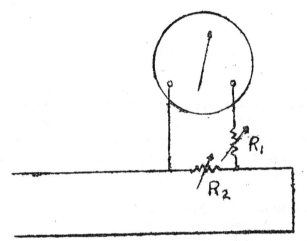

1. The above diagram represents the circuit of a d.c. ammeter. If the value of   1.____
    R_1 is increased while the value of R_2 remains unchanged, the
    A. deflection of the instrument is no longer proportional to the current
    B. range of the ammeter is decreased
    C. range of the ammeter remains the same
    D. range of the ammeter is increased

2. In reference to the above diagram, if the value of R_2 is decreased while the   2.____
    value of R_1 remains unchanged, the
    A. range of the ammeter is increased
    B. range of the ammeter is decreased
    C. range of the ammeter remains the same
    D. deflection of the instrument is no longer proportional to the current

3. In multiple-conductor armored cable construction, a color scheme is used   3.____
    for identifying purposes. The color-coding of a 3-conductor cable should be
    which one of the following?
    A. One white, one red, and one black
    B. Two black and one white
    C. Two white and one black
    D. One white, one black, and one blue

4. To properly make a short Western Union splice, the competent electrician   4.____
    should understand the common splicing rules. The one of the following which
    is NOT a common splicing rule is:
    A. Wires of the same size should be spliced together in line.
    B. A joint, or splice, must be as mechanically strong as the wire itself.
    C. A splice must provide a path for the electric current that will be as good as
       another wire.
    D. All splices must be mechanically and electrically secured by means of
       solder.

Question 5.

DIRECTIONS: Question 5 refers to the following statement.

The ampere-turns acting on a magnetic circuit are given by the product of the turns lined
by the amperes flowing through these turns. Magnetomotive force tends to drive the flux
through the circuit and corresponds to e.m.f. in the electric circuit. It is directly proportional
to the ampere-turns and only differs from the numerical value of the ampere-turns by the
constant factor 1.257, and the product of this factor and the ampere-turns equals the
magnetomotive force. This unit of m.m.f. is the gilbert.

5. One pole of a d.c. motor is wound with 500 turns of wire, through which a   5.____
    current of 2 amperes flows. Under these conditions, the m.m.f., in gilberts,
    acting on this magnetic circuit is *most nearly*
       A. 1,000   B. 1,257   C. 500   D. 628

6. The flux *commonly* used for soldering electrical wire is   6.____
       A. tin chloride   B. zinc chloride
       C. rosin   D. silver amalgam

7. The operation of electrical apparatus such as generators, motors, and   7.____
    transformers depends *fundamentally* on induced
       A. permeance   B. e.m.f.   C. reluctance   D. permeability

8. If an inductive circuit carrying current is short-circuited, the current in the   8.____
    circuit will
       A. cease to flow immediately
       B. continue to flow indefinitely
       C. continue to flow for an appreciable time after the instant of short circuit
       D. increase greatly

9. With reference to a.c. supply circuits, the waves of voltage and current   9.____
    ordinarily encountered in practice are _____ waves.
       A. sine   B. triangular   C. circular   D. rectangular

Questions 10-12.

DIRECTIONS: Questions 10 through 12 are to be answered on the basis of the following diagram.

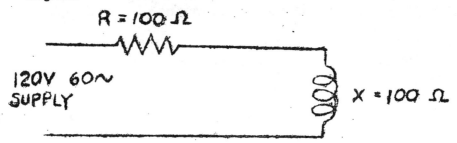

10.   The value of the impedance, in ohms, of the above circuit is *most nearly*   10.____
      A. 200   B. 50   C. 150   D. 140

11.   The current, in amperes, flowing in the above circuit is *most nearly*   11.____
      A. .6   B. 2.4   C. 1.2   D. .85

12.   The power, in watts, consumed in the above circuit is *most nearly*   12.____
      A. 72   B. 144   C. 576   D. 36

13.   The power, in watts, taken by a load connected to a three-phase circuit is   13.____
      generally expressed by
      A. EI P.F. $\sqrt{2}$ B. EI P.F.   C. $\sqrt{3}$ EI P.F.   D. EI/$\sqrt{3}$ P.F.

14.   Three 100-ohm resistances are connected in wye (Y) across a 208-volt,   14.____
      3-phase circuit. The line current, in amperes, is *approximately*
      A. 6.24   B. 3.6   C. 2.08   D. 1.2

15.   An a.c. ammeter is calibrated to read R.M.S. values. This also means that   15.____
      this meter is calibrated to read the _____ value.
      A. average   B. peak   C. effective   D. square

16.   An a.c. current of one ampere R.M.S. flowing through a resistance of 10 ohms   16.____
      has the same heating value as a d.c. current of _____ ampere(s) flowing
      through a _____ resistance.
      A. one; 10-ohm   B. one; 5-ohm   C. two; 10-ohm   D. five; 1-ohm

17.   In the common 3-phase, 4-wire supply system, the voltage (in volts) from   17.____
      line to neutral is *most nearly*
      A. 110   B. 120   C. 208   D. 220

18.   With reference to the preceding question, the neutral line   18.____
      A. does not carry current at any time
      B. carries current at all times
      C. has a potential difference with respect to ground of approximately zero volts
      D. has a potential difference with respect to ground of 208 volts

19. To *reverse* the direction of rotation of a repulsion motor you should   19._____
     A. move the brushes so that they cross the pole axis
     B. interchange the connection of either the main or auxiliary winding
     C. interchange the connections to the armature winding
     D. interchange the connections to the field winding

20. The ordinary direct current series motor does not operate satisfactorily   20._____
with alternating current. One of the MAIN reasons for this is
     A. excessive heating due to eddy currents in the solid parts of the field structure
     B. that the armature current and field current are out of phase with each other
     C. that the field flux lags 120° in time phase with respect to the line voltage
     D. excessive heating due to the low voltage drop in the series field

21. If the full rating of a transformer is 90 KV at 90% power factor, then the   21._____
KVA rating is
     A. 81   B. 90   C. 100   D. 141

22. A 10-ampere cartridge fuse provided with a navy blue label has a voltage   22._____
rating, in volts, of
     A. 220   B. 250   C. 550   D. 600

23. The electrical code states that electrical metallic tubing shall not be used   23._____
for interior wiring systems of more than 600 volts, nor for conductors *larger than* No.
     A. 6   B. 4   C. 2   D. 0

24. The diameter of one strand of an electrical conductor having 7 strands is   24._____
.0305". The size of the conductor, in C.M., is *most nearly*
     A. 13090   B. 10380   C. 6510   D. 4107

25. To *properly* start a 15 HP d.c. compound motor, you should use a   25._____
     A. transformer   B. 4-point starting rheostat
     C. compensator   D. diverter

KEY (CORRECT ANSWERS)

1.	D	11.	D
2.	A	12.	A
3.	A	13.	C
4.	D	14.	D
5.	B	15.	C
6.	C	16.	A
7.	B	17.	B
8.	C	18.	C
9.	A	19.	A
10.	D	20.	A

21.	C
22.	B
23.	D
24.	C
25.	B

TEST 5

DIRECTIONS: Each question or incomplete statement is followed by several suggested answers or completions. Select the one that BEST answers the question or completes the statement. *PRINT THE LETTER OF THE CORRECT ANSWER IN THE SPACE AT THE RIGHT.*

Questions 1-10.

DIRECTIONS: Questions 1 through 10 refer to the material given below. Column I lists definitions of terms used by the electrical code. Column II lists these terms. For each definition listed in Column I, select the term from Column II which it defines and write the letter which precedes the term.

<u>COLUMN I</u>   <u>COLUMN II</u>

1. Current consuming equipment fixed   A. Mains   1.____
    or portable   B. Switchboard
                                               C. Fuse
2. That portion of a wiring system extending D. Outlet   2.____
    beyond the final overcurrent device   E. Service raceway
    protecting the circuit   F. Feeder
                                               G. Isolated
3. Any conductors of a wiring system   H. Appliances   3.____
    between the main switchboard or point   J. Branch circuit
    of distribution and the branch circuit   K. Fitting
    overcurrent device   L. Conductor
                                               M. Enclosed
4. Not readily accessible to persons unless   N. Surrounded   4.____
    special means for access are used   O. Service drop

5. A point on the wiring system at which   5.____
    current is taken to supply fixtures, lamps,
    heaters, motors and current consuming
    equipment

6. The rigid steel conduit that encloses   6.____
    service entrance conductors

7. That portion of overhead service conduc-   7.____
    tors between the last line pole and the first
    point of attachment to the building

8. Conductors of a wiring system between   8.____
    the lines of the public utility company or
    other source of supply and the main
    switchboard or point of distribution

9. A wire or cable or other form of metal
   suitable for carrying electrical energy

9.____

10. Surrounded by a case which will prevent
    accidental contact with live parts

10.____

Questions 11-12.

DIRECTIONS: Questions 11 and 12 are to be answered on the basis of Figure I below.

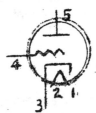

Figure I

11. The above diagram in Figure I is a *commonly* used symbol for a vacuum tube
    and represents which one of the following types of tubes?
    A. Triode   B. Tetrode   C. Pentode   D. Heptode

11.____

12. Tube element No. 5 is *usually* called the
    A. grid   B. plate   C. filament   D. cathode

12.____

Questions 13-14.

DIRECTIONS: Questions 13 and 14 are to be answered on the basis of Figure II below.

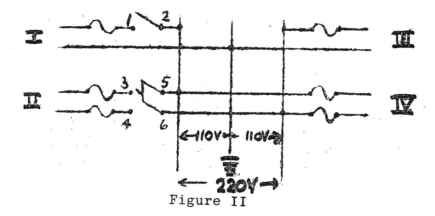

Figure II

13. Circuit No. I in the above diagram
    A. is not properly fused as it should have one fuse in each leg
    B. supplies 220 volts to the load
    C. is grounded if a pair of test lamps light when placed between point 2 and
       ground
    D. supplies 110 volts to the load at the board

13.____

14. Circuit No. II in the above diagram   14.____
    A. is not properly fused as it should have only one fuse in the hot leg
    B. supplies 110 volts to the load at the board
    C. is grounded if a pair of test lamps light up when placed between points 5 and 6
    D. is grounded if, with the switch in the open position, test lamps light up when placed between points 3 and 5

15. To *properly* start a 15 HP, 3-phase induction motor, you should use a   15.____
    A. shunt   B. 4-point starting rheostat
    C. compensator   D. diverter

Questions 16-25.

DIRECTIONS: Questions 16 through 25 refer to the material given below. Column I lists items which are represented by symbols listed in Column II. For each item in Column I, select the appropriate symbol from Column II which it represents and write the letter which precedes the symbol.

COLUMN I   COLUMN II

16. Lighting panel   A.   16.____

17. Special purpose outlet   B.   17.____

18. Floor outlet   C. S_3 18.____

19. Three-way switch   D.   19.____

20. Normally closed contact   E.   20.____

21. Resistor   F.   21.____

22. Watt-hour meter   G.   22.____

23. Two-pole electrically operated contact with blowout coil   H.   23.____

                                     J.

24. Capacitor   24.____

25. Bell   25.____

                                     K.

                                     L.

                                     M.

KEY (CORRECT ANSWERS)

1.	H		11.	A
2.	J		12.	B
3.	F		13.	D
4.	G		14.	D
5.	D		15.	C
6.	E		16.	B
7.	O		17.	D
8.	A		18.	E
9.	L		19.	C
10.	M		20.	F

21.	G
22.	K
23.	J
24.	H
25.	A

TEST 6

DIRECTIONS: Each question or incomplete statement is followed by several suggested answers or completions. Select the one that BEST answers the question or completes the statement. *PRINT THE LETTER OF THE CORRECT ANSWER IN THE SPACE AT THE RIGHT.*

Questions 1-8.

DIRECTIONS: Questions 1 through 8 are to be answered on the basis of the figures below. Each question gives the proper figure to use with that question.

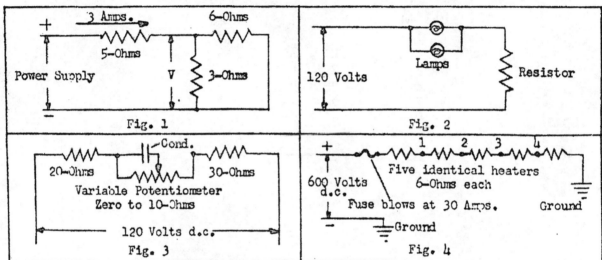

1. In Figure 1, the voltage V is _____ volts.
   A. 27   B. 9   C. 6   D. 3

2. In Figure 1, the current in the 6-ohm resistor is _____ ampere(s).
   A. 3   B. 2   C. 1.6   D. 1

3. In Figure 2, each lamp is to take 1 ampere at 20 volts. The resistor should be _____ ohms.
   A. 100   B. 80   C. 50   D. 40

4. In Figure 3, the MAXIMUM voltage which can be placed across the condenser by varying the potentiometer is _____ volts.
   A. 120   B. 60   C. 40   D. 20

5. In Figure 3, the MINIMUM voltage which can be placed across the condenser by varying the potentiometer is _____ volts.
   A. 60   B. 40   C. 20   D. zero

1.____

2.____

3.____

4.____

5.____

6. In Figure 4, the heater circuit is normally completed through the two ground connections shown. If an accidental ground occurs at point 4, then the number of heaters which will heat up is   6.____
   A. five   B. four   C. one   D. none

7. In Figure 4, the fuse will NOT blow with a ground at point   7.____
   A. 1   B. 2   C. 3   D. 4

8. In Figure 4, if a short occurs from point 2 to point 3, then the number of heaters which will heat up is   8.____
   A. five   B. four   C. two   D. none

Questions 9-16.

DIRECTIONS: Questions 9 through 16 are to be answered on the basis of the wiring diagram below. Refer to this diagram when answering these questions.

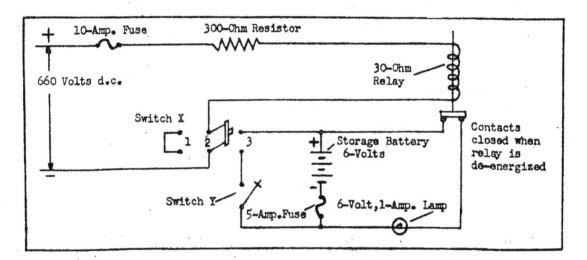

9. Throwing switch X to Position No. 1 will   9.____
   A. charge the battery   B. energize the lamp
   C. energize the relay   D. blow the 5-ampere fuse

10. With switch X in Position No. 1, the 10-ampere fuse will blow if a dead short   10.____
    occurs across the
    A. 300-ohm resistor   B. relay coil
    C. battery   D. lamp

11. With switch X in Position No. 2, the current through the 300-ohm resistor   11.____
    will be
    A. zero   B. 2 amperes   C. 2.2 amperes   D. 10 amperes

12. With switch X in Position No. 3 and switch Y open, the current taken from the battery will be

    A. zero   B. 1 ampere   C. 5 amperes   D. 10 amperes

12.____

13. With switch Y in the open position and the relay contacts open, the

    A. lamp will be lit   B. lamp will be dark
    C. battery will be discharging   D. 5-ampere fuse will be overloaded

13.____

14. The battery will charge with switch X in Position No. _____ and switch Y _____.

    A. 3; closed   B. 3; open   C. 1; closed   D. 1; open

14.____

15. With the relay contacts closed, a dead short across the lamp will

    A. blow the 10-ampere fuse   B. blow the 5-ampere fuse
    C. not blow any fuses   D. cause the battery to charge

15.____

16. When the switches are set to the positions which will charge the battery, the charging current will be *approximately* _____ ampere(s).

    A. ½   B. 2   C. 5   D. 10

16.____

17. The MOST important reason for NOT having a power line splice in a conduit run between boxes is that

    A. it will be impossible to pull the wires through
    B. this would be an unsafe practice
    C. the splice will heat up
    D. the splice would be hard to repair

17.____

18. Goggles would be LEAST necessary when

    A. recharging soda-acid fire extinguishers
    B. chipping stones
    C. putting electrolyte into an Edison battery
    D. scraping rubber insulation from a wire

18.____

19. A commutator and brushes will be found on a(n)

    A. alternator   B. rotary converter
    C. squirrel-cage induction motor   D. wound-rotor induction motor

19.____

20. In a house bell circuit, the pushbutton for ringing the bell is generally connected in the secondary of the transformer feeding the bell. One reason for this is to

    A. save power
    B. keep line voltage out of the pushbutton circuit
    C. prevent the bell from burning out
    D. prevent arcing of the vibrator contact points in the bell

20.____

KEY (CORRECT ANSWERS)

1.	C	11.	A
2.	D	12.	B
3.	C	13.	B
4.	D	14.	A
5.	D	15.	B
6.	B	16.	B
7.	D	17.	B
8.	B	18.	D
9.	C	19.	B
10.	A	20.	B

ELECTRICITY
EXAMINATION SECTION
TEST 1

DIRECTIONS: Each question or incomplete statement is followed by several suggested answers or completions. Select the one that BEST answers the question or completes the statement. *PRINT THE LETTER OF THE CORRECT ANSWER IN THE SPACE AT THE RIGHT.*

1. A unit of inductance is the
    A. microfarad   B. milliohm   C. millihenry   D. micromho

    1._____

2. The resistance which is equivalent to 10 megohms is
    A. 1×10^8 ohms
    C. 1×10^6 ohms
    B. 1×10^7 ohms
    D. 1×10^5 ohms

    2._____

3. A two-microfarad capacitor is connected in parallel with an eight-microfarad capacitor. The TOTAL capacitance of this combination is
    A. 0.25 microfarad
    C. 1.6 microfarads
    B. 0.5 microfarad
    D. 10 microfarads

    3._____

4. A current of 10 milliamperes is
    A. 0.0001 amperes
    C. 0.01 amperes
    B. 0.001 amperes
    D. 0.1 amperes

    4._____

5. If 120 volts are impressed across a resistance of 300 ohms, 5. the power dissipated by the resistance is
    A. 0.4 watt   B. 2.5 watts   C. 36 watts   D. 48 watts

    5._____

6. The number of circular mils in a conductor 0.04 inch in diameter is
    A. 1600 circular mils
    C. 126 circular mils
    B. 1260 circular mils
    D. 40 circular mils

    6._____

7. When an electrical device is connected across a 208-volt, 60-Hertz, A.C. supply, the peak voltage across the device is, most nearly,
    A. 208 volts   B. 295 volts   C. 360 volts   D. 416 volts

    7._____

8. The colors of the three conductors in a 3-conductor cable DS for a 120/208-volt system should be
    A. white, black and green
    C. white, blue and black
    B. white, red and blue
    D. white, black and red

    8._____

9. A 15-ohm resistor is connected in parallel with a 10-ohm resistor. This combination of resistors are in turn connected in series with a 4-ohm resistor. The TOTAL resistance of this combination of three resistors is
    A. 29.0 ohms   B. 10.0 ohms   C. 6.0 ohms   D. 4.2 ohms

    9._____

10. The insulation resistance of a certain conductor is 16 megohms. If the conductor is cut into two equal lengths, the insulation resistance of each length is
    A. 32 megohms   B. 16 megohms   C. 8 megohms   D. 4 megohms

    10._____

11. A certain circuit consists of a reactance with a value of 18 ohms at 60 Hertz connected in series with a 6-ohm resistance. When this circuit is connected to a 120-volt, 60-Hertz, A.C. supply, the current in the circuit is

    A. 20 amperes   B. 15 amperes   C. 12 amperes   D. 10 amperes

11._____

12. A resistance of 2.5 ohms is connected across the terminals of a battery which has an open circuit voltage of 12 volts and an internal resistance of 0.5 ohms. The current in this circuit is, most nearly,

    A. 4.0 amperes   B. 4.8 amperes   C. 6.0 amperes   D. 24 amperes

12._____

13. Assuming that the resistance of a No. 10 (AWG) conductor at 68°F is approximately 1 ohm per 1000 ft., the resistance of 1000 ft., of a No. 13 (AWG) conductor at 68°F is, approximately,

    A. 0.5 ohm   B. 1.26 ohms   C. 2.0 ohms   D. 3.0 ohms

13._____

14. Suppose that the line voltage of a 3-phase circuit is E, the line current, in amperes, is I and the power factor is P.F. The formula for the power consumed, in watts, in this circuit is

    A. $\sqrt{3}$ EI P.F.   B. EI P.F.   C. 3 EI P.F.   D. $\sqrt{2}$ EI P.F.

14._____

15. Assume that a current density of 1000 amperes per square inch is allowable for bus bars. A certain bus bar which has a circular cross section is 1.5 inches in diameter and is 3 feet long. The MAXIMUM allowable current for this bus bar is, most nearly,

    A. 400 amperes   B. 1500 amperes
    C. 1800 amperes   D. 7200 amperes

15._____

16. The color of the label on a 600-volt fuse should be.

    A. blue   B. green   C. red   D. yellow

16._____

17. Of the following, the colors of the three conductors of a 3-conductor cable for a 277/490-volt system used to supply 277-volt fluorescent lights should be

    A. white, brown, and yellow   B. white, black, and yellow
    C. white, red, and orange   D. white, blue, and orange

17._____

18. Although all fuses on a panel are good, the clips on the fuse in circuit No. 1 are much hotter than the clips of the other fuses. The most likely cause of this condition is that

    A. circuit No. 1 is greatly over-loaded
    B. circuit No. 1 is carrying much less than rated load
    C. the fuse of circuit No. 1 is very loose in its clips
    D. the room temperature is abnormally high

18._____

19. Of the following colors, the one that may be used for the 19. ground wire for a piece of portable equipment is

    A. gray   B. green   C. white   D. black

19._____

20. Fixture wire should NOT be smaller than

    A. No. 14   B. No. 16   C. No. 18   D. No. 20

20._____

_____

KEY (CORRECT ANSWERS)

1.	C	11.	C
2.	B	12.	A
3.	D	13.	C
4.	C	14.	A
5.	D	15.	C
6.	A	16.	C
7.	B	17.	A
8.	D	18.	C
9.	B	19.	B
10.	A	20.	C

TEST 2

DIRECTIONS: Each question or incomplete statement is followed by several suggested answers or completions. Select the one that BEST answers the question or completes the statement. *PRINT THE LETTER OF THE CORRECT ANSWER IN THE SPACE AT THE RIGHT.*

1. An example of an adjustable wrench is the   1._____
   A. Bristol wrench   B. Crescent wrench
   C. Allen wrench   D. box wrench

2. The term which is defined by the electrical code as a set of conductors originating at a   2._____
   distribution center other than the main distribution center, and supplying one or more
   branch circuit distribution centers, is a
   A. raceway   B. main   C. sub-feeder   D. service

3. When three No. 10-type R wires are run in the same conduit, 3. the allowable current-   3._____
   carrying capacity of each wire is
   A. 15 amperes   B. 20 amperes   C. 25 amperes   D. 30 amperes

4. Two No. 12-type R conductors in a 3/4-inch conduit are carrying the maximum allowable   4._____
   current to an appliance. It is desired to double the load. Of the following, the BEST way
   to supply this new load is to
   A. run two more No. 12-type R conductors in multiple with the existing conductors
   B. remove the existing conductors and run two No. 10-type R conductors in the conduit
   C. replace the existing conduit and conductors with a 1-inch conduit and two No. 10-type
      R conductors
   D. remove the existing conductors and run two No. 8-type R conductors in the conduit

5. According to the electrical code, No. 1/0 copper conductors in vertical raceways should   5._____
   be supported at intervals of not greater than
   A. 100 feet   B. 80 feet   C. 60 feet   D. 50 feet

6. A universal motor is also a   6._____
   A. squirrel-cage motor   B. synchronous motor
   C. series motor   D. wound-rotor motor

7. In a run of non-metallic conduit between two outlets, the MAXIMUM number of equivalent   7._____
   quarter bends permitted is
   A. 2   B. 3   C. 4   D. 5

8. The MINIMUM number of wattmeters required to measure the power in an unbalanced   8._____
   3-phase, 4-wire system, is
   A. 1   B. 2   C. 3   D. 4

9. An A.C. ammeter which reads 5 amperes full scale and a voltmeter which reads 150 volts   9._____
   full scale are properly connected, without instrument transformers, to various loads on a
   120-volt A.C. circuit. The MAXIMUM load that can be safely measured under these condit-
   ions is
   A. 750 watts at 80% leading power factor
   B. 750 watts at unity power factor
   C. 600 watts at 80% lagging power factor
   D. 600 watts at unity power factor

10. In a single-phase A.C. circuit, the voltage is E, the current is I, the resistance is R, and the wattage is W. A formula which will give the power factor of the circuit is: 10.____

    A. $EI \div RB$.   B. $I^2 \div R$ C. $W \div EI$ D. $EI \div W$

11. A single-phase 100-ampere load is fed from a 120-volt panel board 500 feet away by means of two conductors. Each conductor has a resistivity of 10.5 ohms per circular-mil-foot. The size of conductor that will cause the voltage drop to the load to be most nearly 2 ½ %, is   11.____

    A. 148,000 C M   B. 175,000 C M
    C. 350,000 C M   D. 420,000 C M

12. The method of motor control which is called jogging is the   12.____

    A. quick reversal of the direction of rotation of a motor
    B. repeated closing of the circuit to start a motor from rest in order to get a small movement
    C. using up of the energy in a motor by making it act as a generator with a resistive load
    D. slowing of a motor by using it as a generator to return energy to the power supply system

13. When the armature current drawn by a certain D.C. series motor is 10 amperes-, the torque is 10 pound-feet. If the current is increased to 20 amperes, the torque is   13.____

    A. 5 pound-feet   B. 15 pound-feet
    C. 20 pound-feet   D. 40 pound-feet

14. The proper way to reverse the direction of rotation of a repulsion motor is to   14.____

    A. reverse the connections to the auxiliary field winding
    B. move the brushes to the opposite side of the pole axis
    C. interchange the line leads
    D. interchange the main field connections

15. A D.C. series motor is running at rated load and rated speed. If the entire load is suddenly removed, the   15.____

    A. field strength will increase
    B. armature current will increase
    C. efficiency will increase
    D. motor will start to "race"

16. One way of distinguishing an A.C. series motor from a D.C. series motor of the same horsepower and voltage rating is that the A.C. motor has   16.____

    A. relatively fewer poles
    B. a larger armature
    C. more turns of the same size wire in the field
    D. fewer turns of the same size wire in the armature

17. The proper way to reverse the direction of rotation of a cumulative compound motor without changing its operating characteristics is to   17.____

    A. interchange the connections to the armature
    B. reverse the polarity of the supply
    C. interchange the connections to the shunt field
    D. interchange the connections to the series field

18. A certain ideal transformer has a primary voltage of 2200 volts and a secondary volt-age of 110 volts. The primary-to-secondary-turns ratio of this transformer is
    A. 22 to 1   B. 20 to 1   C. 1 to 11   D. 1 to 20
18._____

19. A light is to be controlled independently from six separate locations. Of the following, the group of switches required to do this is
    A. two 3-way, two S.P.S.T. and two 4-way
    B. three 3-way and three 4-way
    C. four 3-way and two 4-way
    D. two 3-way and four 4-way
19._____

20. A D.C. motor operating at 110 volts and drawing 40 amperes has an efficiency of 80%. The horsepower output of this motor is, most nearly,
    A. 1   B. 3   C. 5   D. 7
20._____

KEY (CORRECT ANSWERS)

1. B	11. C
2. C	12. B
3. D	13. D
4. D	14. B
5. A	15. D
6. C	16. B
7. C	17. A
8. C	18. B
9. D	19. D
10. C	20. C

TEST 3

1. The instrument which should be used to measure the insulation resistance of a motor is a (n)   1._____
   A. ohmmeter   B. megger
   C. ammeter   D. varmeter

2. Of the following, the piece of equipment which should be used to locate a shorted coil in the   armature of a D.C. motor is a   2._____
   A. permeameter   B. varley loop growler
   C. fluxmeter   D. growler

3. Braking a motor by reversing the line polarity is called   3._____
   A. plugging   B. resistance braking
   C. inching   D. regenerative braking

4. The full load-speed of a 120-volt, 60-Hertz, four-pole squirrel cage motor, which has a slip of 6% at full load, is, most nearly,   4._____
   A. 1600 rpm   B. 1700 rpm   C. 1800 rpm   D. rpm

5. The formula for the resistance of one branch of a delta which is equivalent to a given wye   5._____

   is RAB = $\frac{ab+bc+ca}{c}$ If a = b = c = 2 ohms, the value of RAB is, most nearly,
   A. 3 ohms   B. 6 ohms   C. 9 ohms   D. 12 ohms

6. A 3-phase wound-rotor induction motor is running hot and is slower than usual for the load. When stopped, the motor hums and fails to start up again. A possible cause of this condition is that   6._____
   A. the resistance in the rheostat is too low
   B. the brush tension is too great
   C. one phase of the stator is open
   D. the frequency of the supply is too high

7. A 208-volt, 3-phase, A.C. supply is connected to the stator of a motor. D.C. is supplied to its rotor by a small generator directly connected to the end of the motor's shaft. Of the following, it is most likely that this motor is a   7._____
   A. squirrel-cage motor   B. wound-rotor motor
   C. repulsion motor   D. synchronous motor

8. Assume that two single-phase wattmeters are properly connected to measure the power consumed by a 3-phase, 3-wire system. The wattmeters read 1000 watts and 0 watts, respectively. The power factor of the system is   8._____
   A. 0   B. 0.5   C. 0.8   D. 1.0

9. The range of a D.C. ammeter is most often increased by the use of a   9._____
   A. multiplier   B. current transformer
   C. shunt   D. potential transformer

10. According to the electrical code, three-way and four-way switches should be classed as   10._____
    A. D.P. D.T. switches   B. single-pole switches
    C. D.P. S.T. switches   D. three-pole switches

11. The definition of a trip-free circuit breaker is one that is designed   11._____
    A. for remote control from any desired location
    B. to be free from damage by "chattering" of the contacts
    C. to be free from damage of the contacts by arcing
    D. so that it will open even if the handle is manually held down

12. Of the following, the BEST hacksaw blade to use to cut EMT is one having   12._____
    A. 32 teeth per inch   B. 14 teeth per inch
    C. 12 teeth per inch   D. 10 teeth per inch

13. The one of the following fasteners that is BEST to use to secure an outlet box to a brick wall is   13._____
    A. toggle bolts   B. lead expansion anchors
    C. wooden plugs   D. steel masonry nails

14. Of the following, the usual way of extending the range of an A.C. ammeter is to use a   14._____
    A. straight shunt   B. series resistance
    C. current transformer   D. diode

15. In variable-speed induction motors, the phases should be connected in   15._____
    A. series delta for high speed and parallel star for low speed in constant torque motors
    B. parallel star for high speed and series delta for low speed in constant torque motors
    C. parallel star for high speed and series delta for low speed in constant horsepower motors
    D. series star for high speed and parallel star for low speed in constant horsepower motors

16. Of the following, the type of fire extinguisher which is suitable for use on fires in or near electrical equipment is the   16._____
    A. soda-acid fire extinguisher
    B. stored pressure water fire extinguisher
    C. foam fire extinguisher
    D. carbon dioxide fire extinguisher

17. A portable drill is marked with the symbol ▣ . This means that it   17._____
    A. should be used for high voltage circuits
    B. can properly operate at 25-Hertz A.C.
    C. has double insulation
    D. is a D.C. drill

18. Conductors with lead sheaths are run in a 1-inch nonmetallic conduit. The code requires that the minimum radius of the curve to the inner edge of a field bend of this conduit should be   18._____
    A. 6 inches   B. 11 inches
    C. 16 inches   D. 21 inches

19. The minimum permissible radius of the curve of the inner edge of any bend in armored   19._____
cable is   the diameter of the cable.
   A. four times   B. five times
   C. six times   D. eight times

20. Connectors of the "visible type" (i.e., having peep holes) are required when making   20._____
connections between outlet boxes and
   A. flexible conduit   B. electric metallic tubing
   C. armored cable   D. rigid iron conduit

————

KEY (CORRECT ANSWERS)

1. B		11. D
2. D		12. A
3. A		13. B
4. B		14. C
5. B		15. B
6. C		16. D
7. D		17. C
8. B		18. B
9. C		19. B
10. B		20. C

————

TEST 4

DIRECTIONS: Each question or incomplete statement is followed by several suggested answers or completions. Select the one that BEST answers the question or completes the statement. *PRINT THE LETTER OF THE CORRECT ANSWER IN THE SPACE AT THE RIGHT.*

1. The MAXIMUM spacing permitted between the supports of 1-inch rigid nonmetallic Conduit containing RHH wire is   1._____
   - A. 2 1/2 feet
   - B. 3 1/2 feet
   - C. 4 feet
   - D. 5 feet

2. The MINIMUM permitted size of flexible metal conduit containing leads to recessed light fixtures is   2._____
   - A. 1/4 inch
   - B. 3/8 inch
   - C. 1/2 inch
   - D. 5/8 inch

3. A 16-foot extension ladder is to be placed against a vertical wall. According to most safety manuals, the distance between the foot of the ladder and the base of the wall should be   3._____
   - A. less than 1' 0"
   - B. exactly I' 6"
   - C. 1/12 the length of the ladder
   - D, 1/4 the length of the ladder

4. The MAXIMUM voltage defined as low potential is   4._____
   A. 208 volts B. 477 volts C. 600 volts D. 1100 volts

5. In which one of the following locations are types NM and NMC cables permitted?   5._____
   - A. Hoistways
   - B. Battery rooms
   - C. Unfinished basements
   - D. Commercial garages

6. A bank of three single-phase transformers, each having a ratio of 20 to 1, are connected with their primaries in delta and their secondaries in wye. If the low-voltage windings are used as the secondaries, and the line voltage on the secondary side is 480 volts, the line voltage on the primary side is   6._____
   - A. 3,200 volts
   - B. 5,540 volts
   - C. 9,600 volts
   - D. 16,600 volts

7. Of the following tools, the proper one to use to make a hole in a brick wall is a   7._____
   - A. carbon steel drill
   - B. cold chisel
   - C. diamond point chisel
   - D. star drill

8. A light-and-power circuit consists of four wires colored white, black, blue and red, respectively. In order to properly de-energize this circuit, it is necessary to install a switch which simultaneously opens the   8._____
   - A. blue, black, and white wires
   - B. black, red, and white wires
   - C. red, black, and blue wires
   - D. red, white, and blue wires

9. A heavy object should be lifted by first crouching and firmly grasping the object to be lifted.   9._____
Then, the worker should lift
   A. using his back muscles and keeping his legs bent
   B. by straightening his legs and keeping his back as straight as possible
   C. using his arm muscles and keeping his back nearly horizontal
   D. using his arm muscles and keeping his feet close together

10. When mouth-to-mouth resuscitation is administered to an adult, the recommended   10._____
breathing-rate of the rescuer is
   A. 4 breaths per minute
   B. 12 breaths per minute
   C. 25 breaths per minute
   D. 35 breaths per minute

11. The standard number of threads per inch on 1-inch rigid-steel conduit is   11._____
   A. 16 threads per inch
   B. 14 threads per inch
   C. 11 1/2 threads per inch
   D. 8 threads per inch

12. An example of type S fuse is a   12._____
   A. standard ferrule contact cartridge fuse of the renewable type
   B. standard knife-blade contact one-time fuse
   C. dual element time-delay type of standard screw base plug fuse
   D. tamper-resistant type of time-delay plug fuse

13. The method of wiring known as concealed knob-and-tube work   13._____
   A. should not be used in the hollow spaces of walls and ceilings of any building
   B. may be used in the hollow spaces of walls and ceilings of residences
   C. Test 4/KEYS
   D. may be used in the hollow spaces of walls and ceilings of commercial garages
   E. should not be used in the hollow spaces of walls and ceilings of offices

14. The one of the following which is BEST to use to keep a commutator smooth is   14._____
   A. No. 1/0 emery cloth
   B. No. 00 sandpaper
   C. No. 2 steel wool
   D. a wire brush

15. A photoelectric relay used in conjunction with the controls for boiler room equipment uses   15._____
a pentode amplifier.
   The one of the following elements of the pentode which receives the signal is the
   A. plate   B. screen grid
   C. control grid   D. suppressor grid

16. A pair of wires which can be run in multiple is one   16._____
   A. No. 2 type R and one No. 1 type R, each 100 ft. long
   B. one No. 1/0 type R and one No. 1/0 type AA, each 100 ft. long
   C. two No. 2 type AA, each 200 ft. long
   D. two No. 1/0 type R, each 100 ft. long

17. Knobs used in knob-and-tube work are usually made of
    A. molded asbestos
    B. wood
    C. porcelain
    D. steatite

17._____

18. As the speed of a fractional-horsepower, split-phase, single-phase, induction motor of the capacitor-start, induction-run type, increases and approaches full-load speed, the auxiliary winding circuit is
    A. closed by a thermal switch
    B. opened by a thermal switch
    C. closed by a centrifugal switch
    D. opened by a centrifugal switch

18._____

19. The SMALLEST size of wire which is required to have stranded conductors is
    A. No. 10   B. No. 8   C. No. 6   D. No. 4

19._____

20. The MAIN purpose of the electrical code is
    A. economy   B. neatness   C. efficiency   D. safety

20._____

KEY (CORRECT ANSWERS)

1. A	11. C
2. B	12. D
3. D	13. B
4. C	14. B
5. C	15. C
6. B	16. D
7. D	17. C
8. C	18. D
9. B	19. C
10. B	20. D

BASIC ELECTRICITY

FUNDAMENTAL CONCEPTS OF ELECTRICITY
What is Electricity?

The word "electric" is actually a Greek-derived word meaning AMBER. Amber is a translucent (semitransparent) yellowish mineral, which, in the natural form, is composed of fossilized resin. The ancient Greeks used the words "electric force" in referring to the mysterious forces of attraction and repulsion exhibited by amber when it was rubbed with a cloth. They did not understand the fundamental nature of this force. They could not answer the seemingly simple question, "What is electricity?". This question is still unanswered. Though you might define electricity as "that force which moves electrons," this would be the same as defining an engine as "that force which moves an automobile." You would have described the effect, not the force.

We presently know little more than the ancient Greeks knew about the fundamental nature of electricity, but tremendous strides have been made in harnessing and using it. Elaborate theories concerning the nature and behavior of electricity have been advanced, and have gained wide acceptance because of their apparent truth and demonstrated workability.

From time to time various scientists have found that electricity seems to behave in a constant and predictable manner in given situations, or when subjected to given conditions. These scientists, such as Faraday, Ohm, Lenz, and Kirchhoff, to name only a few, observed and described the predictable characteristics of electricity and electric current in the form of certain rules. These rules are often referred to as "laws." Thus, though electricity itself has never been clearly defined, its predictable nature and easily used form of energy has made it one of the most widely used power sources in modern time. By learning the rules, or laws, applying to the behavior of electricity, and by learning the methods of producing, controlling, and using it, you will have "learned" electricity without ever having determined its fundamental identity.

THE MOLECULE

One of the oldest, and probably the most generally accepted, theories concerning electric current flow is that it is comprised of moving electrons. This is the ELECTRON THEORY. Electrons are extremely tiny parts, or particles, of matter. To study the electron, you must therefore study the structural nature of matter itself. (Anything having mass and inertia, and which occupies any amount of space, is composed of matter.) To study the fundamental structure or composition of any type of matter, it must be reduced to its fundamental fractions. Assume the drop of water in figure 1-1 (A) was halved again and again. By continuing the process long enough, you would eventually obtain the smallest particle of water possible-the molecule. All molecules are composed of atoms.

A molecule of water (H_2O) is composed of one atom of oxygen and two atoms of hydrogen, as represented in figure 1-1 (B). If the molecule of water were further subdivided, there would remain only unrelated atoms of oxygen and hydrogen, and the water would no longer exist as such. This example illustrates the following fact-the molecule is the smallest particle to which a substance can be reduced and still be called by the same name. This applies to all substances-liquids, solids, and gases.

When whole molecules are combined or separated from one another, the change is generally referred to as a PHYSICAL change. In a CHEMICAL change the molecules of the substance are altered such that

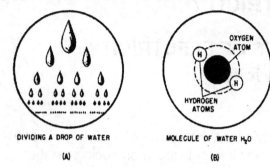

DIVIDING A DROP OF WATER (A)

MOLECULE OF WATER H₂O (B)

Figure 1-1.—Matter is made up of molecules.

new molecules result. Most chemical changes Involve positive and negative ions and thus are electrical in nature. All matter is said to be essentially electrical in nature.

THE ATOM

In the study of chemistry it soon becomes apparent that the molecule is far from being the ultimate particle into which matter may be subdivided. The salt molecule may be decomposed into radically different substancessodium and chlorine. These particles that make up molecules can be isolated and studied separately. They are called ATOMS.

The atom is the smallest particle that makes up that type of material called an ELEMENT. The element retains its characteristics when subdivided into atoms. More than 100 elements have been identified. They can be arranged into a table of increasing weight, and can be grouped into families of material having similar properties. This arrangement is called the PERIODIC TABLE OF THE ELEMENTS.

The idea that all matter is composed of atoms dates back more than 2,000 years to the Greeks. Many centuries passedbefore the study of matter proved that the basic idea of atomic structure was correct. Physicists have explored the interior of the atom and discovered many subdivisions in it. The core of the atom is called the NUCLEUS. Most of the mass of the atom is concentrated in the nucleus. It is comparable to the sun in the solar system, around which the planets revolve. The nucleus contains PROTONS (positively charged particles) and NEUTRONS which are electrically neutral.

Most of the weight of the atom is in the protons and neutrons of the nucleus. Whirling around the nucleus are one or more smaller particles of negative electric charge. THESE ARE THE ELECTRONS. Normally there is one proton for each electron in the entire atom so that the net positive charge of the nucleus is balanced by the net negative charge of the electrons whirling around the nucleus. THUS THE ATOM IS ELECTRICALLY NEUTRAL.

The electrons do not fall into the nucleus even though they are attracted strongly to it. Their motion prevents it, as the planets are prevented from falling into the sun because of their centrifugal force of revolution.

The number of protons, which is usually the same as the number of electrons, determines the kind of element in question. Figure 1-2 shows a simplified picture of several atoms of different materials based on the conception of planetary electrons describing orbits about the nucleus. For example, hydrogen has a nucleus consisting of 1 proton, around which rotates 1 electron. The helium atom has a nucleus containing 2 protons and 2 neutrons with 2 electrons encircling the nucleus. Near the other extreme of the list of elements is curium (not shown in the figure), an element discovered in the 1940's, which has 96 protons and 96 electrons in each atom.

The *Periodic Table of the Elements* is an orderly arrangement of the elements in ascending atomic number (number of planetary electrons) and also in atomic weight (number of protons and neutrons in the nucleus). The various kinds of atoms have distinct masses or

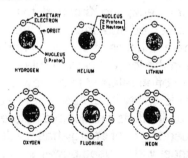

HYDROGEN   HELIUM   LITHIUM

OXYGEN   FLUORINE   NEON

Figure 1-2.—Atomic structure of elements.

weights with respect to each other. The element most closely approaching unity (meaning 1) is hydrogen whose atomic weight is 1.008 as compared with oxygen whose atomic weight is 16. Helium has an atomic weight of approximately 4, lithium 7, fluorine 19, and neon 20, as shown in figure 1-2.

Figure 1-3 is a pictorial summation of the discussion that has just been presented. Visible matter, at the left of the figure, is broken down first to one of its basic molecules, then to one of the molecule's atoms. The atom is then further reduced to its subatomic particlesthe protons, neutrons, and electrons. Subatomic particles are electric in nature. That is, they are the particles of matter most affected by an electric force. Whereas the whole molecule or a whole atom is electrically neutral, most subatomic particles are not neutral (with the exception of the neutron). Protons are inherently positive, and electrons are inherently negative. It is these inherent characteristics which make subatomic particles sensitive to electric force.

When an electric force is applied to a conducting medium, such as copper wire, electrons in the outer orbits of the copper atoms are forced out of orbit and impelled along the wire. The direction of electron movement is determined by the direction of the impelling force. The protons do not move, mainly because they are extremely heavy. The proton of the lightest element, hydrogen, is approximately 1,850 times as heavy as an electron. Thus, it is the relatively light electron that is most readily moved by electricity.

When an orbital electron is removed from an atom it is called a FREE ELECTRON. Some of the electrons of certain metallic atoms are so loosely bound to the nucleus that they are comparatively free to move from atom to atom. Thus, a very small force or amount of energy will cause such electrons to be removed from the atom and become free electrons. It is these free electrons that constitute the flow of an electric current in electrical conductors.

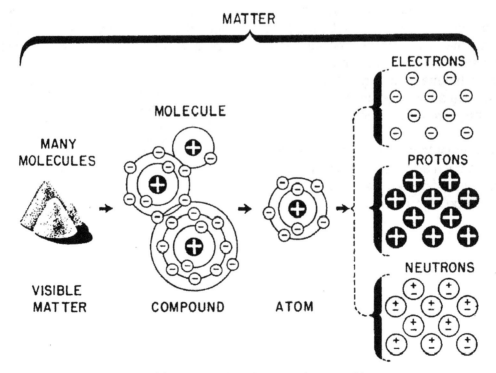

Figure 1-3.—Breakdown of visible matter to electric particles.

4

If the internal energy of an atom is raised above its normal state, the atom is said to be EXCITED. Excitation may be produced by causing the atoms to collide with particles that are impelled by an electric force. In this way, energy is transferred from the electric source to the atom. The excess energy absorbed by an atom may become sufficient to cause loosely bound outer electrons to leave the atom against the force that acts to hold them within. An atom that has thus lost or gained one or more electrons is said to be IONIZED. If the atom loses electrons it becomes positively charged and is referred to as a POSITIVE ION. Conversely, if the atom gains electrons, it becomes negatively charged and is referred to as a NEGATIVE ION. Actually then, an ion is a small particle of matter having a positive or negative charge.

Conductors and Insulators

Substances that permit the free motion of a large number of electrons are called CONDUCTORS. Copper wire is considered a good conductor because it has many free electrons. Electrical energy is transferred through conductors by means of the movement of free electrons that migrate from atom to atom inside the conductor. Each electron moves a very short distance to the neighboring atom where it replaces one or more electrons by forcing them out of their orbits. The replaced electrons repeat the process in other nearby atoms until the movement is transmitted throughout the entire length of the conductor. The greater the number of electrons that can be made to move in a material under the application of a given force the better are the conductive qualities of that material. A good conductor is said to have a low opposition or low resistance to the current (electron) flow.

In contrast to good conductors, some substances such as rubber, glass, and dry wood have very few free electrons. In these materials large amounts of energy must be expended in order to break the electrons loose from the influence of the nucleus. Substances containing very few free electrons are called POOR CONDUCTORS, NONCONDUCTORS, or INSULATORS. Actually, there is no sharp dividing line between conductors and insulators, since electron motion is known to exist to some extent in all matter. Electricians simply use the best conductors as wires to carry current and the poorest conductors as insulators to prevent the current from being diverted from the wires.

Listed below are some of the best conductors and best insulators arranged in accordance with their respective abilities to conduct or to resist the flow of electrons.

Conductors	Insulators
Silver	Dry air
Copper	Glass
Aluminum	Mica
Zinc	Rubber
Brass	Asbestos
Iron	Bakelite

Static Electricity

In a natural, or neutral state, each atom in a body of matter will have the proper number of electrons in orbit around it. Consequently, the whole body of matter comprised of the neutral atoms will also be electrically neutral. In this state, it is said to have a "zero charge," and will neither attract nor repel other matter in its vicinity. Electrons will neither leave nor enter the neutrally charged body should it come in contact with other neutral bodies. If, however, any number of electrons are removed from the atoms of a body of matter, there will remain more protons than electrons, and the whole body of matter will become electrically positive. Should the positively charged body come in contact with another body having a normal charge, or having a negative (too many electrons) charge, an electric current will flow between them. Electrons will leave the more negative body and enter the positive body. This electron flow will continue until both bodies have equal charges.

When two bodies of matter have unequal charges, and are near one another, an electric force is exerted between them because of their unequal charges. However, since they are not in contact, their charges cannot equalize. The existence of such an electric force, where current cannot flow, is referred to as static electricity. "Static" means "not moving." This is also referred to as an ELECTROSTATIC FORCE.

One of the easiest ways to create a static charge is by the friction method. With the friction method, two pieces of matter are rubbed together and electrons are "wiped off" one onto the other. If materials that are good conductors are used, it is quite difficult to obtain a detectable charge on either. The reason for this is that equalizing currents will flow easily in and between the conducting materials. These currents equalize the charges almost as fast as they are created. A static charge is easier to obtain by rubbing a hard nonconducting material against a soft, or fluffy, nonconductor. Electrons are rubbed off one material and onto the other material. This is illustrated in figure 1-4.

When the hard rubber rod is rubbed in the fur, the rod accumulates electrons. Since both fur and rubber are poor conductors, little equalizing current can flow, and an electrostatic charge is built up. When the charge is great enough, equalizing currents will flow in spite of the material's poor conductivity. These currents will cause visible sparks, if viewed in darkness, and will produce a crackling sound.

CHARGED BODIES

One of the fundamental laws of electricity is that LIKE CHARGES REPEL EACH OTHER and UNLIKE CHARGES ATTRACT EACH OTHER. A positive charge and negative charge, being unlike, tend to move toward each other. In the atom the negative electrons are drawn toward the positive protons in the nucleus. This attractive force is balanced by the electron's centrifugal force caused by its rotation about the nucleus. As a result, the electrons remain in orbit and are not drawn into the nucleus. Electrons repel each other because of their like negative charges, and protons repel each other because of their like positive charges.

The law of charged bodies may be demonstrated by a simple experiment. Two pith (paper pulp) balls are suspended near one another by threads, as shown in figure 1-5.

If the hard rubber rod is rubbed to give it a negative charge, and then held against the right-hand ball in part (A), the rod will impart a negative charge to the ball. The right-hand ball will be charged negative with respect to the left-hand ball. When released, the two balls will be drawn together, as shown in figure 1-5 (A). They will touch and remain in contact until the left-hand ball acquires a portion of the negative charge of the right-hand ball, at which time they will swing apart as shown in figure 1-5 (C). If. positive charges are placed on both balls (fig. 1-5 (B)), the balls will also be repelled from each other.

COULOMB'S LAW OF CHARGES

The amount of attracting or repelling force which acts between two electrically charged bodies in free space depends on two things(1) their charges, and (2) the distance between them. The relationship of charge and distance to electrostatic force was first discovered and written by a French scientist named Charles A. Coulomb. Coulomb's Law states that CHARGED BODIES ATTRACT OR REPEL EACH OTHER WITH A FORCE THAT IS DIRECTLY PROPORTIONAL TO THE PRODUCT OF THEIR CHARGES, AND IS INVERSELY PROPOR-

TIONAL TO THE SQUARE OF THE DISTANCE BETWEEN THEM.

ELECTRIC FIELDS

The space between and around charged bodies in which their influence is felt is called an ELECTRIC FIELD OF FORCE. The electric field is always terminated on material objects and extends between positive and negative charges. It can exist in air, glass, paper, or a vacuum. ELECTROSTATIC FIELDS and DIELECTRIC FIELDS are other names used to refer to this region of force.

Fields of force spread out in the space surrounding their point of origin and, in general, DIMINISH IN PROPORTION TO THE SQUARE OF THE DISTANCE FROM THEIR SOURCE.

The field about a charged body is generally represented by lines which are

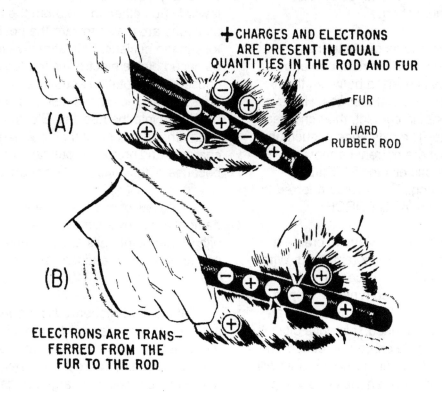

Figure 1-4.—Producing static electricity by friction.

referred to as ELECTROSTATIC LINES OF FORCE. These lines are imaginary and are used merely to represent the direction and strength of the field. To avoid confusion, the lines of force exerted by a positive charge are always shown leaving the charge, and for a negative charge they are shown as entering. Figure 1-6 illustrates the use of lines to represent the field about charged bodies.

Figure 1-6 (A) represents the repulsion of like-charged bodies and their associated fields. Part (B) represents the attraction between unlike-charged bodies and their associated fields.

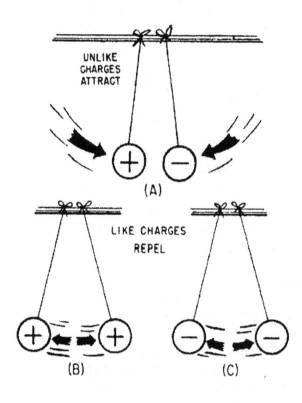

Figure 1-5.—Reaction between charged bodies.

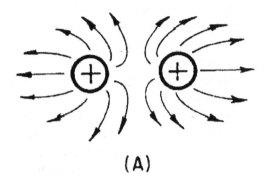

(A)

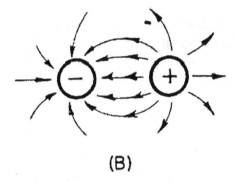

(B)

Figure 1-6.—Electrostatic lines of force.

Magnetism

A substance is said to be a magnet if it has the property of magnetism-that is, if it has the power to attract such substances as iron, steel, nickel, or cobalt, which are known as MAGNETIC MATERIALS. A steel knitting needle, magnetized by a method to be described later, exhibits two points of maximum attraction (one at each end) and no attraction at its center. The points of maximum attraction are called MAGNETIC POLES. All magnets have at least two poles. If the needle is suspended by its middle so that it rotates freely in a horizontal plane about its center, the needle comes to rest in an approximately north-south line of direction. The same pole will always point to the north, and the other will always point toward the south. The magnetic pole that points northward is called the NORTH POLE, and the other the SOUTH POLE.

A MAGNETIC FIELD exists around a simple bar magnet. The field consists of imaginary lines along which a MAGNETIC FORCE acts. These lines emanate from the north pole of the magnet, and enter the south pole, returning to the north pole through the magnet itself, thus forming closed loops.

A MAGNETIC CIRCUIT is a complete path through which magnetic lines of force may be established under the influence of a magnetizing force. Most magnetic circuits are composed largely of magnetic materials in order to contain the magnetic flux. These circuits are similar to the ELECTRIC CIRCUIT, which is a complete path through which current is caused to flow under the influence of an electromotive force.

Magnets may be conveniently divided into three groups.

1. NATURAL MAGNETS, found in the natural state in the form of a mineral called magnetite.

2. PERMANENT MAGNETS, bars of hardened steel (or some form of alloy such as alnico) that have been permanently magnetized.

3. ELECTROMAGNETS, composed of soft-iron cores around which are wound coils of insulated wire. When an electric current flows through the coil, the core becomes magnetized. When the current ceases to flow, the core loses most of its magnetism.

Permanent magnets and electromagnets are sometimes called ARTIFICIAL MAGNETS to further distinguish them from natural magnets.

NATURAL MAGNETS

For many centuries it has been known that certain stones (magnetite, Fe_3O_4) have the ability to attract small pieces of iron. Because many of the best of these stones (natural magnets) were found near Magnesia in Asia Minor, the Greeks called the substance MAGNETITE, or MAGNETIC.

Before this, ancient Chinese observed that when similar stones were suspended freely, or floated on a light substance in a container of water, they tended to assume a nearly north-and-south position. Probably Chinese navigators used bits of magnetite floating on wood in a liquid-filled vessel as crude compasses. At that time it was not known that the earth itself acts like a magnet, and these stones were regarded with considerable superstitious awe. Because bits of this substance were used as compasses they were called LOADSTONES (or lodestones), which means "leading stones."

Natural magnets are also found in the United States, Norway, and Sweden. A natural magnet, demonstrating the attractive force at the poles, is shown in figure 1-7 (A).

ARTIFICIAL MAGNETS

Natural magnets no longer have any practical value because more powerful and more conveniently shaped permanent magnets can be produced artificially. Commercial magnets are made from special steels and alloysfor example, alnico, made principally of aluminum, nickel, and cobalt. The name is derived from the first two letters of the three principal elements of which it is composed. An artificial magnet is shown in figure 1-7 (B).

An iron, steel, or alloy bar can be magnetized by inserting the bar into a coil of insulated wire and passing a heavy direct current through the coil, as shown in figure 1-8 (A). This aspect of magnetism is

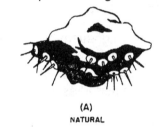

(A)
NATURAL

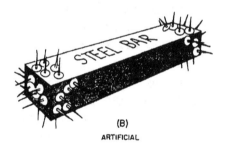

(B)
ARTIFICIAL

Figure 1-7.-(A) Natural magnet; (B) artificial magnet.

treated later in the chapter. The same bar may also be magnetized if it is stroked with a bar magnet, as shown in figure 1-8 (B). It will then have the same magnetic property that the magnet used to induce the magnetism-has namely, there will be two poles of attraction, one at either end. This process produces a permanent magnet by INDUCTION-that is, the magnetism is induced in the bar by the influence of the stroking magnet.

Artificial magnets may be classified as "permanent" or "temporary" depending on their ability to retain their magnetic strength after the magnetizing force has been removed. Hardened steel and certain alloys are relatively difficult to magnetize and are said to have a LOW PERMEABILITY because the magnetic lines of force do not easily permeate, or distribute themselves readily through the steel. Once magnetized, however, these materials retain a large part of their magnetic strength and are called PERMANENT MAGNETS. Permanent magnets are used extensively in electric instruments, meters, telephone receivers, permanent-magnet loudspeakers, andmagnetos. Conversely, substances

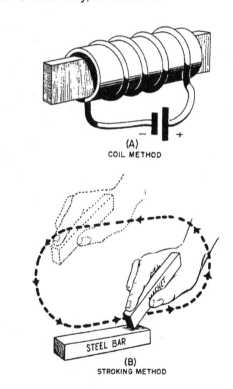

(A)
COIL METHOD

(B)
STROKING METHOD

Figure 1-8.Methods of producing artificial magnets.

that are relatively easy to magnetizesuch as soft iron and annealed silicon steelare said to have a HIGH PERMEABILITY. Such substances retain only a small part of their magnetism after the magnetizing force is removed and are called TEMPORARY MAGNETS. Silicon steel and similar materials are used in transformers where the magnetism is constantly changing and in generators and motors where the strengths of the fields can be readily changed.

The magnetism that remains in a temporary magnet after the magnetizing force is removed is called RESIDUAL MAGNETISM. The fact that temporary magnets retain even a small amount of magnetism is an important factor in the buildup of voltage in self-excited d-c generators.

NATURE OF MAGNETISM

Weber's theory of the nature of magnetism is based on the assumption that each of the molecules of a magnet is itself a tiny magnet. The molecular magnets that compose an unmagne-tized bar of iron or steel are arranged at random, as shown by the simplified diagram of figure 1-9 (A). With this arrangement, the magnetism of each of the molecules is neutralized by that of adjacent molecules, and no external magnetic effect is produced. When a magnetizing force is applied to an unmagnetized iron or steel bar, the molecules become alined so that the north poles point one way and the south poles point the other way, as shown in figure 1-9 (B).

same. If this breaking process could be continued, smaller and smaller pieces would retain their magnetism until each part was reduced to a molecule. It is therefore logical to assume that each of these molecules is a magnet.

A further justification for this assumption results from the fact that when a bar magnet is held out of alinement with the earth's field and is repeatedly jarred, heated, or exposed to a powerful alternating field, the molecular alinement is disarranged and the magnet becomes demagnetized. For example, electric measuring instruments become inaccurate if their permanent magnets lose some of their magnetism because of severe jarring or exposure to opposing magnetic fields.

A theory of magnetism that is perhaps more adequate than the MOLECULAR theory is the DOMAIN theory. Much simplified, this theory may be stated as follows:

In magnetic substances the "atomic" magnets, produced by the movement of the planetary electrons around the nucleus, have a strong tendency to line up together in groups of from 10^{14} to 10^{15} atoms. This occurs without the influence of any external magnetic field. These groups of atoms having their poles orientated in the same direction are called DOMAINS. Therefore,

UNMAGNETIZED STEEL
(A)

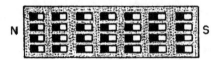
MAGNETIZED STEEL
(B)

Figure 1-9.—Molecular theory of magnetism.

If a bar magnet is broken into several parts, as in figure 1-10, each part constitutes a magnet. The north and south poles of these small magnets are in the same respective directions as those of the original magnet. If each of these parts is again broken, the resulting parts are likewise magnets, and the magnetic orientation is the

throughout each domain an intense magnetic field is produced. These fields are normally in a miscellaneous arrangement so that no external field is apparent when the substance as a whole is unmagnetized. Each tiny domain (10^6 of them may be contained in 1 cubic millimeter) is always magnetized to saturation, and the addition of an external magnetic field does not increase the inherent magnetism of the individual domains.

However, if an external field that is gradually increased in strength is applied to the magnetic substance the domains will line up one by one (or perhaps several at a time) with the external field.

MAGNETIC FIELDS AND LINES OF FORCE

If a bar magnet is dipped into iron filings, many of the filings are attracted to the ends of the magnet, but none are attracted to the center of the magnet. As mentioned previously, the ends of the magnet where the attractive force is the greatest are called the POLES of the magnet. By using a compass, the line of direction of the magnetic force at various points near the magnet may be observed. The compass needle itself is a magnet. The north end of the compass needle always points toward the south pole, S, as shown in figure 1-11 (A), and thus the sense of direction (with respect to the polarity of the bar magnet) is also indicated. At the center, the compass needle points in a direction that is parallel to the bar magnet.

When the compass is placed successively at several points in the vicinity of the bar magnet the compass needle alines itself with the field at each position. The direction of the field is indicated by the arrows and represents the direction in which the north pole of the compass needle will point when the compass is placed in this field. Such a line along which a compass needle alines itself is called a MAGNETIC LINE OF FORCE. As mentioned previously, the magnetic lines of force are assumed to emanate from the north pole of a magnet, pass through the surrounding space, and enter

the south pole. The lines of force then pass from the south pole to the north pole inside the magnet to form a closed loop. Each line of force forms an independent closed loop and does not merge with or cross other lines of force. The lines of force between the poles of a horseshoe magnet are shown in figure 1-11 (B).

The space surrounding a magnet, in which the magnetic force acts, is called a MAGNETIC FIELD. Michael Faraday was the first scientist to visualize the magnet field as being in a state of stress and consisting of uniformly distributed lines of force. The entire quantity of magnetic lines surrounding a magnet is called MAGNETIC FLUX. Flux in a magnetic circuit corresponds to current in an electric circuit.

The number of lines of force per unit area is called FLUX DENSITY and is measured in lines per square inch or lines per square centimeter. Flux density is expressed by the equation

$$B = \frac{\phi}{A}$$

where B is the flux density, ϕ (Greek phi) is the total number of lines of flux, and A is the cross-sectional area of the magnetic circuit. If A is in square centimeters, B is in lines per square centimeter, or GAUSS. The terms FLUX and FLOW of magnetism are frequently used in textbooks. However, magnetism itself is not thought to be a stream of particles in motion, but is simply a field of force exerted in space. A visual representation pf the magnetic field around a magnet can be obtained by placing a plate of glass over a magnet and sprinkling iron filings onto

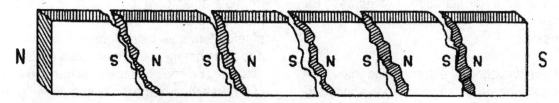

Figure 1-10.—Magnetic poles of a broken magnet.

the glass. The filings arrange themselves in definite paths between the poles.

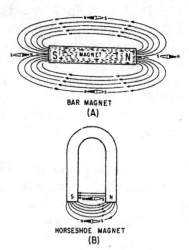

BAR MAGNET
(A)

HORSESHOE MAGNET
(B)

Figure 1-11.—Magnetic lines of force.

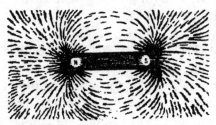

Figure 1-12.—Magnetic field pattern around a magnet.

This arrangement of the filings shows the pattern of the magnetic field around the magnet, as in figure 1-12.

The magnetic field surrounding a symmetrically shaped magnet has the following properties:

1. The field is symmetrical unless disturbed by another magnetic substance.

2. The lines of force have direction and are represented as emanating from the north pole and entering the south pole.

LAWS OF ATTRACTION AND REPULSION

If a magnetized needle is suspended near a bar magnet, as in figure 1-13, it will be seen that a north pole repels a north pole and a south pole repels a south pole. Opposite poles, however, will attract each other.

Thus, the first two laws of magnetic attraction and repulsion are:

1. LIKE magnetic poles REPEL each other.

2. UNLIKE magnetic poles ATTRACT each other.

The flux patterns between adjacent UNLIKE poles of bar magnets, as indicated by lines, are shown in figure 1-14 (A). Similar patterns for adjacent LIKE poles are shown in figure 1-14 (B). The lines do not cross at any point and they act as if they repel each other.

Figure 1-15 shows the flux pattern (indicated by lines) around two bar magnets placed close together and parallel with each other. Figure 1-15 (A) shows the flux pattern when opposite poles are adjacent; and figure 1-15 (B) shows the flux pattern when like poles are adjacent.

The THIRD LAW of magnetic attraction and repulsion states in effect that the force of attraction or repulsion existing between two magnetic poles decreases rapidly as the poles are separated from each other. Actually, the force of attraction or repulsion varies directly as the product of the separate pole strengths and inversely as the square of the distance separating the magnetic

poles, provided the poles are small enough to be considered as points. For example, if the distance between two north poles is increased from 2 feet to 4 feet, the force of

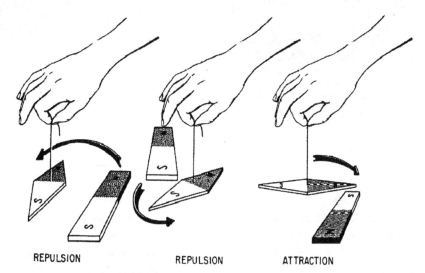

REPULSION   REPULSION   ATTRACTION

Figure 1-13.—Laws of attraction and repulsion.

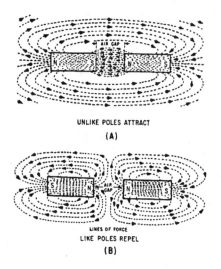

UNLIKE POLES ATTRACT
(A)

LINES OF FORCE
LIKE POLES REPEL
(B)

Figure 1-14.—Lines of force between unlike and like poles.

end of the axis of rotation of the earth. The magnetic axis does not coincide with the geographic axis, and therefore the magnetic and geographic poles are not at the same place on the surface of the earth.

The early users of the compass regarded the end of the compass needle that points in a northerly direction as being a north pole. The other end was regarded as a south pole. On some maps the magnetic pole of the earth towards which the north pole of the compass pointed was designated a north magnetic pole. This magnetic pole was obviously called a north pole because of its proximity to the north geographic pole.

repulsion between them is decreased to one-fourth of its original value. If either pole strength is doubled, the distance remaining the same, the force between the poles will be doubled.

THE EARTH'S MAGNETISM

As has been stated, the earth is a huge magnet; and surrounding the earth is the magnetic field produced by the earth's magnetism. The magnetic polarities of the earth are as indicated in figure 1-16. The geographic poles are also shown at each

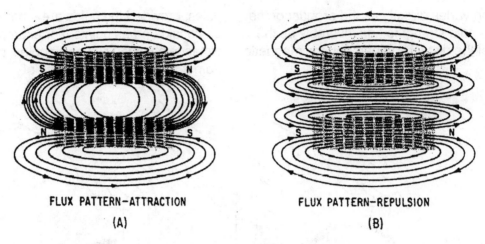

FLUX PATTERN—ATTRACTION
(A)

FLUX PATTERN—REPULSION
(B)

Figure 1-15.—Flux patterns of adjacent parallel bar magnets.

When it was learned that the earth is a magnet and that opposite poles attract, it was necessary to call the magnetic pole located in the northern hemisphere a SOUTH MAGNETIC POLE and the magnetic pole located in the southern hemisphere a NORTH MAGNETIC POLE. The matter of naming the poles was arbitrary. Obviously, the polarity of the compass needle that points toward the north must be opposite to the polarity of the earth's magnetic pole located there.

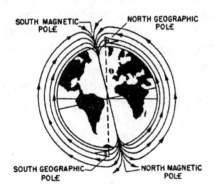

Figure 1-16.—Earth's magnetic poles.

As has been stated, magnetic lines of force are assumed to emanate from the north pole of a magnet and to enter the south pole as closed loops. Because the earth is a magnet, lines of force emanate

from its north magnetic pole and enter the south magnetic pole as closed loops. The compass needle alines itself in such a way that the earth's lines of force enter at its south pole and leave at its north pole. Because the north pole of the needle is defined as the end that points in a northerly direction it follows that the magnetic pole in the vicinity of the north geographic pole is in reality a south magnetic pole, and vice versa.

Because the magnetic poles and the geographic poles do not coincide, a compass will not (except at certain positions on the earth) point in a true (geographic) north-south direction-that is, it will not point in a line of direction that passes through the north and south geographic poles, but in a line of direction that makes an angle with it. This angle is called the angle of VARIATION OR DECLINATION.

MAGNETIC SHIELDING

There is not a known INSULATOR for magnetic flux. If a nonmagnetic material is placed in a magnetic field, there is no appreciable change in flux-that is, the flux penetrates the nonmagnetic material. For example, a glass plate placed between the poles of a horseshoe magnet will have no appreciable effect on the field although glass itself is a good insulator in an electric circuit. If a magnetic material (for example, soft iron) is placed in a magnetic field, the flux may be redirected to take advantage of the greater permeability of the magnetic material as shown in figure 1-17. Permeability is the quality of a substance which determines the ease with which it can be magnetized.

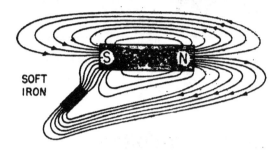

Figure 1-17.—Effects of a magnetic substance in a magnetic field.

The sensitive mechanism of electric instruments and meters can be influenced by stray magnetic fields which will cause errors in their readings. Because instrument mechanisms cannot be insulated against magnetic flux, it is necessary to employ some means of directing the flux around the instrument. This is accomplished by placing a soft-iron case, called a MAGNETIC SCREEN OR SHIELD, about the instrument. Because the flux *is* established more readily through the iron (even though the path is longer) than through the air inside the case, the instrument is effectively shielded, as shown by the watch and soft-iron shield in figure 1-18.

The study of electricity and magnetism, and how they affect each other, is given more thorough coverage in later chapters of this course.

The discussion of magnetism up to this point has been mainly intended to clarify terms and meanings, such as "polarity," "fields," "lines of force," and so forth. Only one fundamental relationship between magnetism and electricity is discussed in this chapter. This relationship pertains to magnetism as used to generate a voltage and it is discussed under the headings that follows.

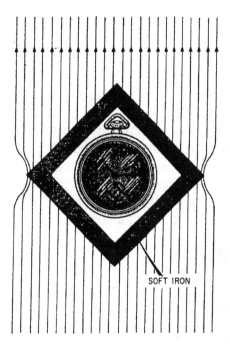

Figure 1-18.—Magnetic shield.

Difference in Potential

The force that causes free electrons to move in a conductor as an electric current is called (1) an electromotive force (e.m.f.), (2) a voltage, or (3) a difference in potential. When a difference in potential exists between two charged bodies that are connected by a conductor, electrons will flow along the conductor. This flow will be from the negatively charged body to the positively charged body until the two charges are equalized and the potential difference no longer exists.

An analogy of this action is shown in the two water tanks connected by a pipe and valve in figure 1-19. At first the valve is closed and all the water is in tank A. Thus, the water pressure across the valve is at maximum. When the valve is opened, the water flows through the pipe from A to B until the water level becomes the same in both tanks. The water then stops flowing in the pipe, because there is no longer a difference in water pressure between the two tanks.

Current flow through an electric circuit is directly proportional to the difference in potential across the circuit, just as the flow of water through the pipe in figure 1-19 is directly proportional to the difference in water level in the two tanks.

A fundamental law of current electricity is that the CURRENT IS DIRECTLY PROPORTIONAL TO THE APPLIED VOLTAGE.

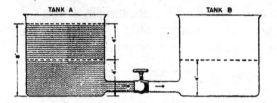

Figure 1-19.—Water analogy of electric difference in potential.

Primary Methods of Producing a Voltage

Presently, there are six commonly used methods of producing a voltage. Some of these methods are much more widely used than others. The methods of utilizing each source will be discussed, and their most common applications will be included. The following is a list of the six most common methods of producing a voltage.

1. FRICTION.-Voltage produced by rubbing two materials together.

2. PRESSURE (Piezoelectricity).-Voltage produced by squeezing crystals of certain substances.

3. HEAT (Thermoelectricity).-Voltage produced by heating the joint (junction) where two unlike metals are joined.

4. LIGHT (Photoelectricity).-Voltage produced by light striking photosensitive (light sensitive) substances.

5. CHEMICAL ACTION.-Voltage produced by chemical reaction in a battery cell.

6. MAGNETISM.-Voltage produced in a conductor when the conductor moves through a magnetic field, or a magnetic field moves through the conductor in such a manner as to cut the magnetic lines of force of the field.

VOLTAGE PRODUCED BY FRICTION

This is the least used of the six methods of producing voltages. Its main application is in Van de Graf generators, used by some laboratories to produce high voltages. As a rule, friction electricity (often referred to as static electricity) is a nuisance. For instance, a flying aircraft accumulates electric charges from the friction between its skin and the passing air.

These charges often interfere with radio communication, and under some circumstances can even cause physical damage to the aircraft. You have probably received unpleasant shocks from friction electricity upon sliding across dry seat covers or walking across dry carpets, and then coming in contact with some other object.

VOLTAGE PRODUCED BY PRESSURE

This action is referred to as piezoelectricity. It is produced by compressing or decompressing crystals of certain substances. To study this form of electricity, you must first understand the meaning of the word "crystal." In a crystal, the molecules are arranged in an orderly and uniform manner. A substance in its crystallized state and in its noncrystallized state is shown in figure 1-20.

For the sake of simplicity, assume that the molecules of this particular substance are spherical (ball-shaped). In the noncrystallized state, in part (A), note that the molecules are arranged irregularly. In the crystallized state, part (B), the molecules are arranged in a regular and uniform manner. This illustrates the major physical difference between crystal and noncrystal forms of matter. Natural crystalline matter is rare; an example of matter that is crystalline in its natural form is diamond, which is crystalline carbon. Most crystals are manufactured.

Crystals of certain substances, such as Rochelle salt or quartz, exhibit peculiar electrical characteristics. These characteristics, or effects, are referred to as "piezoelectric." For instance, when a crystal of quartz is compressed, as in figure 1-20 (C), electrons tend

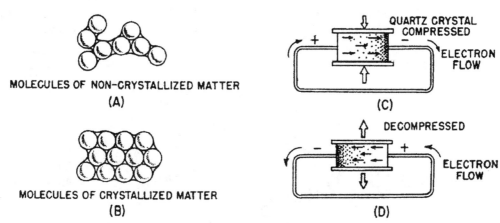

MOLECULES OF NON-CRYSTALLIZED MATTER
(A)

MOLECULES OF CRYSTALLIZED MATTER
(B)

(C)

(D)

Figure 1-20.—(A) Noncrystallized structure, (B) crystallized structure, (C) compression of a crystal, (D) decompression of a crystal.

to move through the crystal as shown. This tendency creates an electric difference of potential between the two opposite faces of the crystal. (The fundamental reasons for this action are not known. However, the action is predictable, and therefore useful.) If an external wire is connected while the pressure and e.m.f. are present, electrons will flow. If the pressure is held constant, the electron flow will continue until the charges are equalized. When the force is removed, the crystal is decompressed, and immediately causes an electric force in the opposite direction, as shown in part (D). Thus, the crystal is able to convert mechanical force, either pressure or tension, to electrical force.

The power capacity of a crystal is extremely small. However, they are useful because of their extreme sensitivity to changes of mechanical force or changes in temperature. Due to other characteristics not mentioned here, crystals are most widely used in radio communication equipment. The more complicated study of crystals, as they are used for practical applications, is left for those courses that pertain to the special ratings concerned with them.

VOLTAGE PRODUCED BY HEAT

When a length of metal, such as copper, is heated at one end, electrons tend to move away from the hot end toward the cooler end. This is true of most metals. However, in some metals, such as iron, the opposite takes place and electrons tend to move TOWARD the hot end. These characteristics are illustrated in figure 1-21. The negative charges (electrons) are moving through the copper away from the heat and through the iron toward the heat. They cross from the iron to the copper at the hot junction, and from the copper through the current meter to the iron at the cold junction. This device is generally referred to as a thermocouple.

Thermocouples have somewhat greater power capacities than crystals, but their capacity is still very small if compared to some other sources. The thermoelectric voltage in a thermocouple depends mainly on the difference in temperature between the hot and cold junctions. Consequently, they are widely used to measure temperature, and as heat-sensing devices in automatic temperature control equipment. Thermocouples generally can be subjected to much greater temperatures than ordinary thermometers, such as the mercury or alcohol types.

VOLTAGE PRODUCED BY LIGHT

When light strikes the surface of a substance, it may dislodge electrons from their orbits around the surface atoms of the substance. This occurs because light has energy, the same as any moving force.

Some substances, mostly metallic ones, are far more sensitive to light than others. That is, more electrons will be dislodged and emitted from the surface of a highly sensitive metal, with a given amount of light, than will be emitted from a less sensitive

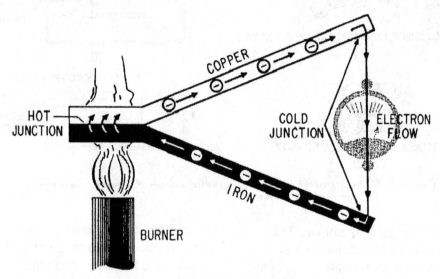

Figure 1-21.—Voltage produced by heat.

substance. Upon losing electrons, the photosensitive (light sensitive) metal becomes positively charged, and an electric force is created. Voltage produced in this manner is referred to as "a photoelectric voltage."

The photosensitive materials most commonly used to produce a photoelectric voltage are various compounds of silver oxide or copper oxide. A complete device which operates on the photoelectric principle is referred to as a "photoelectric cell." There are many sizes and types of photoelectric cells in use, each of which serves the special purpose for which it was designed. Nearly all, however, have some of the basic

features of the photoelectric cells shown in figure 1-22.

The cell shown in part (A) has a curved light-sensitive surface focused on the central anode. When light from the direction shown strikes the sensitive surface, it emits electrons toward the anode. The more intense the light, the greater is the number of electrons emitted. When a wire is connected between the filament and the back, or dark side, the accumulated electrons will flow to the dark side. These electrons will eventually

19

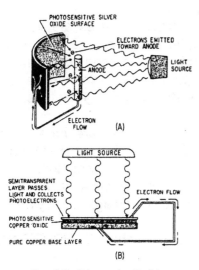

Figure 1-22.—Voltage produced by light.

pass through the metal of the reflector and replace the electrons leaving the light-sensitive surface. Thus, light energy is converted to a flow of electrons, and a usable current is developed.

The cell shown in part (B) is constructed in layers. A base plate of pure copper is coated with light-sensitive copper oxide. An additional layer of metal is put over

the copper oxide. This additional layer serves two purposes:

1. It is EXTREMELY thin to permit the penetration of light to the copper oxide.

2. It also accumulates the electrons emitted by the copper oxide.

An externally connected wire completes the electron path, the same as in the reflector type cell. The photocell's voltage is utilized as needed by connecting the external wires to some other device, which amplifies (enlarges) it to a usable level.

A photocell's power capacity is very small. However, it reacts to light-intensity variations in an extremely short time. This characteristic makes the photocell very useful in detecting or accurately controlling a great number of processes or operations. For instance, the photoelectric cell, or some form of the photoelectric principle, is used in television cameras, automatic manufacturing process controls, door openers, burglar alarms, and so forth.

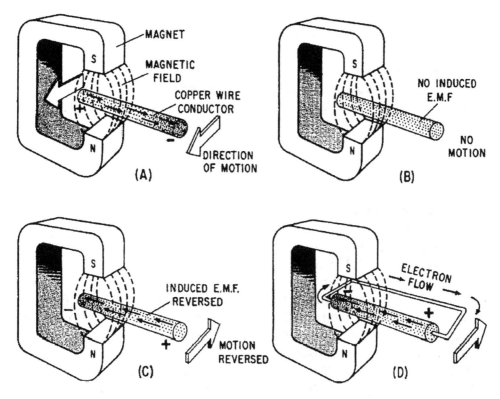

Figure 1-23.—Voltage produced by magnetism.

VOLTAGE PRODUCED BY CHEMICAL ACTION

Up to this point, it has been shown that electrons may be removed from their parent atoms and set in motion by energy derived from a source of friction, pressure, heat, or light. In general, these forms of energy do not alter the molecules of the substances being acted upon. That is, molecules are not usually added, taken away, or split-up when subjected to these four forms of energy. Only electrons are involved. When the molecules of a substance are altered, the action is referred to as CHEMICAL. For instance, if the molecules of a substance combines with atoms of another substance, or gives up atoms of its own, the action is chemical in nature. Such action always changes the , chemical name and characteristics of the substance affected. For instance, when atoms of oxygen from the air come in contact with bare iron, they merge with the molecules of iron. This iron is "oxidized." It has changed chemically from iron to iron oxide, or "rust." Its molecules have been altered by chemical action.

In some cases, when atoms are added to or taken away from the molecules of a substance, the chemical change will cause the substance to take on an electric charge. The process of producing a voltage by chemical action is used in batteries and is explained in chapter 2.

VOLTAGE PRODUCED BY MAGNETISM

Magnets or magnetic devices are used for thousands of different jobs. One of the most useful and widely employed applications of magnets is in the production of vast quantities of electric power from mechanical sources. The mechanical power may be provided by a number of different sources, such as gasoline or diesel engines, and water or steam turbines. However, the final conversion of these source energies to electricity is done by generators employing the principle of electromagnetic induction. These genera-

tors, of many types and sizes, are discussed in later chapters of this course. The important subject to be discussed here is the fundamental operating principle of ALL such electromagnetic-induction generators.

To begin with, there are three fundamental conditions which must exist before a voltage can be produced by magnetism. You should learn them well, because they will be encountered again and again. They are:

1. There must be a CONDUCTOR, in which the voltage will be produced.

2. There must be a MAGNETIC FIELD in the conductor's vicinity.

3. There must be relative motion between the field and the conductor. The conductor must be moved so as to cut across the magnetic lines of force, or the field must be moved so that the lines of force are cut by the conductor.

In accordance with these conditions, when a conductor or conductors MOVE ACROSS a magnetic field so as to cut the lines of force, electrons WITHIN THE CONDUCTOR are impelled in one direction or another. Thus, an electric force, or voltage, is created.

In figure 1-23, note the presence of the three conditions needed for creating an induced voltage:

1. A magnetic field exists between the poles of the C-shaped magnet.

2. There is a conductor (copper wire).

3. There is relative motion. The wire is moved back and forth ACROSS the magnetic field.

In part (A) the conductor is moving TOWARD you. This occurs because of the magnetically induced electromotive force (e.m.f.) acting on the electrons in the copper. The right-hand end becomes negative, and the left-hand end positive. In part (B) the conductor is stopped. This eliminates motion, one of the three required conditions, and there is no longer an induced e.m.f. Consequently, there is no longer any difference in potential between the two ends of the wire. In part (C) the conductor is moving AWAY from you. An induced e.m.f. is again created. However, note carefully that the REVERSAL OF MOTION has caused a REVERSAL OF DIRECTION in the induced e.m.f.

If a path for electron flow is provided between the ends of the conductor, elec-

trons will leave the negative end and flow to the positive end. This condition is shown in part (D). Electron flow will continue as long as the e.m.f. exists. In studying figure 1-23, it should be noted that the induced e.m.f. could also have been created by holding the conductor stationary and moving the magnetic field back and forth.

In later chapters of this course, under the heading "Generators," you will study the more complex aspects of power generation by use of mechanical motion and magnetism.

Electric Current

The drift or flow of electrons through a conductor is called ELECTRIC CURRENT. In order to determine the amount (number) of electrons flowing in a given conductor, it is necessary to adopt a unit of measurement of current flow. The term AMPERE is used to define the unit of measurement of the rate at which current flows (electron flow). The symbol for the ampere is I. One ampere may be defined as the fow of 6.28×10^{18} electrons per second past a fixed point in a conductor

A unit quantity of electricity is moved through an electric circuit when one ampere of current flows for one second of time. This unit is equivalent to 6.28×10^{18} electrons, and is called the COULOMB. The coulomb is to electricity as the gallon is to water. The symbol for the coulomb is Q. The rate of flow of current in amperes and the quantity of electricity moved through a circuit are related by the common factor of time. Thus,

the quantity of electric charge, in coulombs, electricity moved through a circuit are is equal to the product of the current in amperes, I, and the duration of flow in seconds, t. Expressed as an equation, $Q = It$.

For example, if a current of 2 amperes flows through a circuit for 10 seconds the quantity of electricity moved through the circuit is 2 x 10, or 20 coulombs. Conversely, current flow may be expressed in terms of coulombs and time in seconds. Thus, if 20 coulombs are moved through a circuit in 10 seconds, the average current flow is 20/10, or 2 amperes. Note that the current flow in amperes implies the rate of flow of coulombs per second without indicating either coulombs or seconds. Thus a current flow of 2 amperes is equivalent to a rate of flow of 2 coulombs per second.

Resistance

Every material offers some resistance, or opposition, to the flow of electric cur rent through it. Good conductors, such as copper, silver, and aluminum, offer very little resistance. Poor conductors, or insulators, such as glass, wood, and paper, offer a high resistance to current flow.

The size and type of material of the wires in an electric circuit are chosen so as to keep the electrical resistance as low as possible. In this way, current can flow easily through the conductors, just as water flows through the pipe between the tanks in figure 1-19. If the water pressure remains constant the flow of water in the pipe will depend on how far the valve is opened. The smaller the opening, the greater the opposition to the flow, and the smaller will be the rate of flow in gallons per second.

In the electric circuit, the larger the diameter of the wires, the lower will be their electrical resistance (opposition) to the flow of current through them. In the water analogy, pipe friction opposes the flow of water between the tanks. This friction is similar to electrical resistance. The resistance of the pipe to the flow of water through it depends upon (1) the length of the pipe, (2) the diameter of the pipe, and (3) the nature of the inside walls (rough or smooth). Similarly, the electrical resistance of the conductors depends upon (1) the length of the wires, (2) the diameter of the wires, and (3) the material of the wires (copper, aluminum, etc.).

Temperature also affects the resistance of electrical conductors to some extent. In most conductors (copper, aluminum, iron, etc.) the resistance increases with temperature. Carbon is an exception. In carbon the resistance decreases as temperature increases. Certain alloys of metals (manganin and constantan) have resistance that does not change appreciably with temperature.

The relative resistance of several conductors of the same length and cross section is given in the following list with silver as a standard of 1 and the remaining metals arranged in an order of ascending resistance:

Silver...............	1.0
Copper..............	1.08
Gold...............	1.4
Aluminum............	1.8
Platinum............	7.0
Lead...............	13.5

The resistance in an electrical circuit is expressed by the symbol R. Manufactured circuit parts containing definite amounts of resistance are called RESISTORS. Resistance (R) is measured in OHMS. One ohm is the resistance of a circuit element, or circuit, that permits a steady current of 1 ampere (1 coulomb per second) to flow when a steady e.m.f. of 1 volt is applied to the circuit.

GENERAL PRINCIPLES OF WIRING

Section I. DESIGN AND LAYOUT OF INTERIOR WIRING

47. General

The different wiring systems in common use for civilian and armed forces construction are often called open-wire, cable, and conduit systems.

Many installation methods and procedures used in the wiring processes are common to all systems, and these are described in this chapter. In most wiring installations the type of wiring to be installed will be specified on the blueprints. If not so specified the installation method must be determined. In general, the type of wiring used should be similar to that installed in adjacent or nearby buildings.

48. Load Per Outlet

The first step in planning the circuit for any wiring installation is the determination of the connected load per outlet. The load per outlet can be obtained in several different ways:

a. The most accurate method of determining load per outlet is made by obtaining the stated value from the blueprints or specifications.

(1) Commonly, the lighting outlets shown on the blueprints are listed in the specifications along with their wattage rating.

(a) If the lights used are of the incandescent type, this figure represents the total wattage of the lamp.

(b) When fluorescent type lights are specified, the wattage drain (also called load per outlet) should be increased approximately 20 percent to provide for the ballast load. For example, when the fixture is rated as a 2-lamp, 100-watt unit, the actual wattage drain is 200 watts plus approximately 20 watts for each lamp ballast, or a total load of 240 watts.

(2) If the specifications are not available, the blueprints in many cases designate the type of equipment to be connected to specific outlets. Though the equipment ultimately used in the outlet may come from a different manufacturer, equipment standards provide the electrician with assurance that the outlets will use approximately the same wattage. If the equipment is available, the nameplate will list the wattage used or ampere drain. If not, table VII should be used to obtain the average wattage consumption of electrical appliances. Table VIII lists the current requirements for small motors of various horsepower ratings.

b. To provide adequate wiring for systems where the blueprints or specifications do not list any special or appliance loads, the following general rules will apply:

– (1) For heavy duty outlets or mogul size lampholders, the load per outlet should be figured at 5 amperes each.

(2) For all other outlets, both ceiling and wall, the wattage drain (load per outlet) should be computed at 1.5 amperes per outlet.

c. The total outlet load may also be determined on a watts-per-square-foot basis. In this load-determination method, the floor area of the building to be wired is computed from the outside dimensions of the building. This square footage area is then multiplied by the standard watts-per-square-foot requirement based on the type of building to be wired. Table IX lists these constants along with a feeder-demand factor which is explained in paragraph 53 for various types of building occupancies.

49. Type of Distribution

a. The electrical power load in any building cannot be properly circuited until the type and voltage of the central power-distribution system is known. The voltage and the number of wires from the

Table VII. Wattage Consumption of Electrical Appliances

Appliance	Average wattage
Blanket	150
Clock	3
Coffeemaker	550
Chafing dish	600
Dishwasher	100
Egg boiler	250
Fan, 8-inch	30
Fan, 10-inch	35
Fan, 12-inch	50
Frying pan	600
Griddle	450
Grill	600
Heater (radiant)	1000
Heating pad	50
Hotplate	660
Humidifier	500
Immersion heater	300
Iron	1000
Ironer	1320
Mixer	200
Phonograph	40
Range	8000
Refrigerator	250
Radio	100
Roaster	1320
Sewing machine	75
Soldering iron	200
Sunlamp	450
Television	300
Toaster	450
Vacuum cleaner	160
Washing machine	175
Water heater	2000
Waffle iron	660

Table VIII. Motor Currents

Horse-power	Full-load amperes			
	120 v. 1 phase	240 v. 1 phase	208 v. 3 phase	416 v. 3 phase
1/6	3.1	1.6	...	...
1/4	4.4	2.2	...	...
1/2	7.1	3.6	2.1	1.1
3/4	9.8	4.9	3.0	1.5
1	12.5	6.3	3.7	1.9
1 1/2	17.7	8.9	5.3	2.7
2	23.1	11.6	7.0	3.5
3	32.6	16.3	9.6	4.8
5	54.0	27.0	16.0	8.0

powerlines to the buildings are normally shown or specified on the blueprints. However, the electrician should check the voltage and type of distribution at the power-service entrance to every building in which wiring is to be done. This is especially necessary when he is altering or adding circuits. The voltage checks are usually made with an indicating voltmeter at the service-entrance switches or at the distribution load centers. The type of distribution is determined by visual check of the number of wires entering the building.

b. If only two wires enter the building, the service is either direct current or single-phase alternating current. The voltage is determined by an indicating voltmeter.

c. When three wires enter a building the service can either be single-phase, direct-current, or three-phase.

Table IX. Standard Loads for Branch Circuits and Feeders and Demand Factor for Feeders

Occupancy	Standard load, watts per square foot	Feeder demand factor, percent
Armories and auditoriums	1	100%
Banks	2	100%
Barber shops	3	100%
Churches	1	100%
Clubs	2	100%
Dwellings	3	100% for first 3,000 watts, 35% for next 117,000, 25% for excess above 120,000.
Garages	0.5	100%
Hospitals	2	40% for first 50,000 watts, 20% for excess over 50,000.
Office buildings	2	100% for first 20,000 watts, 70% for excess over 20,000.
Restaurants	2	100%
Schools	2	100% for first 15,000 watts, 50% for excess over 15,000.
Stores	3	100%
Warehouses	0.25	100% for first 12,500 watts, 50% for excess over 12,500.
Assembly halls	1	100%

(1) If the power distribution is single-phase alternating current or direct current the test leads over 2 of the wires in the service entrance will give an indicating voltmeter reading that will be exactly twice as much as when the voltmeter leads are applied between any 1 of these 2-wires and the third.

(2) A three-phase distribution system will show no change in voltage between any pair of leads when tested with an indicating voltmeter.

d. Four-wire distribution denotes 3-phase and neutral service. When tested, voltages between the neutral wires and each of the 3 hot wires should be all the same. The voltage readings between any 2 of these 3 wires are similar and should equal the neutral to hot wire voltage multiplied by 1.732. Common operating voltages for this type service are 120 and 208 volts.

50. Grounding

a. *Requirements.*

(1) All electrical systems must have the neutral wire grounded if the voltage between the hot lead and the neutral is less than 150 volts.

(2) It is recommended that all systems have a grounded neutral where the voltage to ground does not exceed 300 volts.

(3) Circuits operating at less than 50 volts need not be grounded, provided the transformer supplying the circuit is connected to a grounded system.

b. *Types of Grounding.*

(1) A system ground is the ground applied to a neutral wire. It reduces the possibility of fire and shock by reducing the voltage of 1 of the wires of a system to 0 volts potential above ground.

(2) An equipment ground is an additional ground which is attached to appliances and machinery located in such places as laundries and basements where wet or humid conditions could create dangerous short circuits. An equipment ground is advantageous in these areas for the appliances can be maintained at zero voltage, and if a short circuit does occur in a hot load, the fuse protection opens the circuit and prevents serious injury to operating personnel.

c. *Methods of Grounding.*

(1) A system ground is provided by the instal-

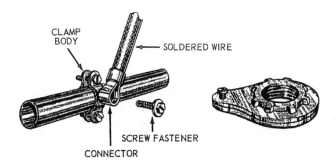

① CLAMP TYPE   ② BUSHING TYPE

Figure 42. Typical grounding fixtures.

lation of a No. 6-gage bare wire connecting the neutral wire either with a water pipe or a ¾-inch conduit driven 8 feet into the ground. The wire is attached to the water pipe or conduit by a special clamp or bushing ground-connector clamp after the pipe or conduit has been filed or sandpapered clean to make a good electrical contact. A clamp type ground-connector has two semicircular sections which encircle the ground rod or conduit and are tightened by a machine screw. A bushing type ground connector clamp is screwed onto the ground rod in a manner similar to installing a bushing on a conduit. Figure 42 shows typical grounding fixtures.

(2) Equipment is grounded through the conduit in a permanent installation by utilizing the system ground, or through the use of a three-wire cord, plug, and matching receptacle. The third wire in the receptacle is attached to either the conduit or the system ground. Similarly, the third prong on the plug is connected to the metal structure of the equipment to be grounded.

d. *Ground Detection.* When testing or inspecting system installations, proper grounding can be determined visually and electrically as follows:

(1) The neutral wire, always grounded, should be a white-colored insulated wire. The equipment ground wire should always be green.

(2) If checked with an indicating voltmeter, the scale should indicate zero when the test prods are placed between the neutral wire and the building water pipes or ground rod.

51. Circuiting the Load

a. If all the power load in a building were con-

Table X. Requirements for Branch Circuits

Rating of circuit	15 amperes	20 amperes	25 amperes	35 amperes	50 amperes
Rubber-insulated conductors 2 or 3 per raceway or cable. Minimum gage number:					
(1) Type R	14	12	10	8	5
(2) Type RP	14	12	10	8	6
(3) Type RH	14	14	12	10	8
Receptacle rating (amperes)	15 (max.)	15 (min.)	20 (min.)	25 (min.)	50 (min.)
Type of lampholders (for exceptions, see National Electrical Code).	Any type.	Heavy duty.	Heavy duty.	Heavy duty.[1]	Heavy duty.[1]
Portable appliances. Maximum individual rating of one appliance, not motor-driven[2] (amperes).	12	15	20	Not permitted.	Not permitted.
Fixed appliances, total rating (amperes):					
(1) If lampholders or portable appliances are also supplied.	6	15	20	25	Combination not permitted.
(2) If fixed appliances only, with one or more being motor-driven, are supplied.	12	15	20	25	Not permitted.
(3) If fixed appliances only, none being motor-driven, are supplied.	15	20	25	35	50[3]

[1] No lampholder may be supplied by this circuit in dwellings.
[2] Can be motor-driven if time-lag fuses are used.
[3] Only appliances permitted on this circuit are fixed cooking appliances or a range and water heater.

nected to a single pair of wires and protected by a single fuse, the entire establishment would be without power in case of a breakdown, a short circuit, or a fuse blowout. In addition the wires would have to be large enough to handle the entire load, and, therefore, too large in some cases to make connections to individual devices. Consequently, the outlets in a building are divided into small groups known as branch circuits. These circuits normally are rated in amperes as shown in table X. This table contains a comparison of the various ampere requirements of the branch circuits with the standard circuit components.

  b. The method of circuiting the building load varies with the size of the building and the power load.

  (1) In a small building with little load, the circuit breakers or fuses are installed at the power-service entrance and the individual circuits are run from this location.

  (2) For buildings of medium size with numerous wiring circuits, the fuse box should be located at the center of the building load so that all the branch runs are short, minimizing the voltage drop in the lines.

  (3) When buildings are large or have the loads concentrated at several remote locations, the ideal circuiting would locate fuse boxes at each individual load center. It is assumed that the branch circuits would be radially installed at each of these centers to minimize the voltage drops in the runs.

  c. The number of circuits required for adequate wiring can be determined by adding the connected load in watts and dividing the total by the wattage permitted on the size of branch circuit selected. The total wattage is obtained from the sum of the loads of each individual outlet determined by one of the three methods outlined in paragraph 48. For example, if 15-ampere, 110-volt circuits are to be used, the maximum wattage permitted on each circuit equals 15 x 110 or 1650 watts. If the total connected load is assumed to be 18,000 watts, $\frac{18000}{1650}$ shows 11.5 circuits are required. Since we cannot have ½ of a circuit, twelve 15-ampere circuits are used to carry the connected load. The number of circuits determined by this method is the basic minimum. For long-range planning in permanent installations, the best practice requires the addition of several circuits to the minimum required, or the installation of the next larger modular-size fusing panel to allow for future wiring additions. If additional circuits over the minimum required are used, reducing the number of outlets per circuit, the electrical installation is more efficient. This is true because the voltage drop in the system is reduced allowing the apparatus to operate more efficiently.

d. Motors which are used on portable appliances are normally disconnected from the power source either by removal of the appliance plug from its receptacle or by the operation of an attached built-in switch. Some large-horsepower motors, however, require a permanent power installation with special controls. Motor switches, some of which are shown in figure 43, are rated in horsepower capacity. In a single motor installation a separate circuit must be run from the fuse or circuit breaker panel to the motor, and individual fuses or circuit breakers installed. For multiple motor installations the National Electrical Code requires that "Two or more motors may be connected to the same branch circuit, protected at not more than 20 amperes at 125 volts or less or 15 amperes at 600 volts or less, if each does not exceed 1 horsepower in rating and each does not have a full load rating in excess of 6 amperes. Two or more motors of any rating, each with individual overcurrent protection (provided integral with the motor start switches or an individual units), may be connected to one branch circuit provided each motor controller and motor-running overcurrent device be approved for group installation and the branch circuit fusing rating be equal to the rating required for the largest motor plus an amount equal to the sum of the full load ratings of the other motors".

52. Balancing the Power Load on a Circuit

The ideal wiring system is planned so that each wiring circuit will have the same ampere drain at all times. Since this can never be achieved, the circuiting is planned to divide the connected load as evenly as possible. Thus, each individual circuit uses approximately the average power consumption for the total system. This will make for minimum service interruption. Figure 44 demonstrates the advantage of a balanced circuit when a 3-wire single-phase, 110–220-volt distribution system is used. The current in the neutral conductor remains 0 as shown.

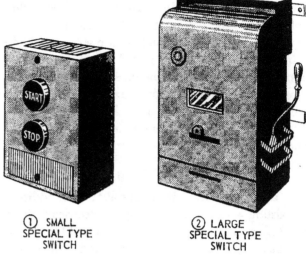

① SMALL SPECIAL TYPE SWITCH   ② LARGE SPECIAL TYPE SWITCH

Figure 43. Motor switches.

This 1 factor reduces the voltage drop in each circuit by 50 percent from what it would be if the load were on two 2-wire circuits.

53. Load Per Building

a. Maximum Demand. In some building installations the total possible power load may be connected to power at the same time. In this case, the generating capacity of the power supply, which must be kept available for these buildings, is equal to the connected load. In the majority of building installations where armed forces personnel will work, the maximum load which the system is required to service is much less than the connected load. This power load which is set at some arbitrary figure below the possible total connected load is called the "maximum demand" of the building.

b. Demand Factor. The ratio of "maximum demand" to total connected load in a building expressed as a percentage is termed demand factor. The determination of building loads can be obtained by the use of standard demand factors as shown in table IX. For example, if the connected load in a warehouse is 22,500 watts, using the demand factors listed in table IX for warehouses the actual building load can be obtained as follows: 100 percent of the first 12,500 watts equals 12,500, 50 percent of the remaining 10,000 watts equals 5,000; therefore, the total building load is 12,500 plus 5,000 watts or 17,500 watts.

54. Balancing the Power Load of a Building

The standard voltage distribution system from a generating station to individual building installations is the 3- or 4-wire, 3-phase type. Distribution transformers as shown in figure 45 on the powerline poles change the voltage to 110 or 220, and are designed to deliver 3-wire single-phase service. These transformers are then connected across the distribution phase leads in a balanced arrangement as shown. Consequently, for maximum transformer efficiency, the building loads assumed for power distribution as shown in figure 45 should also be balanced as previously illustrated in figure 44.

55. Additions to Existing Wiring

a. Circuit Capacity. In the installation of additions to existing wiring in a building the electrician determines first the available extra capacity of the present circuits. This can readily be obtained by ascertaining the fused capacity of the building and subtracting the present connected load. If all the outlets do not have connected loads, their average load should be used to obtain the connected load figure. When the existing circuits have available capacity for new outlets and are located near the additional outlet required, they should be extended and connected to the new outlets.

b. New Circuits. When the existing outlets cannot handle an additional load and a spare circuit has been provided in the local fuse or circuit breaker panel, a new circuit is installed. This is also done if the new outlet or outlets are so located that a new circuit can be installed more economically than an existing circuit extension. Moreover, the installa-

tion of a new circuit will generally decrease the voltage drop on all circuits, resulting in an increase in appliance operating efficiency. Figure 46 illustrates the addition of a new circuit from the spare circuit No. 4 in the circuit breaker panel.

c. New Load Center. In many wiring installations no provisions are made for spare circuits in the fuse panel. Moreover, the location of the new circuit required is often remote from the existing fusing or circuit breaker panel. In this case the most favorable method of providing service to the circuit is to install a new load center at a location close to the circuit outlets. This installation must not overload the incoming service and service-entrance switch. Should such an overload be indicated, the service equipment should also be changed to suit the new requirements. This sometimes can be accomplished in 2-wire systems by pulling in an additional wire from the powerline. This changes the service from 2-wire to 3-wire at 110 to 220 volts. In these cases the fuse or circuit breaker box should also be changed and enlarged to accommodate the increased circuit capacity. Figure 47 schematically illustrates the installation of an additional load center for a new circuit.

d. Concealed Installations. The addition of outlets in a building with finished interior walls having enclosed air spaces entails the use of a fish wire and drop chain. Figure 48 shows the addition of a wire run for an outlet accomplished by a drop from the attic space or as a riser from the basement. First

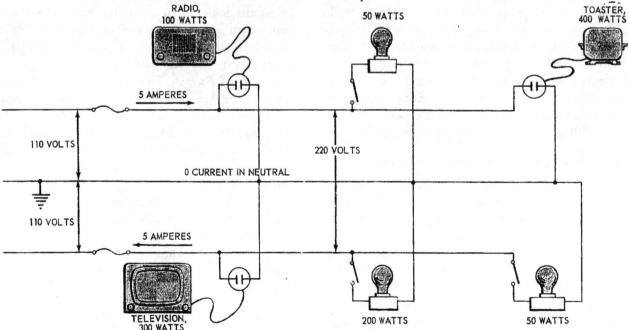

Figure 44. Diagram showing circuit balancing.

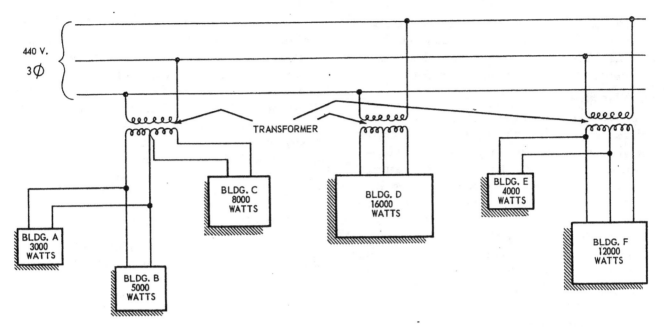

Figure 45. Diagram showing building load balancing.

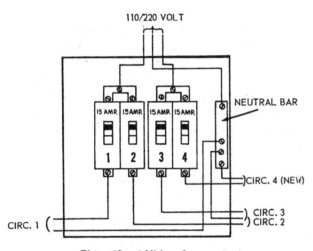

Figure 46. Addition of a new circuit.

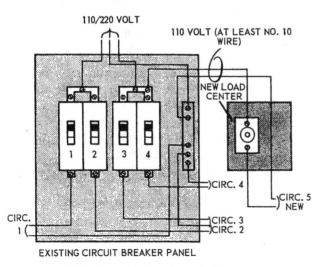

Figure 47. Addition of new load center.

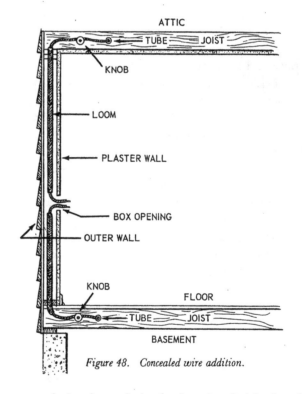

Figure 48. Concealed wire addition.

an opening is made in the interior finished wall at the desired outlet position. If the attic circuit is to be tapped, holes are drilled in the top plates of the wood studding, and a drop chain is lowered inside the wall and pulled through the box opening. The wire to be installed is then attached to the chain and pulled through, completing the rough-in operation for the outlet. Similarly when a wire is to be pulled in from the basement, a stiff wire, called a fish wire, is used. After drilling through the rough floor and bottom plate of the studding the fish wire is pushed up from the basement until it is grasped at the box opening. The wire to be pulled is then attached and pulled through the inner wall section.

56. Wire Size

a. Wire sizes No. 14 and larger are classified in accordance with their maximum allowable current-carrying capacity based on their physical behavior when subjected to the stress and temperatures of operating conditions. Fourteen-gage wire is the smallest wire size permitted for use in interior wiring systems.

b. The determination of the wire size to be used in circuits is dependent on the voltage drop coincident with each size. The size of the conductor used as a feeder to each circuit is also based on voltage drop, and should be selected so that the voltage drop from the branch circuit supply to the outlets will not be more than 3 percent for power loads and 1 percent for lighting loads. Table XI which is based on an allowable 3 percent voltage drop, lists the wire sizes required for various distances between supply and load, at the difference amperages.

c. Table XI also lists the service-wire requirements and capacities. The minimum gage for service-wire installation is No. 8 except for installations consisting of a single branch circuit in which case they shall not be smaller than the conductors of a branch circuit and in no case smaller than No. 12. Though this may seem to contradict the minimum wire size listed, the service-wire sizes are increased because they must not only meet the voltage-drop requirement but also be inherently strong enough to support their own weight, plus any additional loading caused by climatic conditions (ice, branches, and so on).

57. Special Switches

a. Three-Way Switching. A single-pole switch controls a light or a receptacle from only one location. When lights have to be controlled from more than one location, a 3-way switch is used. Three-way switches can be identified by a common terminal, normally color-coded darker than the other terminals and located alone at the end of the switch housing. A schematic wiring diagram of a 3-way switch with 3-wire cable is shown in figure 49. In the diagram terminals A and A′ are the common terminals, and switch operation connects them either to B or C and B′ and C′ respectively. Either switch will operate to close or open the circuit, turning the lights on or off.

b. Four-Way Switching. Occasionally it is necessary to control an outlet or light from more than 2 locations. Two 3-way switches plus a 4-way switch for each location where control is desired and required in addition to that normally available in a 3-way circuit as illustrated in figure 50 (i. e., 3 control points, one 4-way switch, 4 control points, two 4-way switches). In figure 50 the switches must be installed with the 4-way units connected between the two 3-way units, and the 3-wire cable installed between the switches.

58. Wiring For Hazardous Locations

Hazardous locations requiring special wiring considerations are divided into four classes by the National Electric Code.

a. Class I. For locations in which highly flammable gasses and liquids are manufactured, used, or handled, such as hydrogen, gasoline, alcohol, etc., all wiring must be in rigid metal conduit with explosion-proof fittings. All equipment such as circuit breakers, fuses, motors, generators, controllers, etc., must be totally inclosed in explosion-proof housings.

b. Class II. In locations where combustible dust is likely to be thrown into suspension in the air in sufficient quantities to produce explosive mixtures, such as flour mills, grain elevators, coal pulverizing plants, etc., the wiring must be in rigid conduit with threaded fittings. All equipment must be in dust-proof cabinets with motors and generators totally inclosed or in totally inclosed fan-cooled housings.

c. Class III. Locations in which easily ignitible fibers or materials producing combustible flyings are handled or used, such as textile mills, cotton gins, or woodworking plants, require wiring of the same type as in Class II. If the atmosphere is such that lint and flyings will collect on motors or generators they must be inclosed as in Class II.

d. Class IV. In locations where easily combustible fibers are stored, such as warehouses for cotton waste, hemp, Spanish moss, excelsior, etc., all of the type of wiring described in this manual may be used. Open wiring is permitted when the conductors are protected where they are not run in roof spaces or well out of reach of mechanical damage. Rotating machines must be inclosed as in Class II.

59. Installation in Hazardous Locations

The Code further specifies standards for particular types of installations. For example, some of these special requirements for hospital operating room installation are listed in *a* through *f* below:

Table XI. Voltage Drop Tables

Wire size for 120-volt single-phase circuit

Load (amps.)	Minimum wire size (AWG)	Service wire size (AWG)	Wire size (AWG) — Distance one way from supply to load (ft.)												
			50	75	100	125	150	175	200	250	300	350	400	450	500
15	14	10	14	12	10	8	8	6	6	6	4	4	4	2	2
20	14	10	12	10	8	8	6	6	6	4	4	2	2	2	2
25	12	8	10	8	8	6	6	4	4	4	2	2	2	1	1
30	12	8	10	8	6	6	4	4	4	2	2	1	1	0	0
35	12	6	8	6	6	4	4	4	2	2	1	1	0	0	2/0
40	10	6	8	6	6	4	4	2	2	2	1	0	0	2/0	2/0
45	10	6	8	6	4	4	2	2	2	1	0	0	2/0	2/0	3/0
50	10	6	8	6	4	4	2	2	2	1	0	2/0	2/0	3/0	3/0
55	8	4	6	4	4	2	2	2	1	0	2/0	2/0	3/0	3/0	4/0
60	8	4	6	4	4	2	2	1	1	0	2/0	3/0	3/0	4/0	4/0
65	8	4	6	4	4	2	2	1	0	2/0	2/0	3/0	4/0	4/0	
70	8	4	6	4	2	2	1	1	0	2/0	2/0	3/0	4/0	4/0	
75	6	4	6	4	2	2	1	0	0	2/0	3/0	4/0	4/0		
80	6	4	6	4	2	2	1	0	0	2/0	3/0	4/0	4/0		
85	6	4	4	4	2	1	1	0	2/0	3/0	3/0	4/0			
90	6	2	4	2	2	1	0	0	2/0	3/0	4/0	4/0			
95	6	2	4	2	2	1	0	2/0	2/0	3/0	4/0				
100	4	2	4	2	2	1	0	2/0	2/0	3/0	4/0				

Wire size for 220-volt three-phase circuits

Load (amps.)	Minimum wire size (AWG)	Service wire size (AWG)	Wire size (AWG) — Distance one way from supply to load (ft.)												
			100	150	200	250	300	350	400	500	600	700	800	900	1,000
15	14	12	14	12	10	8	8	8	6	6	6	4	4	4	2
20	14	10	12	10	8	8	6	6	6	4	4	4	2	2	2
25	12	8	10	8	8	6	6	6	4	4	2	2	2	2	1
30	12	8	10	8	6	6	6	4	4	2	2	2	1	1	0
35	12	8	10	8	6	6	4	4	4	2	2	1	1	0	0
40	10	6	8	6	6	4	4	4	2	1	1	1	0	0	2/0
45	10	6	8	6	6	4	4	2	2	2	1	0	0	2/0	2/0
50	10	6	8	6	4	4	2	2	2	1	0	0	2/0	2/0	3/0
55	8	6	8	6	4	4	2	2	2	1	0	2/0	2/0	3/0	3/0
60	8	6	6	6	4	2	2	2	1	0	0	2/0	3/0	3/0	4/0
65	8	4	6	4	4	2	2	2	1	0	2/0	2/0	3/0	3/0	4/0
70	8	4	6	4	4	2	2	1	1	0	2/0	3/0	3/0	4/0	4/0
75	6	4	6	4	2	2	2	1	0	2/0	2/0	3/0	4/0	4/0	
80	6	4	6	4	2	2	1	1	0	2/0	3/0	3/0	4/0	4/0	
85	6	4	6	4	2	2	1	0	0	2/0	3/0	4/0	4/0		
90	6	4	6	4	2	2	1	0	0	2/0	3/0	4/0	4/0		
95	6	4	6	4	2	1	1	0	2/0	3/0	3/0	4/0			
100	4	2	4	2	2	1	0	0	2/0	3/0	4/0	4/0			
125	4	2	4	2	1	0	2/0	2/0	3/0	4/0					
150	2	2	2	2	0	2/0	2/0	3/0	4/0						
175	2	1	2	1	0	2/0	3/0	4/0	4/0						
200	1	0	1	0	2/0	3/0	4/0	4/0							
225	0	0	0	0	2/0	3/0	4/0								
250	2/0	2/0	2/0	2/0	3/0	4/0									
275	3/0	3/0	3/0	3/0	3/0	4/0									
300	3/0	3/0	3/0	3/0	4/0										
325	4/0	4/0	4/0	4/0											

Table is based upon approximately 3% voltage drop.

Table XI. Voltage Drop Tables—Continued

Wire size for 240-volt three-phase circuits.

Load (amps.)	Minimum wire size (AWG)	Service wire size (AWG)	Wire size (AWG) Distance one way from supply to load (ft.)												
			100	150	200	250	300	350	400	500	600	700	800	900	1,000
15	14	10	14	12	10	9	8	6	6	6	4	4	4	2	2
20	14	10	12	10	8	8	6	6	6	4	4	2	2	2	2
25	12	8	10	8	8	6	6	4	4	4	2	2	2	1	1
30	12	8	10	8	6	6	4	4	4	2	2	1	1	0	0
35	12	6	8	6	6	4	4	4	2	2	1	1	0	2/0	2/0
40	10	6	8	6	6	4	4	2	2	2	1	0	0	2/0	3/0
45	10	6	8	6	4	4	2	2	2	1	0	2/0	2/0	3/0	3/0
50	10	6	8	6	4	4	2	2	2	1	0	2/0	2/0	3/0	3/0
55	8	4	6	4	4	2	2	2	1	0	2/0	2/0	3/0	3/0	4/0
60	8	4	6	4	4	2	2	1	1	0	2/0	3/0	3/0	4/0	4/0
65	8	4	6	4	4	2	2	1	0	2/0	2/0	3/0	4/0	4/0	
70	8	4	6	4	2	2	1	1	0	0	2/0	3/0	4/0	4/0	
75	6	4	6	4	2	2	1	0	0	2/0	3/0	4/0	4/0		
80	6	4	6	4	2	2	1	0	0	2/0	3/0	4/0	4/0		
85	6	4	4	4	2	1	1	0	2/0	3/0	3/0	4/0			
90	6	2	4	2	2	1	0	0	2/0	3/0	4/0	4/0			
95	6	2	4	2	2	1	0	2/0	2/0	3/0	4/0				
100	4	2	4	2	2	1	0	2/0	2/0	3/0	4/0				
125	4	2	4	2	1	0	2/0	3/0	3/0	4/0					
150	2	1	2	1	0	2/0	3/0	4/0	4/0						
175	2	0	2	0	2/0	3/0	4/0	4/0							
200	1	0	1	0	2/0	3/0	4/0								
225	1/0	2/0	1/0	2/0	3/0	4/0									
250	2/0	2/0	2/0	2/0	3/0	4/0									
275	3/0	3/0	3/0	3/0	4/0										
300	3/0	3/0	3/0	3/0	4/0										
325	4/0	4/0	4/0	4/0											

Table is based on approximately 3% voltage drop.

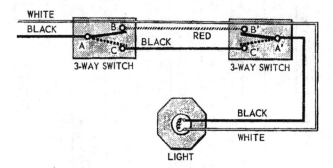

Figure 49. Three-way switch wiring.

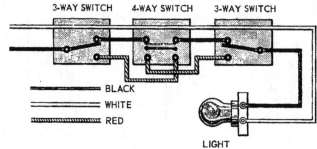

Figure 50. Four-way switch wiring.

a. All equipment installed in the operating room must be explosion proof and provided with a suitable equipment ground.

b. In anaesthetizing locations, an ungrounded electrical distribution system is required to reduce the hazards of electric shocks and arcs in the event of insulation failure. Alternating-current circuits shall be insulated from the conventionally grounded alternating supply by means of one or more transformers which isolate the circuits electrically from the main feeder line. Direct-current circuits shall be insulated from their grounded feeders by means of a motor generator set or suitable battery system.

c. All service equipment including switch and panel boards must be installed in nonhazardous locations.

d. Ceiling suspended lighting fixtures shall be suitably protected against mechanical injury.

e. Explosion-proof switches, receptacles, motors or similar conduit installations must be isolated from the rest of the conduit runs by sealing fittings. This type fitting has a removable plug which permits the insertion of a sealing compound, sealing off the points of possible explosion from the remaining conduit areas.

f. Nonmetallic tools such as rubber head hammers and spark free drills must always be used when making electrical repairs or installations in the area.

Section II. BASIC PROCEDURES COMMON TO ALL WIRING

60. Splices

A spliced wire must be as good a conductor as a continuous conductor. Figure 51 shows many of the variations of splicing used to obtain an electrically-secure joint. Though splices are permitted wherever accessible in wiring systems they should be avoided whenever possible. The best wiring practice (including open wiring systems) is to run continuous wires from the service box to the outlets. Under no conditions should splices be made in conductors encased in conduit.

61. Solderless Connectors

Figure 52 illustrates several types of connectors used in place of splices because of their ease of installation. Since heavy wires are difficult to tape and solder properly, split-bolt connectors (fig. 52 ①) are commonly used for wire joining. Figure 52 ②

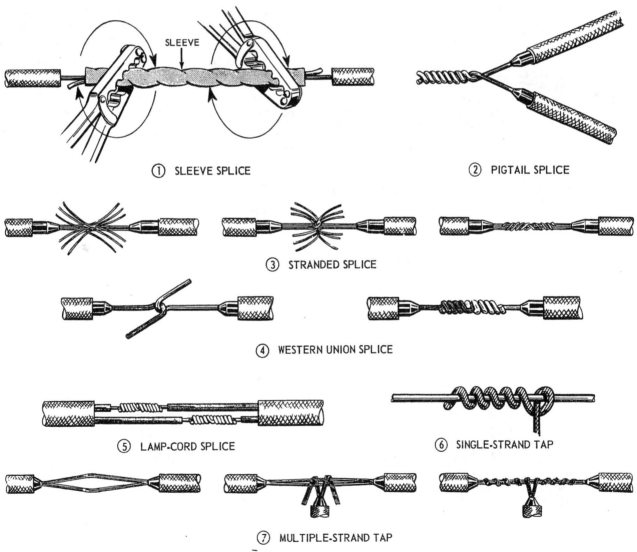

① SLEEVE SPLICE ② PIGTAIL SPLICE

③ STRANDED SPLICE

④ WESTERN UNION SPLICE

⑤ LAMP-CORD SPLICE ⑥ SINGLE-STRAND TAP

⑦ MULTIPLE-STRAND TAP

Figure 51. Typical wire splices and taps.

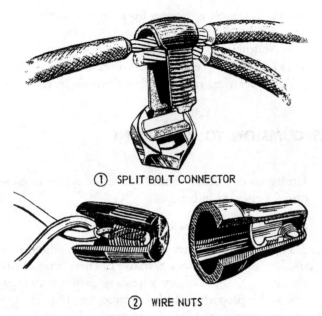

① SPLIT BOLT CONNECTOR

② WIRE NUTS

Figure 52. Solderless connectors.

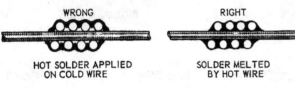

WIRE SOLDER

SOLDERING
COPPER

① APPLICATION OF SOLDER

WRONG   RIGHT

HOT SOLDER APPLIED   SOLDER MELTED
ON COLD WIRE   BY HOT WIRE

② RIGHT AND WRONG SOLDER JOINT

Figure 53. Soldering and solder joints.

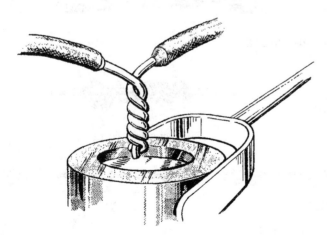

Figure 54. Dip soldering.

illustrates several types of solderless connectors popularly called wire nuts, which are used for connecting small-gage and fixture wire. One design shown consists of a funnel-shaped metal-spring insert molded into a plastic shell, into which the wires to be joined are screwed. The other type shown has a removable insert which contains a setscrew to clamp the wires. The plastic shell is screwed onto the insert to cover the joint.

62. Soldering

a. All splices must be soldered before they are considered to be as good as the original conductor. The primary requirements for obtaining a good solder joint are a clean soldering iron, a clean joint, and a nonacid flux. These requirements can be satisfied by using pure rosin on the joint, or by using a rosin-core solder.

b. To insure a good solder joint, the electric heated or copper soldering iron should be applied to the joint until the joint melts the solder by its own heat. Figure 53 2 shows the difference between a good and bad solder joint. The bad joint has a weak crystalline structure.

c. Figure 54 illustrates dip soldering. This method of soldering is frequently used by experienced electricians because of its convenience and relative speed for soldering pigtail splices. These splices are the most common type used in interior wiring.

63. Taping Joints

a. Every soldered joint must be covered with a coating of rubber, or varnished cambric, and friction tape to replace the wire insulation of the conductor. In taping a spliced solder joint (fig. 55) the rubber or cambric tape is started on the tapered end of the wire insulation and advanced toward the other end, with each succeeding wrap, by overlap-

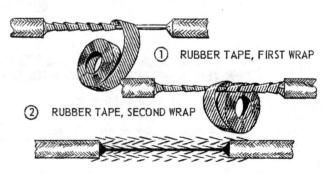

① RUBBER TAPE, FIRST WRAP

② RUBBER TAPE, SECOND WRAP

③ RUBBER AND FRICTION TAPED JOINT

Figure 55. Rubber- and friction-tape insulating.

ping the windings. This procedure is repeated from one end of the splice to the other until the original insulation thickness has been restored. The joint is then covered with several layers of friction tape.

b. Though the method in *a* above for taping joints is still considered to be standard, the scotch electrical tape, which serves as an insulation and a protective covering, should be used whenever available. This tape materially reduces the time required to tape a joint, and reduces the space needed by the joint because a satisfactory protective and insulation covering can be achieved with single-layer taping.

64. Insulation and Making Wire Connections

a. When attaching a wire to a switch or an electrical device or when splicing it to another wire, the wire insulation must be removed to bare the copper conductor. Figure 56 ① shows the right and wrong way to remove insulation. When the wire-stripping tool is applied at right angles to the wire, there is danger that the wire may be nicked and thus weakened. This may result in a short circuit. Consequently the cut is made at an angle to the conductor. After the protective insulation is removed, the conductor is scraped or sanded thoroughly to remove all traces of insulation and oxide on the wire.

b. Figures 56 ② and ③ show the correct method of attaching the trimmed wire to terminals. The

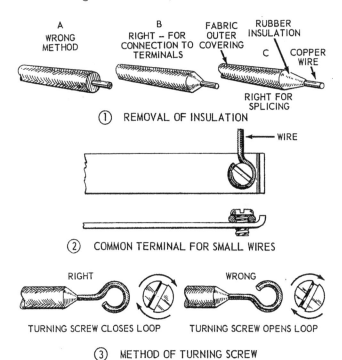

Figure 56. Removing insulation and attaching wire to terminals.

wire loop is always inserted under the terminal screw, as shown, so that the tightening process tends to close the loop. The loop is made so that the wire insulation terminates close to the terminal.

65. Job Sequence

a. General. The installation of interior wiring is generally divided into two major divisions called roughing-in and finishing. Roughing-in is the installation of the outlet boxes, cable, wire, and conduit. Finishing is the installation of the switches, receptacles, covers, fixtures, and the completion of the service. The interval between these two work periods is used by other trades for plastering, inclosing walls, finishing floors, and trimming.

b. Roughing-In.

(1) The first step in the roughing-in phase of a wiring job is the mounting of outlet boxes. The mounting can be expedited if the locations of all boxes are first marked on the studs and joists of the building.

(2) All of the boxes are mounted on the building members on their own or by special brackets. For concealed installation, all boxes must be installed with the forward edge or plaster ring of the boxes flush with the finished walls. Figure 25 illustrates typical box mountings.

(3) The circuiting and installation of wire for open wiring, cable, or conduit should be the next step. This involves the drilling and cutting-out of the building members to allow for the passage of the conductor or its protective covering. The production-line method of drilling the holes for all runs, as the installations between boxes are called, at one time, and then installing all of the wire, cable, or conduit, will expedite the job.

(4) The final roughing-in step in the installation of conduit systems is the pulling-in of wires between boxes. This can also be included as the first step in the finishing phase, and requires care in the handling of the wires to prevent the marring of finished wall or floor surfaces.

c. Finishing.

(1) The splicing, soldering, and taping of joints in the outlet boxes is the intial step in the completion phase of a wiring job.

(2) Upon completion of the first finishing step, the proper leads to the terminals of

switches, ceiling and wall outlets, and fixtures are then installed.

(3) The devices and their cover plates are then attached to the boxes. The fixtures are generally supported by the use of special mounting brackets called fixture studs or hickeys.

(4) The service-entrance cable and fusing or circuit breaker panels are then connected and the circuits fused.

(5) The final step in the wiring of any building requires the testing of all outlets by the insertion of a test prod or test lamp, the operation of all switches in the building, and the loading of all circuits to insure proper circuiting has been installed.

OPEN WIRING, KNOBS, AND TUBES

Section I.   INSTALLATION

66. Advantages and Uses

Open wiring is permitted by the National Electrical Code for interior use.   A cost comparison of the four basic types of wiring indicates open wiring to be the most economical.   This is true only because the costs of the materials used in installation are comparatively low when compared to the other systems.   If the labor costs were computed, this system may be equal or higher in cost than the other methods of installation, especially when a great amount of damage-protection installation is needed.   Installations of open wiring, however, are very common during wartime periods of material shortages.

67. Materials

a. Conductors.   Conductors for open wiring in dry places may be any one of the rubber-covered (R, RP, RH, or RHT), slow-burning, weatherproof (SBW), varnish-cambric (V), or thermoplastic (T or TW) types.   In damp locations, conductors should always be of the rubber-covered type.

b. Insulators.   Insulators should be free of projections or sharp edges that might cut into and injure the insulation.   They are commonly made of porcelain.   Loom, which is a flexible nonmetallic tubing, is also used to protect the electrical conductors.

c. Boxes and Devices.   Boxes and devices used with open wiring are described in paragraph 31.

68. Wire Spacing

In an exposed installation of knob-and-tube wiring, the wires must be separated from each other by at least 2½ inches.   They must be spaced at least ½ inch from the building surface in a dry location, and at least 1 inch when in a wet or damp location.   In a concealed installation the wires must be separated a distance of at least 3 inches and must be supported at least 1 inch from the mounting surface.   The minimum spacing of wires in straight runs and at right angle turns is illustrated in figures 57 and 58.

69. Support Spacing

a. Run Spacing.   When wiring is run over exposed flat surfaces, the knobs and cleats should be spaced no further than 4½ feet apart as shown in figure 59.

b. Tap Spacing.   A support should be installed within 6 inches of a wire tap or takeoff.   The wire of the tap circuit should always be secured to this support to insure a strain-free tap.

c. Support Spacing from Boxes.   Supports should be installed within 12 inches of an outlet box.   The wires to the box should be installed loosely so that there is no strain on the terminal connections.

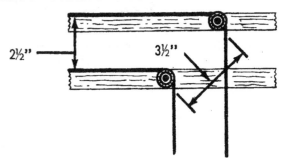

Figure 57.   Wire spacing for exposed work.

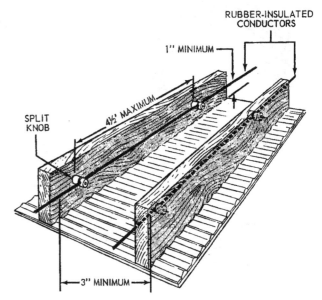

Figure 58.   Minimum wire spacing for concealed installation.

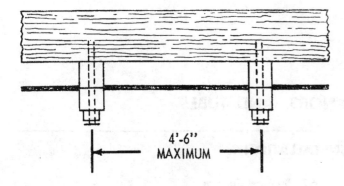

Figure 59. Knob and cleat spacing.

70. Installation

a. Typical Installation. Figure 60 shows a typical exposed knob-and-tube installation for a hospital unit, and demonstrates the circuiting and the methods of installing the conductors to each of the outlets.

b. Knobs and Cleats.

    (1) Split knobs are used to support wire sizes 10 through 14 and can support 1 or 2 wires. They are used as 2-wire supports at splices and taps. Figure 61 ① illustrates the use of split knobs.

    (2) Solid knobs are employed to support wire size No. 8 or larger. The wires must be supported on the solid knobs by tying. The conductors used for tying must have the same insulation as the supported conductors. A porcelain solid knob is shown in figure 61 ②.

    (3) Two- or three-wire cleats are also used in supporting wire sizes No. 10 to 14. Single cleats must be used for wire size No. 8 or larger. Cleats are available which support the wires at distances of ½ to 1 inch from the surface on which the cleats are mounted.

    (4) The installation steps used in mounting the split knobs or cleats for supporting wires are shown in figure 61. In the first operation, leather washers, to cushion the porcelain, are threaded on the nails of a 2-wire cleat. In the second step 2 wires are placed in the grooves of the cleat base section and the cleat head and nails are positioned above the wires. The third step shows the cleat in supporting position after the wires have been pulled tight and the nails driven firmly into the wood.

c. Wire Protectors.

    (1) *Tubes.* When conductors pass through

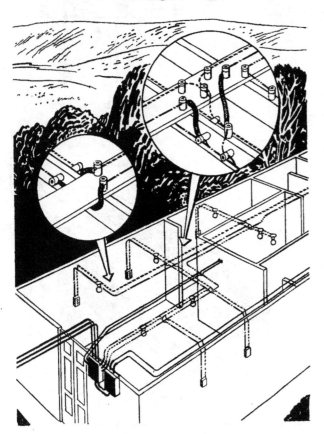
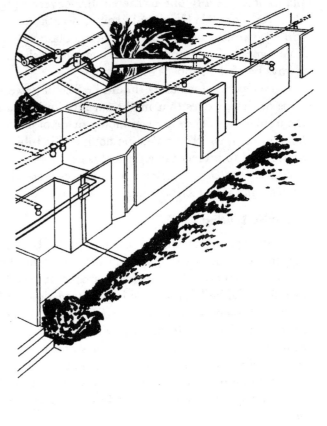

Figure 60. Typical knob-and-tube installation

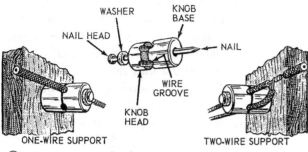

① PORCELAIN SPLIT KNOB SUPPORTING ONE OR TWO WIRES

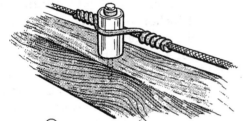

② PORCELAIN SOLID KNOB

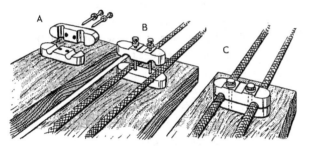

③ PORCELAIN CLEATS SUPPORTING TWO PARALLEL WIRES

Figure 61. Knob and cleat installation.

studs, joists, floors, walls, or partitions they must be protected by porcelain tubes installed in the hole through the supporting members. These tubes are available in standard sizes ranging from 1 to 24 inches long and ⁵⁄₁₆ to 1½ inch inner diameter. The tubes must be long enough to extend through the entire wall. If the wall is too thick to use porcelain bushings, standard iron pipe or conduit may be used, provided insulated bushings are installed at each end of the pipe. The holes in which the tubes are to be installed should be drilled at an angle so that the tube head can be placed on the high side of the hole to prevent it from being dislodged by gravity. The tubes may also be used to protect wires at points of crossover. As the tube is installed on the wire closest to the supporting surface, it is always installed on the inner wire, thus preventing the outer wires from making contact with the mounting surface.

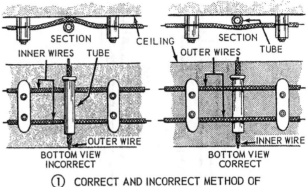

① CORRECT AND INCORRECT METHOD OF INSTALLING PROTECTIVE TUBE FOR WIRE CROSSOVER

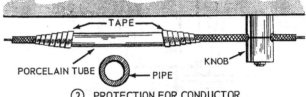

② PROTECTION FOR CONDUCTOR PASSING OVER PIPE

Figure 62. Protective tubes for conductors.

Figure 62 illustrates the proper and improper use of tubes at points of wire crossover and also the use of a tube installation for protecting an electrical conductor passing over a pipe. Conductors passing through timber cross braces in plastered partitions must be protected by an additional tube extending at least 3 inches above the timber. The extra tubes (fig. 63) protect the conductors from plaster accumulation, which collects on the horizontal cross members when plastering.

(2) *Loom.* In some installations where it is difficult to support wires on knobs and cleats, the wires may be encased in a continuous flexible tubing, commonly called loom. This tubing which is fabricated of woven varnished cambric, should be supported on the building by means of knobs, spaced approximately 18 inches apart. Any such run should not exceed a distance of 15 feet. Loom is also used to insulate wires at crossovers when they are installed closer than ½ inch to supporting timbers, when 2 or more wires are spaced less than 2½ inches apart, or upon entry to an outlet box. Outlet boxes used in open wiring are designed for the secure clamping of the loom wire to the box. Figure 64 illustrates typical uses of loom.

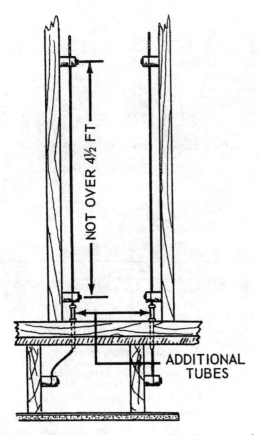

Figure 63. *Additional tubes to protect against plaster accumulation.*

least 1 inch but not more than 2 inches outside of the conductors. This method of installation is used when the wires are threaded through the joists and rafters. In some installations the wires have to be installed on the running boards with protective sides called railings.

(2) *Railings.* Railings should be at least ⅞ inch thick and when used alone are at least as high as the insulating supports. When used with running boards they are at least 2 inches high. Figure 65 ② illustrates the installation of railings with and without a running board.

(3) *Boxing.* The preferred method of protecting open wiring on walls within 7 feet of the floor is called boxing. This method requires the installation of railings with a cover spaced at least 1 inch from the conductor. In this installation, the boxing should be closed at the top and bushings installed to protect the entering and leaving wire leads.

(4) *Protection limitations.* As previously outlined and illustrated the labor and expense of installing damage protection in open wiring is extensive. Consequently, open wiring installations should be limited to wiring layouts whose outlet locations do not require damage protection. Nonconforming installations may be made in emergencies where the possibility of mechanical damage is not present.

e. Three-Wire Installations. The installation of wires in groups of 3 on joists and running boards requires that those surfaces be at least 7 inches wide to insure wire spacing of 2½ inches and a space of 1 inch for wood clearance beyond each outside wire. When joists are not large enough, 1 wire may be run on

d. Damage Protection.

(1) *Running boards.* When conductors are installed where they may be subject to mechanical damage, protective shields called running boards must be used. Exposed open wiring located within 7 feet of the floor is considered to be subject to mechanical injury. The required installations of a running board on the rafters and below joists for preventing such injury is pictured in figure 65 ①. Running boards must be at least ½ inch thick and must extend at

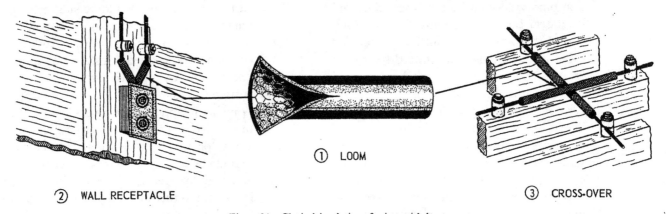

② WALL RECEPTACLE   ① LOOM   ③ CROSS-OVER

Figure 64. *Typical insulation of wires with loom.*

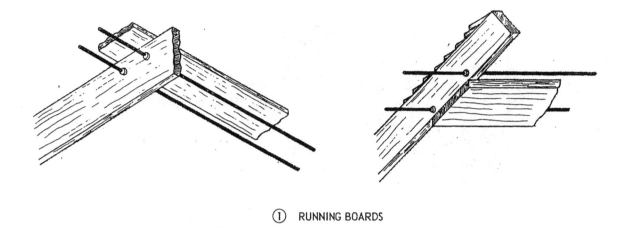

① RUNNING BOARDS

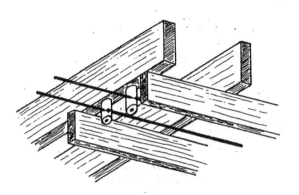
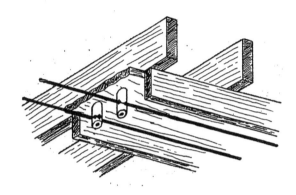

② RAILINGS

Figure 65. Protection for wiring subject to damage.

the top of the joist and the other 2 wires on the sides. Typical installations of 3 wires on joists and running boards are shown in figure 66.

f. Concealed Installation. Concealed knob-and-tube wiring consists of conductors supported in the hollow spaces of walls and ceilings. The wiring is installed in buildings under construction after the floors and studdings are in place, but before lathing or any other construction is completed. The wires are attached to devices in boxes which must have their front edges mounted flush with the finished surface. To facilitate this type of installation, the boxes are generally mounted on brackets or wooden cleats as shown in figure 67.

71. Connection to Devices

a. Figure 68 shows the procedure used in connecting electrical lighting devices to an open wiring circuit. The base of the porcelain lamp socket is first fastened by wood screws to the mounting member. The wires are then stripped of insulation and looped

around the screw terminals. Finally, the porcelain head is attached to the base.

b. A typical duplex receptacle installation for an open wiring installation (fig. 69) illustrates the required knob mounting 12 inches from the box, and the placement of loom over the wire at the box entry. The standard mounting height of a receptacle is either 1 foot or 4 feet above the floor depending upon the location of the outlet.

c. The installation and connection of lampholders commonly used in exposed open wiring is shown in figure 70. The pigtail socket has permanently attached leads of No. 14 wire size or larger. These are paired, but are not twisted together unless they are longer than 3 feet. The pendant lampholder is a device to which the lamp cord is attached and supported by means of an underwriters knot. Both the pendant and pigtail lampholder sockets are keyless (no switch) and are operated by wall switches to prevent additional strain on the lead wires supporting the sockets.

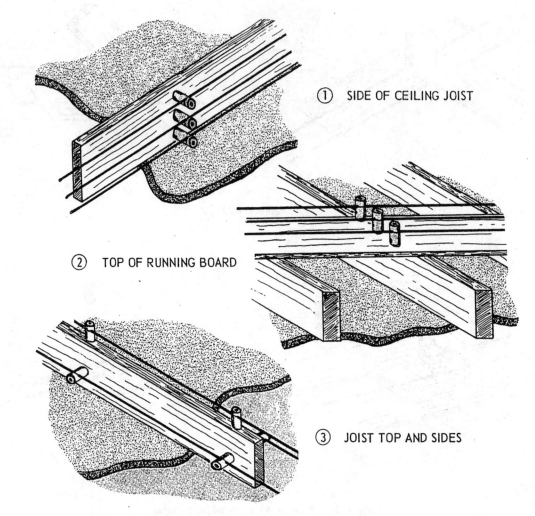

① SIDE OF CEILING JOIST

② TOP OF RUNNING BOARD

③ JOIST TOP AND SIDES

Figure 66. Knob mounting for three-wire circuits.

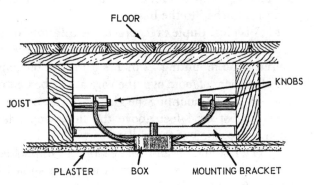

FLOOR

KNOBS

JOIST

PLASTER   BOX   MOUNTING BRACKET

Figure 67. Installation of box in plaster.

d. Figure 71 illustrates a typical service-entrance installation and figure 72 shows the procedures in circuit breaker wiring. If a service-entrance switch were used instead of a main circuit breaker, a separate fuse cabinet would be required to provide individual circuit protection. The wires from the powerline should be secured to the building at least 10 feet from the ground for normal installations. When the service entrance is located above a road-

way this height should be increased to 18 feet. If the building is not high enough to meet these requirements, the entrance height may be less, provided all conductors within 8 feet of the ground are rubber-insulated. The line wires at the service entrance to a building should be spaced at least 6 inches apart and should be supported at least 2 inches from the building by service-entrance insulators or brackets. Upon entering the building, the line wires should be threaded upward through slanting noncombustible tubes so that moisture will not follow the conductor into the service-entrance switch.

e. Motors are often located with permanent power leads of exposed open wiring, requiring extensive damage protection. To minimize both time and expense the tap from the open-wiring ceiling circuits should be made with armored cable or conduit. Figure 73 shows a diagrammatic installation of the power connections and operating switch for a three-phase motor connected to exposed knob-and-tube wiring.

Figure 68. Porcelain fittings used with knob and tube wiring.

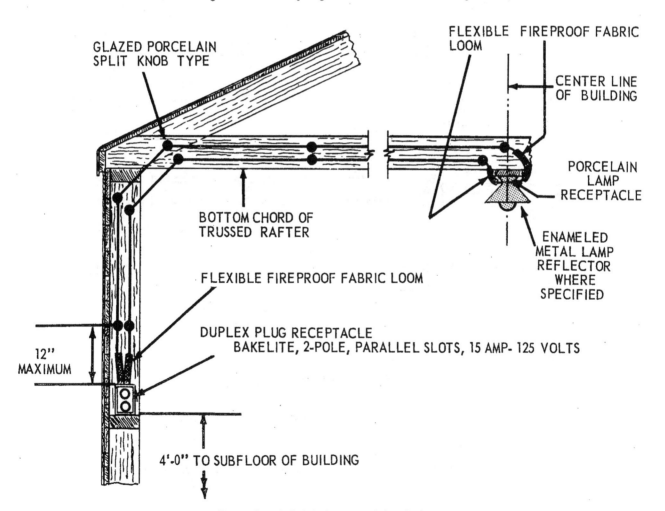

GLAZED PORCELAIN
SPLIT KNOB TYPE

FLEXIBLE FIREPROOF FABRIC
LOOM

CENTER LINE
OF BUILDING

BOTTOM CHORD OF
TRUSSED RAFTER

PORCELAIN
LAMP
RECEPTACLE

ENAMELED
METAL LAMP
REFLECTOR
WHERE
SPECIFIED

FLEXIBLE FIREPROOF FABRIC LOOM

DUPLEX PLUG RECEPTACLE
BAKELITE, 2-POLE, PARALLEL SLOTS, 15 AMP- 125 VOLTS

12"
MAXIMUM

4'-0" TO SUBFLOOR OF BUILDING

Figure 69. Typical duplex receptacle installation.

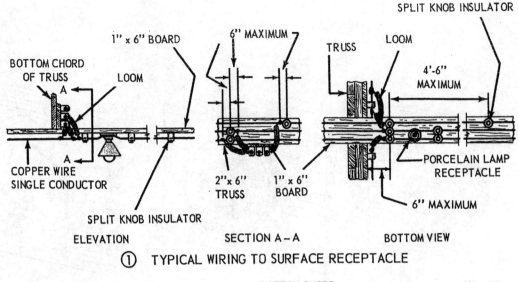

SPLIT KNOB INSULATOR

BOTTOM CHORD OF TRUSS
LOOM
1" x 6" BOARD
6" MAXIMUM
TRUSS
LOOM
4'-6" MAXIMUM
COPPER WIRE SINGLE CONDUCTOR
SPLIT KNOB INSULATOR
2" x 6" TRUSS
1" x 6" BOARD
PORCELAIN LAMP RECEPTACLE
6" MAXIMUM

ELEVATION   SECTION A – A   BOTTOM VIEW

① TYPICAL WIRING TO SURFACE RECEPTACLE

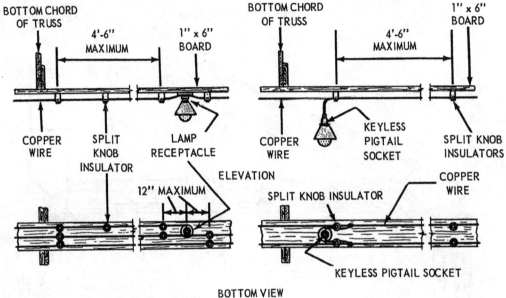

BOTTOM CHORD OF TRUSS
4'-6" MAXIMUM
1" x 6" BOARD
COPPER WIRE
SPLIT KNOB INSULATOR
LAMP RECEPTACLE
12" MAXIMUM

BOTTOM CHORD OF TRUSS
4'-6" MAXIMUM
1" x 6" BOARD
COPPER WIRE
KEYLESS PIGTAIL SOCKET
SPLIT KNOB INSULATORS
ELEVATION
SPLIT KNOB INSULATOR
COPPER WIRE
KEYLESS PIGTAIL SOCKET

BOTTOM VIEW

② TERMINATION OF WIRES AT RECEPTACLE   ③ TYPICAL PIGTAIL-SOCKET WIRING

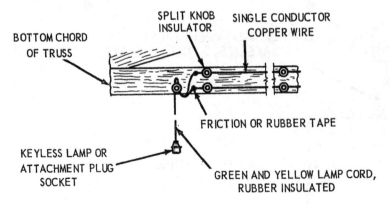

SPLIT KNOB INSULATOR
SINGLE CONDUCTOR COPPER WIRE
BOTTOM CHORD OF TRUSS
FRICTION OR RUBBER TAPE
KEYLESS LAMP OR ATTACHMENT PLUG SOCKET
GREEN AND YELLOW LAMP CORD, RUBBER INSULATED

ELEVATION

④ PENDANT-CONNECTOR INSTALLATION DETAIL

Figure 70. Lampholder installations.

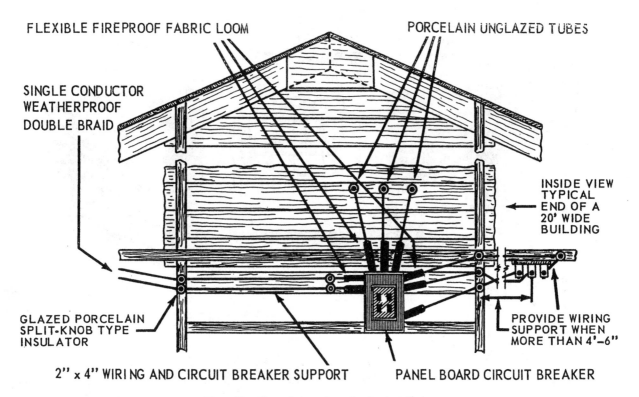

FLEXIBLE FIREPROOF FABRIC LOOM

PORCELAIN UNGLAZED TUBES

SINGLE CONDUCTOR WEATHERPROOF DOUBLE BRAID

INSIDE VIEW TYPICAL END OF A 20' WIDE BUILDING

GLAZED PORCELAIN SPLIT-KNOB TYPE INSULATOR

PROVIDE WIRING SUPPORT WHEN MORE THAN 4'-6"

2" x 4" WIRING AND CIRCUIT BREAKER SUPPORT

PANEL BOARD CIRCUIT BREAKER

Figure 71. Typical main circuit breaker installation.

72. Additions to Existing Wiring

a. Circuiting. Additions to existing circuits require analysis to determine whether additional circuit capacity is needed to handle the new load. These considerations are the same as those required for other types of installations and are outlined in paragraph 55.

b. Wire Connection.

(1) *Where to connect.* An open wiring system has a distinct advantage over the other wiring methods in that wires for new or additional outlets can be attached to the circuit runs by merely making tap splices in the wire runs, or by extending the circuit from an outlet box. However, the electrician in planning these additional outlets in the existing circuits should be careful to have the shortest possible wire runs. This will result in attaining the lowest voltage drop.

(2) *How to connect.* First make sure the circuit is dead. This is a primary safety rule for all electricians working in existing wiring

systems. This can be done by removing the fuse, tripping the circuit breaker to the OFF position, or pulling the service-entrance switch and disconnecting the entire building from power before commencing work. A voltage tester or test lamp is also used to doublecheck the circuit upon which work is to be done. The wires must then be connected and supported in the same manner as outlined for an original building installation.

c. Connections to Other Types of Wiring. Conduit and cable wiring cannot be installed with splices in the conduit or cable runs. Consequently, all splicing and connections must be made within the confines of an outlet, junction, or fuse box. Therefore, when open wiring is combined with one of the other wiring systems the transition from one system to another must be made in one of these boxes. Since standard outlet, junction, or fuse boxes are used, open wiring must be encased in loom at the box entry. An example combining knob-and-tube wiring and conduit wiring is illustrated in figure 74.

Section II. EXPEDIENT WIRING

73. Use

There are many applications where electrical wiring installations are needed for temporary use. One

example is a forward area installation. A complete installation including knobs, tubes, cleats, and damage protection would require too much time and would be impractical. Consequently, expedient wir-

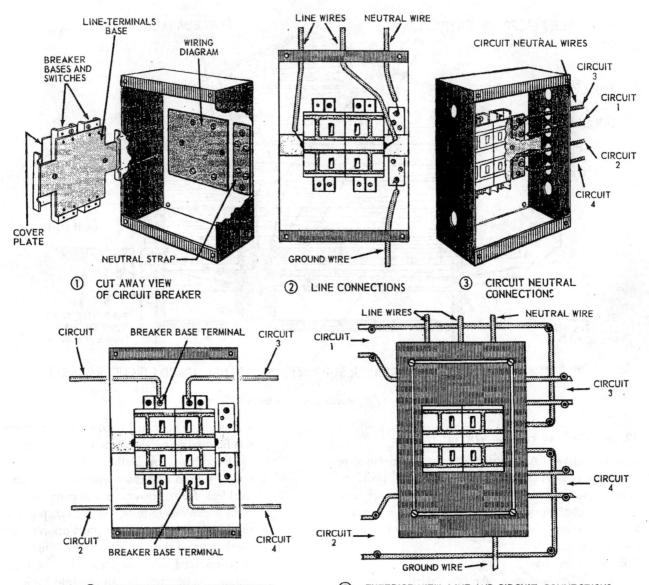

① CUT AWAY VIEW OF CIRCUIT BREAKER   ② LINE CONNECTIONS   ③ CIRCUIT NEUTRAL CONNECTIONS

④ CIRCUIT HOT WIRE CONNECTIONS   ⑤ EXTERIOR VIEW- LINE AND CIRCUIT CONNECTIONS

Figure 72. Typical circuit breaker wiring.

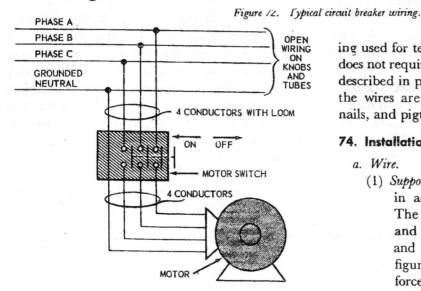

Figure 73. Motor connection.

ing used for temporary buildings and forward areas does not require the mounting and protective devices described in paragraphs 66 through 72. Generally the wires are attached to building members with nails, and pigtail sockets are used for outlets.

74. Installation

a. *Wire.*

(1) *Supports.* The wire sizes should be selected in accordance with normal installations. The wires should be laid over ceiling joists and fastened by nails driven into the joists and then bent over the wire as shown in figure 75. The nails should exert enough force to firmly grip the wire without injuring the insulation. If loom is available, it

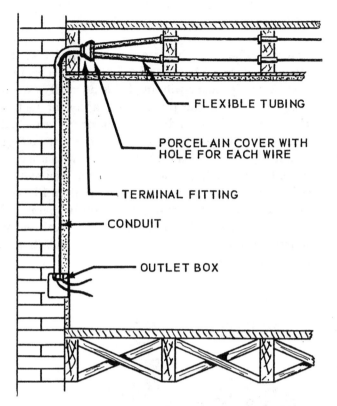

Figure 74. *Changing from knob-and-tube to conduit wiring.*

FLEXIBLE TUBING

PORCELAIN COVER WITH HOLE FOR EACH WIRE

TERMINAL FITTING

CONDUIT

OUTLET BOX

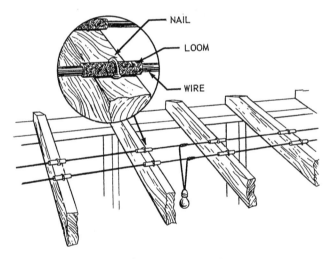

NAIL

LOOM

WIRE

Figure 75. *Expedient wiring.*

should be installed to protect the wire at the nail support. This is particularly essential if the wooden joists are wet. If possible, expedient wiring installations

Section III. BELL WIRING

75. Installation

Signal equipment may occasionally be supplied for 110-volt operation, in which case it must be installed

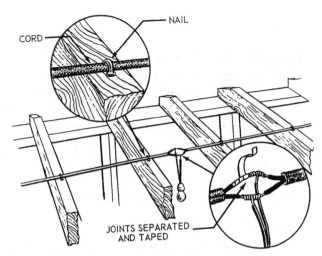

NAIL

CORD

JOINTS SEPARATED AND TAPED

Figure 76. *Expedient-wiring cord installation.*

should be fastened to joists or studs at a distance of at least 7 feet above the floor. This will prevent accidental injury to the system or personnel which might result from the absence of damage protection.

(2) *Spacing.* The spacing of wires should be the same as that outlined for exposed knob and tube wiring.

(3) *Joints, splices, and taps.* Joints, splices, taps, and connections are made as outlined in paragraphs 60 through 65 with the exception of the procedures outlined for soldering and taping. In expedient wiring, soldering is omitted and only friction tape is used as a protective covering on the connections.

(4) *Fixture drops.* Fixture drops, preferable pigtail sockets, are installed by tapping their leads to wires, as shown in figure 75, and then taping the taps. The sockets are supported by the tap wires.

b. Cord. Figure 76 illustrates the application of a two-conductor cord in an expedient-wiring installation. The cord used should always be of the rubber-covered type and fastened securely to prevent the possibility of short circuits. The outer rubber sheathing should be removed at the point of fixture attachment and the fixture leads tapped into the conductor, purposely maintaining the separation between taps as shown. Each tap then should be individually taped.

in the same manner as outlets and sockets operating on this voltage. Most bells and buzzers are rated to operate on 8, 12, 18, or 24 volts ac or dc. These operating voltages are known as low-voltage or low-energy circuits. They can be installed with minimum consideration for circuit insulation since there is no danger of shock to personnel or fire due to short circuits. The wire commonly used is insulated with several layers of paraffin impregnated cotton or with a thermoplastic covering. Upon installation, these wires are attached to building members with small insulating staples and are threaded through building construction members without insulators.

76. Battery Operation

Early installations of low-voltage signal systems were powered by 6-volt dry cells. For example, 2 of these batteries were installed in series to service a 12-volt system. If the systems involved a number of signals over a large area, 1 or more batteries were added in series to offset the voltage drop. Though this type of alarm or announcing system is still being used and installed in some areas, it is a poor method because the batteries used as a power source require periodic replacement.

77. Transformer Operation

The majority of our present-day buzzer and bell signal systems operate from a transformer power source. The transformers are equipped to be mounted on outlet boxes and are constructed so that the 110-volt primary-winding leads normally extend from the side of the transformer adjacent to box mounting. These leads are permanently attached to the 110-volt power circuits, and the low-voltage secondary-winding leads of the transformer are connected to the bell circuit in a manner similar to a switch-and-light combination. If more than 1 buzzer and push button is to be installed they are paralleled with the first signal installation. A typical wiring schematic diagram for this type of installation is shown in figure 77.

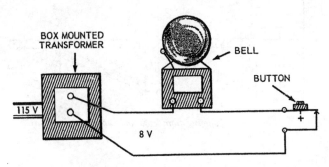

Figure 77. Bell and buzzer wiring.

ELECTRICAL TERMS AND FORMULAS

CONTENTS

ELECTRICAL TERMS AND FORMULAS

Terms

AGONIC.—An imaginary line of the earth's surface passing through points where the magnetic declination is 0°; that is, points where the compass points to true north.

AMMETER.—An instrument for measuring the amount of electron flow in amperes.

AMPERE.—The basic unit of electrical current.

AMPERE-TURN.—The magnetizing force produced by a current of one ampere flowing through a coil of one turn.

AMPLIDYNE.—A rotary magnetic or dynamo-electric amplifier used in servomechanism and control applications.

AMPLIFICATION.—The process of increasing the strength (current, power, or voltage) of a signal.

AMPLIFIER.—A device used to increase the signal voltage, current, or power, generally composed of a vacuum tube and associated circuit called a stage. It may contain several stages in order to obtain a desired gain.

AMPLITUDE.—The maximum instantaneous value of an alternating voltage or current, measured in either the positive or negative direction.

ARC.—A flash caused by an electric current ionizing a gas or vapor.

ARMATURE.—The rotating part of an electric motor or generator. The moving part of a relay or vibrator.

ATTENUATOR.—A network of resistors used to reduce voltage, current, or power delivered to a load.

AUTOTRANSFORMER.—A transformer in which the primary and secondary are connected together in one winding.

BATTERY.—Two or more primary or secondary cells connected together electrically. The term does not apply to a single cell.

BREAKER POINTS.—Metal contacts that open and close a circuit at timed intervals.

BRIDGE CIRCUIT.—The electrical bridge circuit is a term referring to any one of a variety of electric circuit networks, one branch of which, the "bridge" proper, connects two points of equal potential and hence carries no current when the circuit is properly adjusted or balanced.

BRUSH.—The conducting material, usually a block of carbon, bearing against the commutator or sliprings through which the current flows in or out.

BUS BAR.—A primary power distribution point connected to the main power source.

CAPACITOR.—Two electrodes or sets of electrodes in the form of plates, separated from each other by an insulating material called the dielectric.

CHOKE COIL.—A coil of low ohmic resistance and high impedance to alternating current.

CIRCUIT.—The complete path of an electric current.

CIRCUIT BREAKER.—An electromagnetic or thermal device that opens a circuit when the current in the circuit exceeds a predetermined amount. Circuit breakers can be reset.

CIRCULAR MIL.—An area equal to that of a circle with a diameter of 0.001 inch. It is used for measuring the cross section of wires.

COAXIAL CABLE.—A transmission line consisting of two conductors concentric with and insulated from each other.

COMMUTATOR.—The copper segments on the armature of a motor or generator. It is cylindrical in shape and is used to pass power into or from the brushes. It is a switching device.

CONDUCTANCE.—The ability of a material to conduct or carry an electric current. It is the reciprocal of the resistance of the material, and is expressed in mhos.

CONDUCTIVITY.—The ease with which a substance transmits electricity.

CONDUCTOR.—Any material suitable for carrying electric current.

CORE.—A magnetic material that affords an easy path for magnetic flux lines in a coil.

COUNTER E.M.F.—Counter electromotive force; an e.m.f. induced in a coil or armature that opposes the applied voltage.

CURRENT LIMITER.—A protective device similar to a fuse, usually used in high amperage circuits.

CYCLE.—One complete positive and one complete negative alternation of a current or voltage.

DIELECTRIC.—An insulator; a term that refers to the insulating material between the plates of a capacitor.

197

ELECTRICAL TERMS AND FORMULAS

DIODE.—Vacuum tube—a two element tube that contains a cathode and plate; semiconductor—a material of either germanium or silicon that is manufactured to allow current to flow in only one direction. Diodes are used as rectifiers and detectors.

DIRECT CURRENT.—An electric current that flows in one direction only.

EDDY CURRENT.—Induced circulating currents in a conducting material that are caused by a varying magnetic field.

EFFICIENCY.—The ratio of output power to input power, generally expressed as a percentage.

ELECTROLYTE.—A solution of a substance which is capable of conducting electricity. An electrolyte may be in the form of either a liquid or a paste.

ELECTROMAGNET.—A magnet made by passing current through a coil of wire wound on a soft iron core.

ELECTROMOTIVE FORCE (e.m.f.).—The force that produces an electric current in a circuit.

ELECTRON.—A negatively charged particle of matter.

ENERGY.—The ability or capacity to do work.

FARAD.—The unit of capacitance.

FEEDBACK.—A transfer of energy from the output circuit of a device back to its input.

FIELD.—The space containing electric or magnetic lines of force.

FIELD WINDING.—The coil used to provide the magnetizing force in motors and generators.

FLUX FIELD.—All electric or magnetic lines of force in a given region.

FREE ELECTRONS.—Electrons which are loosely held and consequently tend to move at random among the atoms of the material.

FREQUENCY.—The number of complete cycles per second existing in any form of wave motion; such as the number of cycles per second of an alternating current.

FULL-WAVE RECTIFIER CIRCUIT.—A circuit which utilizes both the positive and the negative alternations of an alternating current to produce a direct current.

FUSE.—A protective device inserted in series with a circuit. It contains a metal that will melt or break when current is increased beyond a specific value for a definite period of time.

GAIN.—The ratio of the output power, voltage, or current to the input power, voltage, or current, respectively.

GALVANOMETER.—An instrument used to measure small d-c currents.

GENERATOR.—A machine that converts mechanical energy into electrical energy.

GROUND.—A metallic connection with the earth to establish ground potential. Also, a common return to a point of zero potential. The chassis of a receiver or a transmitter is sometimes the common return, and therefore the ground of the unit.

HENRY.—The basic unit of inductance.

HORSEPOWER.—The English unit of power, equal to work done at the rate of 550 foot-pounds per second. Equal to 746 watts of electrical power.

HYSTERESIS.—A lagging of the magnetic flux in a magnetic material behind the magnetizing force which is producing it.

IMPEDANCE.—The total opposition offered to the flow of an alternating current. It may consist of any combination of resistance, inductive reactance, and capacitive reactance.

INDUCTANCE.—The property of a circuit which tends to oppose a change in the existing current.

INDUCTION.—The act or process of producing voltage by the relative motion of a magnetic field across a conductor.

INDUCTIVE REACTANCE.—The opposition to the flow of alternating or pulsating current caused by the inductance of a circuit. It is measured in ohms.

INPHASE.—Applied to the condition that exists when two waves of the same frequency pass through their maximum and minimum values of like polarity at the same instant.

INVERSELY.—Inverted or reversed in position or relationship.

ISOGONIC LINE.—An imaginary line drawn through points on the earth's surface where the magnetic deviation is equal.

JOULE.—A unit of energy or work. A joule of energy is liberated by one ampere flowing for one second through a resistance of one ohm.

KILO.—A prefix meaning 1,000.

LAG.—The amount one wave is behind another in time; expressed in electrical degrees.

LAMINATED CORE.—A core built up from thin sheets of metal and used in transformers and relays.

LEAD.—The opposite of LAG. Also, a wire or connection.

ELECTRICAL TERMS AND FORMULAS

LINE OF FORCE.—A line in an electric or magnetic field that shows the direction of the force.

LOAD.—The power that is being delivered by any power producing device. The equipment that uses the power from the power producing device.

MAGNETIC AMPLIFIER.—A saturable reactor type device that is used in a circuit to amplify or control.

MAGNETIC CIRCUIT.—The complete path of magnetic lines of force.

MAGNETIC FIELD.—The space in which a magnetic force exists.

MAGNETIC FLUX.—The total number of lines of force issuing from a pole of a magnet.

MAGNETIZE.—To convert a material into a magnet by causing the molecules to rearrange.

MAGNETO.—A generator which produces alternating current and has a permanent magnet as its field.

MEGGER.—A test instrument used to measure insulation resistance and other high resistances. It is a portable hand operated d-c generator used as an ohmmeter.

MEGOHM.—A million ohms.

MICRO.—A prefix meaning one-millionth.

MILLI.—A prefix meaning one-thousandth.

MILLIAMMETER.—An ammeter that measures current in thousandths of an ampere.

MOTOR-GENERATOR.—A motor and a generator with a common shaft used to convert line voltages to other voltages or frequencies.

MUTUAL INDUCTANCE.—A circuit property existing when the relative position of two inductors causes the magnetic lines of force from one to link with the turns of the other.

NEGATIVE CHARGE.—The electrical charge carried by a body which has an excess of electrons.

NEUTRON.—A particle having the weight of a proton but carrying no electric charge. It is located in the nucleus of an atom.

NUCLEUS.—The central part of an atom that is mainly comprised of protons and neutrons. It is the part of the atom that has the most mass.

NULL.—Zero.

OHM.—The unit of electrical resistance.

OHMMETER.—An instrument for directly measuring resistance in ohms.

OVERLOAD.—A load greater than the rated load of an electrical device.

PERMALLOY.—An alloy of nickel and iron having an abnormally high magnetic permeability.

PERMEABILITY.—A measure of the ease with which magnetic lines of force can flow through a material as compared to air.

PHASE DIFFERENCE.—The time in electrical degrees by which one wave leads or lags another.

POLARITY.—The character of having magnetic poles, or electric charges.

POLE.—The section of a magnet where the flux lines are concentrated; also where they enter and leave the magnet. An electrode of a battery.

POLYPHASE.—A circuit that utilizes more than one phase of alternating current.

POSITIVE CHARGE.—The electrical charge carried by a body which has become deficient in electrons.

POTENTIAL.—The amount of charge held by a body as compared to another point or body. Usually measured in volts.

POTENTIOMETER.—A variable voltage divider; a resistor which has a variable contact arm so that any portion of the potential applied between its ends may be selected.

POWER.—The rate of doing work or the rate of expending energy. The unit of electrical power is the watt.

POWER FACTOR.—The ratio of the actual power of an alternating or pulsating current, as measured by a wattmeter, to the apparent power, as indicated by ammeter and voltmeter readings. The power factor of an inductor, capacitor, or insulator is an expression of their losses.

PRIME MOVER.—The source of mechanical power used to drive the rotor of a generator.

PROTON.—A positively charged particle in the nucleus of an atom.

RATIO.—The value obtained by dividing one number by another, indicating their relative proportions.

REACTANCE.—The opposition offered to the flow of an alternating current by the inductance, capacitance, or both, in any circuit.

RECTIFIERS.—Devices used to change alternating current to unidirectional current. These may be vacuum tubes, semiconductors such as germanium and silicon, and dry-disk rectifiers such as selenium and copper-oxide.

RELAY.—An electromechanical switching device that can be used as a remote control.

RELUCTANCE.—A measure of the opposition that a material offers to magnetic lines of force.

RESISTANCE.—The opposition to the flow of current caused by the nature and physical dimensions of a conductor.

RESISTOR.—A circuit element whose chief characteristic is resistance; used to oppose the flow of current.

RETENTIVITY.—The measure of the ability of a material to hold its magnetism.

RHEOSTAT.—A variable resistor.

SATURABLE REACTOR.—A control device that uses a small d-c current to control a large a-c current by controlling core flux density.

SATURATION.—The condition existing in any circuit when an increase in the driving signal produces no further change in the resultant effect.

SELF-INDUCTION.—The process by which a circuit induces an e.m.f. into itself by its own magnetic field.

SERIES-WOUND.—A motor or generator in which the armature is wired in series with the field winding.

SERVO.—A device used to convert a small movement into one of greater movement or force.

SERVOMECHANISM.—A closed-loop system that produces a force to position an object in accordance with the information that originates at the input.

SOLENOID.—An electromagnetic coil that contains a movable plunger.

SPACE CHARGE.—The cloud of electrons existing in the space between the cathode and plate in a vacuum tube, formed by the electrons emitted from the cathode in excess of those immediately attracted to the plate.

SPECIFIC GRAVITY—The ratio between the density of a substance and that of pure water, at a given temperature.

SYNCHROSCOPE—An instrument used to indicate a difference in frequency between two a-c sources.

SYNCHRO SYSTEM.—An electrical system that gives remote indications or control by means of self-synchronizing motors.

TACHOMETER.—An instrument for indicating revolutions per minute.

TERTIARY WINDING.—A third winding on a transformer or magnetic amplifier that is used as a second control winding.

THERMISTOR.—A resistor that is used to compensate for temperature variations in a circuit.

THERMOCOUPLE.—A junction of two dissimilar metals that produces a voltage when heated.

TORQUE.—The turning effort or twist which a shaft sustains when transmitting power.

TRANSFORMER.—A device composed of two or more coils, linked by magnetic lines of force, used to transfer energy from one circuit to another.

TRANSMISSION LINES.—Any conductor or system of conductors used to carry electrical energy from its source to a load.

VARS.—Abbreviation for volt-ampere, reactive.

VECTOR.—A line used to represent both direction and magnitude.

VOLT.—The unit of electrical potential.

VOLTMETER.—An instrument designed to measure a difference in electrical potential, in volts.

WATT.—The unit of electrical power.

WATTMETER.—An instrument for measuring electrical power in watts.

Formulas

Ohm's Law for d-c Circuits

$$I = \frac{E}{R} = \frac{P}{E} = \sqrt{\frac{P}{R}}$$

$$R = \frac{E}{I} = \frac{P}{I^2} = \frac{E^2}{P}$$

$$E = IR = \frac{P}{I} = \sqrt{PR}$$

$$P = EI = \frac{E^2}{R} = I^2R$$

Resistors in Series

$$R_T = R_1 + R_2 \cdots$$

Resistors in Parallel
Two resistors

$$R_T = \frac{R_1 R_2}{R_1 + R_2}$$

More than two

$$\frac{1}{R_T} = \frac{1}{R_1} + \frac{1}{R_2} + \frac{1}{R_3}$$

ELECTRICAL TERMS AND FORMULAS

R-L Circuit Time Constant equals

$$\frac{L \text{ (in henrys)}}{R \text{ (in ohms)}} = t \text{ (in seconds), or}$$

$$\frac{L \text{ (in microhenrys)}}{R \text{ (in ohms)}} = t \text{ (in microseconds)}$$

R-C Circuit Time Constant equals

R (ohms) X C (farads) = t (seconds)

R (megohms) x C (microfarads) = t (seconds)

R (ohms) x C (microfarads) = t (microseconds)

R (megohms) x C (micromicrofrads = t (microseconds)

Comparison of Units in Electric and Magnetic Circuits.

	Electric circuit	Magnetic circuit
Force	Volt, E or e.m.f.	Gilberts, F, or m.m.f.
Flow	Ampere, I	Flux, Φ, in maxwells
Opposition	Ohms, R	Reluctance, R
Law	Ohm's law, $I = \frac{E}{R}$	Rowland's law $\Phi = \frac{F}{R}$
Intensity of force	Volts per cm. of length	$H = \frac{1.257IN}{L}$, gilberts per centimeter of length
Density	Current density— for example, amperes per cm^2.	Flux density—for example, lines per cm^2., or gausses

Capacitors in Series
Two capacitors

$$C_T = \frac{C_1 C_2}{C_1 + C_2}$$

More than two

$$\frac{1}{C_T} = \frac{1}{C_1} + \frac{1}{C_2} + \frac{1}{C_3}...$$

Capacitors in Parallel

$$C_T = C_1 + C_2...$$

Capacitive Reactance

$$X_c = \frac{1}{2\pi f C}$$

Impedance in an R-C Circuit (Series)

$$Z = \sqrt{R^2 + X_c^2}$$

Inductors in Series

$$L_T = L_1 + L_2 ... \text{ (No coupling between coils)}$$

Inductors in Parallel
Two inductors

$$L_T = \frac{L_1 L_2}{L_1 + L_2} \text{ (No coupling between coils)}$$

More than two

$$\frac{1}{L_T} = \frac{1}{L_1} + \frac{1}{L_2} + \frac{1}{L_3} ... \text{ (No coupling between coils)}$$

Inductive Reactance

$$X_L = 2\pi f L$$

Q of a Coil

$$Q = \frac{X_L}{R}$$

Impedance of an R-L Circuit (series)

$$Z = \sqrt{R^2 + X_L^2}$$

Impedance with R, C, and L in Series

$$Z = \sqrt{R^2 + (X_L - X_C)^2}$$

Parallel Circuit Impedance

$$Z = \frac{Z_1 Z_2}{Z_1 + Z_2}$$

Sine-Wave Voltage Relationships
Average value

$$E_{ave} = \frac{2}{\pi} \times E_{max} = 0.637 E_{max}$$

ELECTRICAL TERMS AND FORMULAS

Effective or r.m.s. value

$$E_{eff} = \frac{E_{max}}{\sqrt{2}} = \frac{E_{max}}{1.414} = 0.707E_{max} = 1.11E_{ave}$$

Maximum value

$$E_{max} = \sqrt{2}E_{eff} = 1.414E_{eff} = 1.57E_{ave}$$

Voltage in an a-c circuit

$$E = IZ = \frac{P}{I \times P.F.}$$

Current in an a-c circuit

$$I = \frac{E}{Z} = \frac{P}{E \times P.F.}$$

Power in A-C Circuit
Apparent power = EI
True power

$$P = EI \cos \theta = EI \times P.F.$$

Power factor

$$P.F. = \frac{P}{EI} = \cos \theta$$

$$\cos \theta = \frac{\text{true power}}{\text{apparent power}}$$

Transformers
Voltage relationship

$$\frac{E}{E} = \frac{N}{N} \text{ or } E = E \times \frac{N}{N}$$

Current relationship

$$\frac{I_p}{I_s} = \frac{N_s}{N_p}$$

Induced voltage

$$E_{eff} = 4.44 \, BAfN10^{-8}$$

Turns ratio equals

$$\frac{N_p}{N_s} = \sqrt{\frac{Z_p}{Z_s}}$$

Secondary current

$$I_s = I_p \frac{N_p}{N_s}$$

Secondary voltage

$$E_s = E_p \frac{N_s}{N_p}$$

Three Phase Voltage and Current Relationships
With wye connected windings

$$E_{line} = 1.732E_{coil} = \sqrt{3}E_{coil}$$

$$I_{line} = I_{coil}$$

With delta connected windings

$$E_{line} = E_{coil}$$

$$I_{line} = 1.732I_{coil}$$

With wye or delta connected winding

$$P_{coil} = E_{coil}I_{coil}$$

$$P_t = 3P_{coil}$$

$$P_t = 1.732E_{line}I_{line}$$

(To convert to true power multiply by $\cos \theta$)

Synchronous Speed of Motor

$$\text{r.p.m.} = \frac{120 \times \text{frequency}}{\text{number of poles}}$$

GREEK ALPHABET

Name	Capital	Lower Case	Designates
Alpha	A	α	Angles.
Beta	B	β	Angles, flux density.
Gamma . . .	Γ	γ	Conductivity.
Delta	Δ	δ	Variation of a quantity, increment.
Epsilon . . .	E	ϵ	Base of natural logarithms (2.71828).
Zeta	Z	ζ	Impedance, coefficients, coordinates.
Eta	H	η	Hysteresis coefficient, efficiency, magnetizing force.
Theta	Θ	θ	Phase angle.
Iota	I	ι	
Kappa	K	κ	Dielectric constant, coupling coefficient, susceptibility.
Lambda . . .	Λ	λ	Wavelength.
Mu	M	μ	Permeability, micro, amplification factor.
Nu	N	ν	Reluctivity.
Xi	Ξ	ξ	
Omicron . . .	O	o	
Pi	Π	π	3.1416
Rho	P	ρ	Resistivity.
Sigma	Σ	σ	
Tau	T	τ	Time constant, time-phase displacement.
Upsilon . . .	Υ	υ	
Phi	Φ	φ	Angles, magnetic flux.
Chi	X	χ	
Psi	Ψ	ψ	Dielectric flux, phase difference.
Omega	Ω	ω	Ohms (capital), angular velocity ($2\pi f$).

COMMON ABBREVIATIONS AND LETTER SYMBOLS

Term	Abbreviation or Symbol
alternating current (noun)	a.c.
alternating-current (adj.)	a-c
ampere	a.
area	A
audiofrequency (noun)	AF
audiofrequency (adj.)	A-F
capacitance	C
capacitive reactance	X_c
centimeter	cm.
conductance	G
coulomb	Q
counterelectromotive force	c.e.m.f.
current (d-c or r.m.s. value)	I
current (instantaneous value)	i
cycles per second	c.p.s.
dielectric constant	K,k
difference in potential (d-c or r.m.s. value)	E
difference in potential (instantaneous value)	e
direct current (noun)	d.c.
direct-current (adj.)	d-c
electromotive force	e.m.f.
frequency	f
henry	h.
horsepower	hp.
impedance	Z
inductance	L
inductive reactance	X_L
kilovolt	kv.
kilovolt-ampere	kv.-a.
kilowatt	kw.
kilowatt-hour	kw.-hr.
magnetic field intensity	H
magnetomotive force	m.m.f.
megohm	M
microampere	μ a.
microfarad	μ f.
microhenry	μ h.
micromicrofarad	$\mu\mu$ f.
microvolt	μ v.
milliampere	ma.
millihenry	mh.
milliwatt	mw.
mutual inductance	M
power	P
resistance	R
revolutions per minute	r.p.m.
root mean square	r.m.s.
time	t
torque	T
volt	v.
watt	w.

CPSIA information can be obtained
at www.ICGtesting.com
Printed in the USA
LVHW060209070921
697185LV00020B/235

9 781731 802255